W9-BXA-098

Francisco brings abundant insight to his story. Few motion pictures have had a cast and crew of such wonderfully talented—and eccentric—people working on it. From Bogie, who until then had been type-cast as a two-bit gangster, to Bergman, stunningly beautiful and on the threshold of becoming a major star, to the incredible supporting cast of Paul Henreid, Claude Rains, Peter Lorre, Sydney Greenstreet, and Conrad Veidt. All of this was overseen by the charismatic Hungarian director Michael Curtiz. (Curtiz's mangled English was legendary. "The next time I send a dumb sum of a beetch, I go myself," was one of his chronic complaints.)

Filled with solid film history as well as entertaining gossip, YOU MUST REMEMBER THIS offers everything movie lovers could ask for, as it gloriously re-creates the special magic and mystique of a film that has touched us all.

Photo by Vito Torelli

With a solid background as a successful actor on stage, film, and television, CHARLES FRANCISCO is well qualified to report on the subject. He served as a combat correspondent during the Korean war and later reported on a wide variety of subjects as a radio-TV newsman in Chicago and New York. Author of *The Radio City Music Hall,* Mr. Francisco resides in New York City.

You Must Remember This...

BOOKS BY CHARLES FRANCISCO

THE RADIO CITY MUSIC HALL:
An Affectionate History of the World's Greatest Theater

YOU MUST REMEMBER THIS . . .
The Filming of Casablanca

You Must Remember This....

The Filming of Casablanca

Charles Francisco

Prentice-Hall, Inc., Englewood Cliffs, New Jersey

Printed in the United States of America
Prentice-Hall International, Inc., London
Prentice-Hall of Australia, Pty. Ltd., Sydney
Prentice-Hall of Canada, Ltd., Toronto
Prentice-Hall of India Private Ltd., New Delhi
Prentice-Hall of Japan, Inc., Tokyo
Prentice-Hall of Southeast Asia Pte. Ltd., Singapore
Whitehall Books Limited, Wellington, New Zealand
10 9 8 7 6 5 4 3 2 1

Library of Congress Cataloging in Publication Data

Francisco, Charles
  You must remember this.

  Includes index.
  1. Casablanca. [Motion picture] I. Title.
PN1997.C3523F7   1980   791.43'72   80-18823
ISBN 0-13-977058-5

For Dot and Sylvia

. . . The fundamental things apply.

Acknowledgments

Putting together the pieces of the *Casablanca* puzzle was a job made easier and more enjoyable by the generosity of a number of individuals and research institutions. My deepest thanks go to Murray Burnett, Joan Alison, Paul Henreid, and Hal Wallis whose personal reflections helped in my quest to bring the filming back to life. I am also indebted to Maxine Fleckner and her staff at the Wisconsin Center for Film and Theater Research, as well as the helpful people at the American Film Institute, the Academy of Motion Picture Arts and Sciences, and the Lincoln Center Library for the Performing Arts. Much of the material in this book was gleaned from the valuable files of these worthy organizations. Public acknowledgment must also be made of the editorial and technical aid of Suzanne Francisco who "moonlights" as my wife.

You Must Remember This...

One

Wisps of fog, stirred by the twin propellers of the waiting aircraft, floated somberly above the rain-slickened landing strip. The man in the trench coat peered intently at the beautiful young woman at his side. The firm voice belied the forlorn look in his eyes.

"Last night we said a great many things. You said I was to do the thinking for both of us. Well, I've done a lot of it since then and it all adds up to one thing—you're getting on that plane with Victor where you belong. . . . Inside of us we both know you belong with Victor. You're part of his work, the thing that keeps him going. If that plane leaves the ground and you're not with him, you'll regret it. Maybe not today, maybe not tomorrow—but soon, and for the rest of your life. . . . I've got a job to do, too. Where I'm going you can't follow. What I've got to do you can't be a part of. Look, I'm no good at being noble, but it doesn't take much to see that the problems of three little people don't amount to a hill of beans in this crazy world. Someday you'll understand that. Here's looking at you, kid."

And the lines worked as well in the 1972 movie as they had in the one released thirty years earlier. The new motion picture was called *Play It Again, Sam,* and the man in the trench coat was Woody Allen. His "moving" speech drew the loudest laugh of the picture. The lines worked beautifully in *Play It Again, Sam,* because they were the culmination of Allen's wacky efforts to go against type and become the living reincarnation of his hero, Humphrey Bogart, as he had played Rick Blaine in the 1942 film version of *Casablanca.* The words spoken by Bogart in that movie were among the most romantic ever delivered by any actor in any film, and the insecure, bespectacled Allen had been waiting all his life for an opportunity to say them in "real life."

Like millions of other movie buffs around the world, Allen had long been entranced by the special magic of *Casablanca* and its legendary star. Unlike most movie fans, he had decided to do something about his dream. Not yet established as America's most prolific writer-director-star, Allen was already breaking ground by using a movie to pay tribute to another movie. In his comedic brilliance, Allen used the mystique of *Casablanca* to create a character with whom millions could identify. Bogart and *Casablanca* had become a great deal more than actor and film—together they had become a genuine part of American folklore, and Allen was well aware of it.

Countless thousands of motion pictures have been released since the opening credits of *Casablanca* first reached the screen. Most of these films have been more costly to produce, a few have been better directed and acted, but none has continued to grow in popularity like the simple World War II classic which starred Humphrey Bogart, Ingrid Bergman, and Paul Henreid. *Casablanca* occupies a unique position in the history of film.

A relatively low-budget picture about a bitter, expatriate American in an out-of-the-way North African port city early in World War II would seem to have little chance of retaining its popularity for so long. It wasn't consciously made as an art film or a future movie classic. It was strictly a film of its time, the product of a studio which was devoutly dedicated to the business of selling entertainment. *Casablanca* wasn't filmed with the grandiose settings or sweeping plots of many other films which preceded and followed it. It didn't even utilize the biggest box-office names on the Warner lot. Yet, this unique motion picture continues to be the favorite of millions of moviegoers around the world while other fine films have all but faded from memory.

There are very few days of the year when *Casablanca* isn't appearing somewhere. It continues to be a top-rated feature on the movie schedules of television stations throughout the United States and abroad, and it also attracts hordes of devoted paying customers of all ages in a number of movie theaters around the world. Since the early 1970s, Station WPIX-TV (Channel 11) has owned the television rights to *Casablanca* in the New York market. WPIX executives confirm that *Casablanca* remains a powerful and consistent tool for improving ratings and selling time. Usually shown twice a year and scheduled during rating periods or at times when the networks concentrate on major news events that an independent station cannot adequately cover, *Casablanca* consistently delivers a sizable audience.

In the 1970s, *Casablanca* made the *Motion Picture Almanac*'s list of the "Great Hundred," but the best rankings were yet to come. A bold headline in the *Los Angeles Times* of August 25, 1973, announced, "*Casablanca* ranks as Warner Brothers' most popular film in fifty years." The story revealed the results of a nationwide poll commissioned by Leslee Productions. Those polled were asked to respond to a 65-page questionnaire which took six and a half hours to fill out. The respondents were not told they would be judging only films released by Warner Brothers.

The questionnaire was as intricate as it was long. Participants were asked to rate the films on four factors— enjoyability, popularity, cinematic significance, and impact. A total of 1,600 films were rated, and a thorough computer analysis of the results showed *Casablanca* the clear-cut winner. More than thirty years after its release, it was rated the best film ever! Although only Warner films were judged, the list of runners-up proved *Casablanca* won its race against some very stiff competition.

The Maltese Falcon (1941) finished second, *Who's Afraid of Virginia Woolf* (1966) was third, Tennessee Williams' *A Streetcar Named Desire* (1951) placed fourth, and *The Treasure of Sierra Madre* (1948) was named fifth best. Three of the five films starred Humphrey Bogart, and only his *Maltese Falcon* pre-dated *Casablanca.*

An even more interesting poll illustrating the impact and lasting power of *Casablanca* was conducted several years later. To celebrate its tenth anniversary, the prestigious American Film Institute (AFI) announced plans for the largest survey ever conducted in the history of the American motion-picture industry. Its aim was simple—to pinpoint the ten best American films of all time. The AFI had all the resources necessary for such an undertaking within its own membership of 35,000. The national membership represented a wide cross section of those vitally interested in cinema as a business and an art form. The 35,000 voters were industry people—producers, directors, performers, technicians—as well as critics, media standouts, authors, academicians, students, and other dedicated film buffs.

The guidelines were simple. Each member was asked to list his first five choices in order of preference. Any American film of any period or type was eligible. To encourage the potentially passive to participate, the institute enclosed a list of 341 pictures generally ranked among the greatest. But the members were not bound to choose from this list; they were encouraged to make their own *personal* choices without interference from anyone.

A point system would be used to tabulate the results, and a distinguished accounting firm was hired for the job. The governing board of the AFI was astounded at the response. More than 1,100 movie titles were returned with the selections. The vote had proved to be more independent and democratic than anyone had hoped and now another vote would be necessary. The accountants meticulously tallied the points, and the fifty most popular films were determined. Another ballot was then sent to each of the 35,000 members with a request that he or she select five in order of preference from the new list of fifty.

To emphasize the importance of the survey on the tenth anniversary of its founding, the American Film Institute made grand plans. It would reveal its list of the best American films of all time before President Jimmy Carter and a national television audience at the John F. Kennedy Center for the

4

Performing Arts in Washington, D.C., in November 1977. In a sense, the occasion would be a coming-of-age celebration for American film. The film industry would salute itself with an evening of entertainment and serious reflection before the President of the United States in the glamor and prestige of the nation's capital.

The long-awaited list of the best American films stirred a great deal of controversy, proving, if nothing else, that the AFI survey was conducted most democratically. It also reflected a preoccupation of today's film buffs with the products of their own generations. Nearly half of the fifty pictures selected had been released no later than 1960; twelve of them were products of the 1970s. The cartoon-like *Star Wars,* released during the year of the vote, was judged better than *All About Eve* of 1950, and *One Flew Over the Cuckoo's Nest* of 1975 finished well ahead of *The Best Years of Our Lives* of 1946.

With so many great films of the past (including those of Charlie Chaplin and Frank Capra) failing to make the top ten, it seemed likely that an unpretentious, low-budget movie like *Casablanca* would be entirely ignored. But it wasn't. *Casablanca* was voted the third best American film of all time—a close runnerup to *Gone With the Wind* and *Citizen Kane* in the first two places. Bogart's *The African Queen,* released in 1952, finished fourth ahead of the 1940 classic *The Grapes of Wrath.*

That *Gone With the Wind* was named the best American film of all time was hardly a surprise. For many years it had been the highest-grossing film ever made. It was a lavish full-color film version of one of the best-selling, most-loved novels in American history. It had a superstar cast with Clark Gable, Vivien Leigh, Olivia De Havilland, Leslie Howard, and others. Its plot centered on a very colorful and trying time in the history of the nation, and it had flourished in numerous reissues since 1939. Likewise, *Citizen Kane,* though never popular with a mass audience, had become an elitist favorite which was quickly elevated to "art film" status after its 1941 release. It had been a breakthrough film proving that a creative genius like the young Orson Welles could elevate the movie form from one of entertainment to art.

But *Casablanca* was something else again. The rea-

5

sons for its unexpected popularity puzzled many. Its leading male and female characters owned neither plantations nor newspapers. Its straightforward story line was not enhanced by the romantic chivalry of a war on horseback, nor was its prevailing mood colored by the intellectual stimulation of the machinations of the rich and powerful. Its creators had only hoped it would meet with general approval from the vast movie audience in the year of its release. Yet, some thirty-five years later, 35,000 supposedly knowledgeable motion-picture enthusiasts had named it the third best movie of all time!

However, the polls are only the tip of the iceberg that is the incredible, growing popularity of *Casablanca*. It remains the rarest of films because it has been adopted as their own by the children and grandchildren of those who saw it during its original release in the early 1940s. *Casablanca* and its leading actors, particularly Humphrey Bogart, have gone beyond the bounds of enormous popularity into that strange, undefinable realm of cultism.

In the mid-1970s, an original *Casablanca* poster (which cost Warner Brothers pennies to print) was sold to a collector for $450. A Washington, D.C., newspaper article of the 1960s declared Bogart "a bigger star than ever, a decade after his death." Long before Farrah Fawcett entered the market, a photo blow-up of Bogie clad in his *Casablanca* trench coat helped launch the poster business into a huge industry. His "Rick Blaine" poster joined those of the Beatles and other rock stars on the walls of college students who had been born long after *Casablanca* was released.

It seems fair to say that Bogart's wearing of a trench coat in the unforgettable final scene of *Casablanca* did more for the perpetuation of that garment than the actions of the entire British Army in the trenches of World War I. By the same token, the lion's share of the credit for keeping *Casablanca* "alive" must go to the generations of college students since the 1940s. During the late forties and fifties, universities decided to look at cinema as a serious art form and featured *Casablanca* and other noteworthy movies in film classics programs on campus. Others, recognizing the commercial potential of the appeal of old films, opened small theaters adjacent to campuses for the exhibition of special movies. *Casablanca* has been the overwhelming favorite.

From Berkeley to Madison to Cambridge, the collegians still flock to art houses for showings of *Casablanca.* "*Casablanca* clubs" have sprung up on many campuses, and a study taken a few years ago revealed that many club members had seen the film twenty to fifty times each. *Casablanca* even became the subject of a thesis for a master's degree at the University of Illinois during the 1970s.

In the turbulent 1960s and early 1970s, when college students across the land were openly revolting (in the adjectival as well as verbal sense in the minds of many highly placed officials) against a government they did not trust and a war they detested, *Casablanca* continued to ride high in the esteem of most of them. It was a situation which continues to confound the experts. To the students, war was anathema, yet the film reflected the values of a war-time America united as it had never been in its history. Bogie's Rick Blaine waged a war within himself between his philosophy of "I stick my neck out for nobody" and his basic sense of right and wrong. However, in the end he picked up a gun to strike a blow for freedom. In view of the criticism college students endured as dissidents during the 1960s and members of the "Me Generation" of the 1970s, it seems remarkable that the moral and political stance of *Casablanca* would continue to be moving to the overwhelming majority of them.

The philosophical values of *Casablanca* showed up in a most unlikely place in early 1974. A reporter for the staid *New York Times* used them in illustrating a story about the seamy Watergate scandal in Washington, D.C. He compared the way Bogie's character handled the ethical battle inside himself in the *Casablanca* story with the manner in which the Watergate figures coped with their real-life dilemmas.

The impact of *Casablanca,* perhaps more appropriately, also left its mark on the world of architecture. Hard by the historic Brattle Theatre in Cambridge adjacent to the Harvard campus, students began to flock in the late 1970s to a hangout called Rick's Place. They can catch *Casablanca* at the Brattle and then retire to Rick's for a drink and a few

7

daydreams of themselves as Bogie or Bergman. The duplication of Bogie's *Casablanca* "gin joint" is not just a college-town phenomenon. Ornate copies of Rick's café abound in Philadelphia and elsewhere, including a drinking and dining establishment called Play It Again Sam in Las Vegas. In late 1979 McDonald's announced plans for construction of an authentic replica of Rick's Café Americain as its newest fast-food outlet in the heart of Hollywood near Sunset and Vine.

Perhaps the most elaborate architectural salute to *Casablanca* is located in a Holiday Inn on the lakefront of the city of Chicago. In the city where jazz came of age after its trip up the Mississippi from New Orleans, Rick's Café Americain is Chicago's premiere jazz room. In establishing a style for the piano playing of the character Sam in *Casablanca,* Warner Brothers wanted a sound reminiscent of jazz great Teddy Wilson. Today, a man can don a snap-brim hat and trench coat and saunter through the lobby of the elegant skyscraper hotel on Lake Shore Drive and catch the musical improvisations of the real Teddy Wilson and others.

A true *Casablanca* fan will have no difficulty locating the special nightclub inside the huge hotel. A large-scale model of the movie café's front door, with its ornate neon sign saying "Rick's Café Americain," will beckon. The entrance is an exact duplicate of the original movie set. Inside the café, the architecture and the ambience have been retained. Only Rick and the other characters from the movie are missing. The old "gin joint" lives!

Another re-creation of the Rick's Café set would show up on network television in early December 1979. Although she would later win three Academy Awards for her acting, Ingrid Bergman's glowing performance as Ilsa Lund in *Casablanca* wasn't even selected for a nomination in 1942. Yet, when Variety Clubs International honored her in an "All-Star Tribute," the fete was held on stage nine of the Warner Studios in Burbank, and she was introduced on the set of Rick's Café with *Casablanca* co-star Paul Henreid and two other surviving members of the original cast ushering her on. Frank Sinatra represented his old friend Bogart and sang the picture's haunting love song, "As Time Goes By," while Miss Bergman sat at Dooley Wilson's battered piano.

8

Criticism is, of course, a highly individual and inexact science and/or art form. Many motion-picture scholars will debate the argument that *Casablanca* is undoubtedly the best American motion picture of all time. Few will question the fact that it was *one* of the best and certainly one of the most popular films ever made. Its appeal has been universal and its longevity unparalleled. There is no argument that *Casablanca* is an excellent motion picture from virtually every possible point of view.

Many film experts, in trying to explain the success of *Casablanca,* have resorted to an almost mystical view of its creation. They talk about "the right chemistry"—the right place at the right time,—as if they were describing a surprisingly long-lived marriage that grew out of a love-at-first-sight meeting. They shake their heads in awe at the unusual good fortune that brought the proper producer, director, writers, musicians, studio, stars, and supporting cast together to create a small masterpiece out of what was intended to be just another commercial, wartime entertainment.

The Hollywood of 1942 had its share of "accidental geniuses" making colossal blunders, even as it has them today. The first announcement of the impending production of *Casablanca* illustrates what "could have been." In early 1942 the Hollywood trade paper *Box Office Barometer* ran a small squib stating that Warner Brothers was planning to start production on a new melodrama with the working title *Casablanca.* The article went on to say that the director and writers had not yet been assigned, but the leading roles would be played by Ronald Reagan, Ann Sheridan, and Dennis Morgan!

Casablanca could have easily become a cheap "spin-off" of an exotic melodrama like *Algiers* with George Raft and Hedy Lamarr as its stars. It would surely have lost some of its timeless sheen if it had retained its original title, *Everybody Comes to Rick's.*

Decades have passed since *Casablanca* was shown at its first sneak preview in Huntington Beach, California. The tough, sometimes cynical story—the bittersweet love affair—the dry cracks and memorable phrases—Bogie—"Play it again, Sam"—the unforgettable music—all have become the stuff on which legends are built. Millions of words have been written and spoken about the film in scholarly forums, newspapers, and magazines. Today, too few of those directly responsible for the creation of *Casablanca* are still with us, and because of that, the true story of the making of this fabled motion picture has been largely crowded out by speculation and fantasy.

Casablanca has withstood the rigors of time and survived as one of America's favorite movies not because of any known act of Divine Providence, but rather because the story was placed in the hands of an unusual, dedicated group of film artists and craftsmen. That the images and sound on the finished reels of film came together in such a simple, honest, and polished manner in no way reflects the chaos and feverish struggle that went into the process of preparation and filming on the fifty-day shooting schedule.

As compelling as the story line of *Casablanca* remains today, the true account of the actual filming of the picture also deserves a telling. That untold story is interesting and complex in its own right. As time goes by—you must remember this.

Two

What was to become *Casablanca* made its first tentative entry into the world of film within hours of the Japanese attack on Pearl Harbor, December 7, 1941. A yellowed memorandum from the Warner Brothers story department, dated December 8, 1941, outlines the basic *Casablanca* plot and signals the beginning of one of Hollywood's most memorable efforts.

Despite (or perhaps because of) the growing realization that their nation must inevitably enter the war that had already ravaged Europe and much of Asia, American movie fans had made 1941 a banner year for the motion-picture industry. The movies were America's most popular entertainment. Television, although a practical reality, would not be publicly feasible for a number of years. Only radio offered any organized competition for the mass entertainment market. Nearly every family in the United States had one of the wooden boxes, and programs like *Jack Armstrong, Fibber Magee and Mollie,* and *One Man's Family* kept them listening.

President Franklin Delano Roosevelt had been inaugurated recently to an unprecedented third term in office, and business was booming. After the agonies of the long Depression, most people preferred to try and ignore the unsettling news from abroad while their spirits kept time to the jingle of

11

coins in their pockets. The gearing-up for a possible war and the Lend-Lease program for Britain, faced with an imminent invasion from Nazi Germany, was helping to create thousands of new jobs. In 1941 the average American was still unable to afford the promised "two cars in every garage," but there was finally money enough for a "chicken in (most) every pot." An occasional night out seemed to be everyone's God-given right. And in 1941 "a night out" meant a night at the movies for most people.

The flickering images on the big screen weren't reverently referred to as "film" or "cinema" by the paying customers of that era. They were *movies,* plain and simple. But a ticket to view them was the "little man's" trip to the psychiatrist, his hashish, his vacation to faraway places. The movies were entertaining, taught lofty values, and inspired achievement, and this variety of benefits could be partaken of for about 25.2 cents per trip—the average price of a movie ticket in 1941.

According to industry estimates, some 85 million Americans trooped into their neighborhood motion-picture theaters *each week* during that year. There were 19,750 movie theaters in the forty-eight United States, or nearly twice the number that exist in the fifty states of today. Even with those low affordable prices, Americans spent more than $809 million on movie tickets—nearly 20 percent of their total recreation spending—yet their money bought them a sizable evening or afternoon of entertainment. Oftentimes the bill included two feature films (the long-lamented double feature with an "A" and a "B" movie), a cartoon, and a newsreel. The movie newsreel, equivalent to today's pictorial TV news, allowed the people to see as well as hear world figures such as Roosevelt, Churchill, Hitler, and Mussolini. So many films were released that each new one played an average of only three and a half days at a given theater.

The increasing popularity of the movies created a demand for new film product, and the movie mills of southern California worked overtime to meet that need. During 1941, 492 American-made films were released, and many of them were memorable. This was the year of *Blood and Sand, Blossoms in the Dust, Citizen Kane, Dumbo, Fantasia, Here*

12

Comes Mr. Jordan, Hold Back the Dawn, How Green Was My Valley, The Little Foxes, The Maltese Falcon, Meet John Doe, One Foot in Heaven, The Philadelphia Story, The Road to Zanzibar, Sergeant York, Sun Valley Serenade, Suspicion, and *Sweater Girl,* among others.

The motion-picture industry of that era was exactly what the name implied—an entity unto itself, owned and operated by men whose only business was the creation and dissemination of movies to an eager public. Unlike today, the studios were not divisions of huge companies with interests in many diversified businesses. Metro-Goldwyn-Mayer, Paramount, Warner Brothers, Twentieth Century-Fox, Columbia, United Artists, RKO, and Universal were the industry giants with their own production facilities, distribution organizations, and in some cases their own string of movie theaters. Important contributions were also made by prestigious independent companies like Goldwyn and Selznick. Two minor studios, Republic and Monogram, churned out dozens of Westerns, comedies, and who-dun-its for the Saturday matinee crowd.

The year 1941 was one of artistic and financial success for Warner Brothers, the studio from which *Casablanca* would come. In the 1930s the four Warners had extended themselves to the verge of bankruptcy, often using stock options instead of cash to expand the business. But at the close of 1941, Warner Brothers could boast of an operating profit of $5,429,302 from a gross of $102,293,170. The studio had an impressive list of stars, contract players, producers, directors, and screenwriters, as well as an additional payroll of 3,654 behind-the-scenes workers.

Harry, Albert, Sam, and Jack Warner had entered the motion-picture business in the early years of the century when the movies were a curiosity instead of an industry. Their Jewish parents, Ben and Pearl Warner, fled the cossack raids in Poland to start a new life in America in the 1880s. Eventually, the elder Warners brought their children to Youngstown, Ohio, where Mr. Warner opened a meat market. The second youngest of the brothers, Sam, would prove to be the most daring and imaginative of the four. In 1905, he announced that he had an opportunity to buy one of the new-fangled movie projection machines at the bargain price of $1,000.

13

After pooling all of their financial resources, the entire family was still short of the needed cash until Ben Warner agreed to "hock" the family's delivery horse.

The Warner Brothers film empire had a low-key beginning in a rented store on the main street of the small town of Niles, Ohio. Within two years its financial prospects had improved to the point that the Warners would expand their enterprise from simple film exhibition into the more lucrative business of distribution throughout the eastern United States. By 1911, the Warners were willing to risk some of their surplus capital on a film production of their own creation. With Jack as the screenwriter and Sam as director, the younger brothers shot two films in St. Louis. The Warners made other films in succeeding years, shooting most of them at the old Biograph Studios in New York.

The "moving picture business" was obviously a growth industry, and the Warners were in it to stay. In 1919, with brothers Harry and Albert supervising financial matters in the East, Sam and Jack rented a broken-down studio at Eighteenth and Main in Los Angeles. They later shot films at another rented studio in Culver City and began to make monthly payments on a ten-acre parcel of land at Sunset and Bronson in Hollywood. It was on this lot that they built their first private studio complex with an appropriate sign bearing the soon-to-be famous legend, "Warner Brothers Pictures."

The Warner Brothers' holdings began to assume imperial shape with the acquisition of the Vitagraph Company in 1925 and the steady gobbling up of hundreds of motion picture and presentation houses across the country. But the tremendous cash outlays for acquisitions also put the company on shaky financial ground, and it took a dog and a radio station to switch the entries from red to black in the financial ledgers. A series of films with the original canine star Rin-Tin-Tin fattened the Warner bankroll. The two younger Warners also got on the radio bandwagon and talked their brothers into building the studios and transmitter of Radio Station KFWB on the Sunset Boulevard movie lot.

Their involvement in broadcasting led directly to Warner Brothers' greatest single contribution to the early arts and sciences of the motion picture. Within weeks of the opening of KFWB, Sam and Jack were pressing Harry and Albert to invest some of the company money in an experimental sound system for film. Warners signed an historic partnership agreement with Western Electric in June 1926, and Sam Warner went to Bell Laboratories in New York to work on perfecting the sound system while Jack began production on the first film to utilize it. *Don Juan,* with a music-only sound track running less than an hour, opened in New York to unanimous rave reviews on August 6, 1926.

Warner Brothers had clearly stolen a beat on every studio in Hollywood by bringing sound to film. But neither Warner Brothers nor any other studio had pictures that talked. The race was on in earnest, and Warners' Vitaphone system was well in the lead. With Sam still working on the laboratory process in New York, Jack began preparing the hit Broadway play *The Jazz Singer* as the very first talkie. With Al Jolson doing the scant talking and singing, *The Jazz Singer* opened in New York on October 6, 1927, and the world of the movies was changed forever. The scientific triumph was tempered by tragedy when Sam Warner, the most creative of the brothers and the moving force behind the new process, died just twenty-four hours before the picture opened.

The loss of Sam Warner left Jack as the sole head of the motion-picture operation in Hollywood. Brothers Harry and Albert never became actively involved in production matters, preferring to preside over the business end of the corporation. Warner Brothers made the ultimate leap forward in 1928 when, buoyed by the financial success and prestige garnered from the introduction of talking pictures, Warners bought the First National Studio in Burbank, a sprawling cluster of huge new sound stages located just beyond the Hollywood Hills in the San Fernando Valley. Warner Brothers was now a major studio in every sense of the word.

Jack Warner became king of the new studio, working with renewed vigor from the biggest office on the lot, increasing production to forty or more films per year, experimenting with new kinds of movie themes, and importing scores of young actors and actresses from the legitimate stages of New York and elsewhere. Signed to long-term contracts, some performers fell by the wayside when Warner refused to pick up their options; others became major stars as members of the legendary Warner Brothers stock company.

At the time *Casablanca* was filmed, the term *studio system* would be defined by actors as a financially secure but artistically stifling arrangement in which performers were almost totally dependent on the whims of the studio head. At Warner Brothers that omnipotence was the prerogative of Jack L. Warner. More than any other Hollywood mogul, Warner seemed to be in a continuous state of war with the stars who worked for him. In time, MGM would boast of "more stars than there are in the heavens," but Jack Warner's foresight in signing a number of "castoffs" and "unknowns" would enable him to build a roster of superb dramatic talent that was second to none.

With the aid of his top associates, Warner nursed to stardom such box-office luminaries of the 1930s and early 1940s as Bette Davis, Joan Crawford, Errol Flynn, James Cagney, Olivia De Havilland, Edward G. Robinson, Paul Muni, Joan Blondell, Dick Powell, Ruby Keeler, George Arliss, Ida Lupino, Pat O'Brien, Claude Rains, Barbara Stanwyck, Ronald Reagan, Ann Sheridan, Jane Wyman, and many others.

Warner Brothers' "bread and butter" product of the 1930s was the genre which became known popularly as the "gangster movie." This type of film became the training ground for stars like Cagney, Robinson, and George Raft. Character actors in the Warner stock company became familiar faces to the public in these action films, although it would take them longer to achieve the star status of a Flynn or a Cagney. This roster included John Garfield, Raymond Massey, Alan Hale, Peter Lorre, and the most chilling "killer" of them all, Humphrey Bogart. As the popularity of gangster movies declined toward the end of the decade, studio executives began to seek other ways to use these men's talents. Yet the actors were seldom consulted.

The studio system became an escalating source of bitter resentment between many of the contract players and the studio chiefs. The studios spent millions of dollars developing and promoting its stars, and the stars became the magnets which drew customers to the ticket window. An increasing number of performers felt they deserved more consideration from their employers. But Jack Warner reasoned that many of his contract players had been virtually unknown when he found them—nobody *forced* them to sign a contract—and neither heaven nor hell could persuade him to bow to their "outrageous" demands. Their names were on the dotted line, and they belonged to Warner to utilize in any legitimate way he chose. They would perform in the roles and properties to which they were assigned, and they would continue to collect the agreed-upon salary unless he chose to increase it. At the same time, Warner reserved the right to loan them to other studios for huge sums if he so decided.

In 1936 Bette Davis made headlines in newspapers around the world when she became the first star to sue the head of a studio in an attempt to end what she considered the virtual stranglehold the Warners held on her professional life. Before signing with Warner Brothers, Davis had appeared in a number of Broadway plays and made a few uninspired films at Universal. That studio was preparing to drop her because of its belief that "she has no sex appeal whatsoever." Jack Warner, listening to his advisers, thought she had an innate talent and "star quality" and signed her to a long-term contract. In less than three years she brought Warner Brothers Pictures its first Oscar as best actress for her performance in *Dangerous,* and her salary was gratefully raised to $5,000 per week from its original base of $300.

But the volatile actress wasn't seeking more money in her suit against Jack Warner. Her grievance concerned a situation which was even more infuriating to the chief of Warner Brothers Pictures. She wanted a voice in selecting the roles she was obliged to play. She flatly refused to star in a picture called *God's Country and the Woman.* Warner considered the Davis suit an obvious attempt by a performer to sidestep her legal contract and usurp the powers of the filmmaker in deciding the pictures he should produce and the performers he should utilize in any given role.

Warner failed in his attempt to soft-talk Davis out of her stand and resorted to the standard studio punishment: clamping her on suspension without pay until she agreed to his demands. But Davis was a fighter *par excellence,* and she took her boss by surprise when she accepted an offer of work in England where she filed a lawsuit to terminate the contract. The British court, to the relief of every studio head, eventually ruled in Warner's favor. Bette Davis was forced to return to Warner Brothers, more or less on the studio's terms.

It wasn't until shortly after the release of *Casablanca* that a Warner star was finally able to weaken the studio's ironclad control over its actors. Olivia De Havilland, backed by the Screen Actors Guild, won her 1943 court case against Warner Brothers. The court ruled that no studio or producer could sign a contract with an actor for a period of longer than seven years. It also stipulated that any suspensions against the performer could not be used to extend the contract. Warner would later admit that the revision of the suspension clause was an important victory for "some" actors because De Havilland, Davis, Cagney, and Humphrey Bogart had weathered "about twenty-five suspensions without pay between them."

Despite his reputation as the most tightfisted of all the Hollywood moguls, Warner was able to mollify many of his stars by giving them healthy salary increases without pressure from the courts.

The Warner studio released at least as many bad pictures as good ones, but prospects for Warner Brothers Pictures had never been brighter as 1941 drew to a close. The studio had produced forty-eight features during the year, the profit picture was probably the best in the company's history, and the prestige of the WB logo would be strengthened by such releases as *Yankee Doodle Dandy, Kings Row,* and *Now, Voyager,* which seemed likely to be candidates for nominations at the 1942 Academy Awards.

Although they had been lifetime Republicans, Warner and his older brothers had been among the first of the Hollywood elite to jump aboard the Roosevelt bandwagon in the New Yorker's first successful presidential campaign. Jack Warner considered himself a "personal friend of the President" and a man with inside knowledge about the country's future. He had volunteered to cooperate with the administration in helping to prepare the public for war, as he would later volunteer for active military service as an army filmmaker. Between 1936 and 1941 Warner Brothers would win four

Oscars for special short subject films dealing with patriotic themes. With the deteriorating position of the Allies in the war in Europe, by 1941 Warner was convinced that the United States was about to become the last bulwark against the spread of fascism and was determined that more Warner films would deal with that theme in the future.

In the long run, Jack Warner's insatiable quest for prestige and his eye for talent would prove to be his strong points as the head of a major studio. He was possibly most adept at selecting unusually capable people to work behind the cameras. In his early days in Hollywood he hired an eager but inexperienced young man to coauthor the screenplay for the initial Rin-Tin-Tin movie. The novice writer was Darryl F. Zanuck, who would later open a rival studio which would become the ambitious Twentieth Century-Fox. Mark Hellinger, Harry Rapf, Lewis Milestone, and Alexander Korda were also once members of the Warner production staff.

Warner became increasingly meticulous in signing the other key artists and craftsmen who would build the prestige of Warner Brothers Pictures. He wanted only the best, and he was willing to pay for quality. Howard Hawks, Mervyn LeRoy, William Dieterle, Frank Borzage, Ernst Lubitsch, Willie Wyler, John Huston, and Michael Curtiz were all on the list of fine film directors who did much of their early work on the Warner lot.

Jack Warner was never bashful about taking the lion's share of the credit for the success of the studio he headed. But a quick scan of his list of chief assistants reveals the error in the final truth of his assumption. The making of a great motion picture is a collective art form which precludes the success of a single film being predicated on the genius of an individual, be he studio mogul, *auteur,* or star. Because Warner was overly protective of his stature as chief executive of the Burbank studios, the enormous contributions of his closest subordinates were often unknown to the general public.

One of the most respected and least applauded members of the Warner team in 1941 was a man named Harold Brent Wallis. For ten of the thirteen years Wallis had worked at Warner Brothers, he had wielded a strong creative influence over every Warner production. Even his administrative power at the studio was second only to that of Jack L. Warner. As studio manager and chief of production, Hal B. Wallis was Warner's closest adviser. In 1941 he worked out a new arrangement with the studio which would prove to be an immediate boon to both Warner Brothers and Wallis. It would enable Wallis to concentrate on the supervision and planning of a motion picture he would make in 1942, the second film he had scheduled under his new contract. That film would ultimately prove to be a very special motion picture— *Casablanca.*

Three

At the dawn of the 1980s, Hal B. Wallis had earned his position as one of the elder statesmen of the motion-picture industry. In his nearly sixty years in Hollywood, he had been a vital part of the film business as it grew to enormous popularity, faltered, and started a comeback. In an era when the producer was the creative coordinator of a film project rather than a simple fundraiser, Hal Wallis was one of the very best.

Wallis has produced more than two hundred films during his career, most of them box-office smashes and many of them artistic triumphs. He was the man who introduced the zany antics of Dean Martin and Jerry Lewis in a series of films for Paramount during the late forties and early fifties. Later he brought Elvis Presley to Hollywood and made the King of Rock'n'Roll a tremendous movie attraction during Hollywood's lowest period. Still later, he engineered the drive for John Wayne's only Oscar by casting the Western star in *True Grit*.

Films produced by Wallis have been honored with best picture nominations by the Academy of Motion Picture Arts and Sciences as far back as 1932 for Warners' *I Am a Fugitive from the Chain Gang*. Such Wallis-produced films as *Yankee Doodle Dandy; Now, Voyager; Come Back Little Sheba; The Rose Tattoo; Anne of a Thousand Days;* and

Becket were all highly acclaimed. But no motion picture on that list of more than two hundred has ever achieved the popularity of *Casablanca*. *Casablanca* bears the Wallis stamp from beginning to end.

Like so many of his contemporaries, Hal Wallis was largely a self-taught man both in general education and in the business of making motion pictures—he learned by doing. Except for the ill health of his mother, Wallis might never have begun a career in show business. Born in Chicago around the turn of the century, Wallis fell victim to a dilemma faced by most young men of his time. The responsibility of contributing to the income of his family forced him to choose employment over high school. He worked first as an office boy in a Chicago real estate firm before finding what he considered a real career opportunity as a traveling salesman.

In the second decade of the twentieth century, technology had made electrical energy for home heating a promising new business, and Wallis became one of its most enthusiastic advocates. He learned how to sell and did well peddling his company's wares throughout Missouri, Kansas, and Nebraska. Barely out of his teens, with a future in the electrical heating business, he was forced to change his plans with little advance notice. When his mother became seriously ill and her doctors prescribed a warmer, drier climate, young Hal was forced to join the family on their exodus to southern California. He quickly discovered that the milder climate was excellent for his mother's health and disastrous for his future in the electrical heating business. He had to find another field of endeavor.

Wallis had always been a devotee of the arts and spent every spare moment reading and educating himself far beyond his formal schooling. He hoped to find work that would reward him intellectually and financially. The movie business was the most publicized and interesting of all possible occupations in the still-sleepy Los Angeles of 1922. Grand movie "palaces" were springing up all over Los Angeles for the exhibition of the fascinating silent films of Charlie Chaplin, Buster Keaton, and others. Wallis was already a movie fan, intrigued by the mystery of the process behind films, and so he reasoned that with all the studios being built on vacant land among the orange groves on the outskirts of central Los Angeles, the motion-picture business was bound to expand dramatically in the years ahead. He made up his mind to get his foot in the door somewhere and become a part of the new industry.

Using his intelligence as well as all the tricks and charm he had learned as a traveling salesman, Wallis began a concentrated effort to find himself a niche in the picture business. When the break finally came, it was through the back door. He met a man named H. L. Gumbiner, who operated a chain of movie theaters. Gumbiner was impressed with the enthusiastic Wallis and named him manager of the Garrick Cinema in downtown Los Angeles.

The Garrick was an important house in Los Angeles, and because of that Wallis was soon able to make valuable contacts among the top distributors in the business as well as some of the people who were actually producing the films. Sam and Jack Warner were then personally involved in both ends of the business, and it was only natural that Wallis would meet them. The Warners, particularly Sam, took a liking to the young man from Chicago, and Sam invited Hal Wallis to join the studio team.

Wallis had no training in public relations or promotion other than what he had learned as an exhibitor at the Garrick, but Sam Warner found him a man of ideas with a gift "of the gab." He made Wallis an assistant to Charles Kurtzman, who was then the head of publicity for Warner Brothers in Hollywood. Wallis plunged into his new occupation with a gusto that astounded even the workaholic Sam and Jack Warner. Within three months, the Warners named Wallis to replace Kurtzman as top man in their publicity department.

The job proved to be another valuable course in the cinematic education of Hal Wallis. He had broken into the business as manager of a movie theater and had moved on into the fringe area of film production. Now he was suddenly the man most responsible for creating a public thirst to view the Warner product. It was Wallis who dreamed up the idea of praising the expertise of Warner's director Ernst Lubitsch by dubbing it "The Lubitsch Touch." His job was a challenge, he was learning, and he was eager to move on into areas where he could exert some creative influence on actual films.

With his brother Sam's death in 1927, Jack Warner was alone in watching over the growth of Warner Brothers' Hollywood operation. Needing input from someone he could trust, Warner realized that the competent and loyal Hal Wallis fit the bill perfectly. When Warners bought the First National studio complex in 1928, Hal B. Wallis was named studio manager, and a very short time later he was given the additional responsibility of succeeding C. Graham Baker as production executive. Still a young man, Wallis had attained his goal of reaching a position of authority in both the creative and business ends of making motion pictures.

His job as virtual second-in-command to Jack Warner on production matters at the studio would not be permanent. True to his rambunctious style, Warner neglected to give Wallis any notice of his impending demotion. One morning in 1931 Wallis arrived at his office to find a workman removing his nameplate from the door. He had been in his position for three years, but now he was being replaced by another early Warner associate. The new Warner production chief would be Darryl Francis Zanuck.

Eventually, Jack Warner explained that Zanuck was taking over Wallis' former job as part of the agreement in the Warner Brothers—First National merger. Warner also assured Wallis there would always be a place for his talent on the Warner lot. Wallis took the demotion with graciousness, because it allowed him the opportunity to become a full-time producer at the studio. During the next three years he produced a number of successful films, including *I Am a Fugitive from the Chain Gang* and a musical called *Gold Diggers of 1933* that still delights fans of "high camp" on occasional TV showings.

True to his word, Jack Warner returned Wallis to his post of Warner Brothers chief of production in 1934 when Darryl F. Zanuck resigned to work full-time on the formation of Twentieth Century-Fox. Wallis was eminently better qualified for the job the second time around. In little more than a decade he had acquired impressive credits in a still-infant industry. His education had been impeccable—as a theater manager, a publicist, a studio manager, a producer, and as the chief of production of one of the world's largest film companies.

Although Jack Warner received most of the credit for the success of Warner Brothers' studio operations during the years between 1934 and 1942, Hal Wallis was the hard-working creative power behind the throne. As chief of production, it was his responsibility to oversee the production of every Warner film released during that period. Wallis' youth helped him weather the often twelve- to eighteen-hour days he put in on the job.

Warner, of course, had veto power on every aspect of the studio operation, but it was Wallis who had the first responsibility of approving scripts, assigning producers, directors, writers, and cameramen, in addition to supervising all casting. His days were taken up with story and casting conferences, viewing the daily rushes, approving the final editing of films, negotiating with agents, and the countless other details involved with producing motion pictures at a major Hollywood studio of the period. He thrived on the work, and his record was spectacular.

During the seven years of Wallis' second tenure as chief of production, Warners released a total of 371 films. Several of the best of that number were personally produced by Hal Wallis. In that seven-year period Warner motion pictures garnered eighty-six nominations in various categories from the Academy of Motion Picture Arts and Sciences and came away with thirty-five Oscars. With Wallis at the helm as production chief, the Warner profit picture improved from $700,000 in 1935 to $5.5 million at the close of 1941.

But Wallis' job was as frustrating as it was rewarding. To paraphrase Harry S Truman, the buck stopped at the desk of Hal Wallis even though his decision wasn't always final. In the background loomed the omnipotent presences of the brothers Warner and their well-known interest in "the bottom line." What the Warners giveth, they could taketh away. In addition, Jack Warner failed to be a consistent backer of his production chief in the inevitable squabbles for position and power inside the huge studio.

In his memoirs, published more than twenty years after the release of *Casablanca,* Jack Warner gave his own view of one such situation during Wallis' term in executive office. Referring to a film called *Border Town,* Warner wrote,

Mark Hellinger was the producer on this film. Mark had more knowledge in one finger than our studio manager Hal Wallis could squeeze out of fifty whole bodies, and because Wallis was jealous there was constant friction between the two men. I put a stop to this by making Mark Hellinger a producer who was not under Wallis' control, and thereafter he made some great pictures, including High Sierra, They Drive by Night *and* Naked City.

That incident and others like it caused Wallis to re-evaluate his goals and his position on the Warner lot. Eventually, it would prompt him to sever his connections with the studio. He was a sensitive man who had little use for Hollywood politics or its social scene—his work was his hobby and the only serious one he had other than collecting works of art. The motion-picture business had changed greatly since he had regained the reins as production chief at Warners—and so had the world.

Much of the world was at war by the beginning of the 1940s, and although Wallis had never been very much interested in world politics, he had lived through a turbulent period of America's growth and had a strong social conscience. The federal government had reinstated the draft, the country was mobilizing, and there was little likelihood that the United States could stay out of the conflict. Wallis, like other major executives of the Hollywood studios, had been well briefed by the Roosevelt administration on the important contributions the movie industry could make in the areas of preparedness and morale-building in the trying times ahead.

Well past the age of obligatory military service, Wallis knew there was a contribution he could make to a potential effort against the totalitarian forces shaking the earth on the far sides of the Atlantic and Pacific. Now, more than ever, the film industry could inform and uplift the populace as well as entertain it.

Rather than renegotiate his contract for another term, in late 1941 Wallis decided to move in a new direction and was pleasantly surprised when Jack Warner agreed that the idea seemed a good one. After weeks of negotiations between Wallis and Warner and their respective attorneys and agents, Hal Wallis was ready to begin a new phase of his illustrious career which would carry him to greater fame and success than he had ever achieved as Warner's second-in-command at Burbank.

The eventual deal with Warners was rather unusual at the time. Wallis would continue to work under the WB logo, and he would have access to the full production and distribution facilities of the Warner studio. In addition, through hard negotiations, he won the right to first call on all Warner story material as well as the services of every artist at the studio. Wallis would be held personally responsible for a limited number of Warner films each year and, in an important concession by Jack Warner, each of these films would carry a large-sized, prominently displayed legend, "A Hal B. Wallis Production."

The first motion picture to carry the Hal B. Wallis production label was a so-called woman's picture that would eventually become one of the top ten grossing films of 1942. The film, *Now, Voyager,* would also win an Oscar nomination for Bette Davis and prove to be a memorable screen introduction for her co-star, Paul Henreid. By December 1941, Wallis was in production on *Now, Voyager.* He was sure it would be an entertaining, polished film, but it hardly reflected the lofty, long-term goals he had set for himself under his new contract. That was brought home to him after the shocking events which took place across the blue Pacific on Sunday, December 7, 1941.

The first week of December 1941 had been heavy with work on *Now, Voyager,* and Wallis decided to seek a little rest and relaxation on the weekend. His friend Michael Curtiz had invited him to spend a few hours on the Curtiz ranch to get away from his business problems and vent his frustrations on a favorite sport, skeet shooting. Two other Warner luminaries, Mr. and Mrs. George Brent (she was the glamorous Ann Sheridan), would also be present for the relaxed get-together.

It was John Meredith Lucas, Mike Curtiz' stepson, who broke the startling news that ended the party: The Japanese had attacked Pearl Harbor in the Hawaiian Islands. The moment that the American nation had been dreading for months had arrived—in a way that precious few of its 131,669,275 citizens could have anticipated. The skeet shooting on the Curtiz ranch was immediately abandoned in favor of the radio reports of the deadly shooting some 3,000 miles away.

On Monday morning, December 8, normal production was halted at Warner Brothers. Workers in the sound stages, editing and makeup rooms, scenery docks, and myriad administrative offices joined their fellow Americans in clustering around radio sets to listen to the broadcast of President Franklin D. Roosevelt in his address to a joint session of Congress. Describing the Japanese sneak attack as a "stab in the back," the President asked the legislative branch of government for a formal declaration of war. His proposal was quickly ratified, and the United States of America became a country unified as never before. Americans were faced with a stern test of their collective courage in the most destructive life-and-death struggle the world has ever known.

It's ironic that *Casablanca,* by far the most popular of all World War II movies, began its cinematic birth process on the day that FDR asked for his declaration of war. A reader named Stephen Karnot, sobered by the Roosevelt speech, returned to his cubicle in the Warner Brothers story department in Burbank and began to sort through a pile of novels, short stories, and other manuscripts until a neatly typed, bulky package caught his eye. The title page informed him that he was holding *Everybody Comes to Rick's*—a play in three acts by Murray Burnett and Joan Alison. The title made it sound like a pleasant divertissement, and, besides, the play's literary agent, Anne Watkins, had a good reputation. So Karnot decided to plunge in and see what *Everybody Comes to Rick's* had to offer.

Reading, along with an ability to write an honest synopsis of what he had read, was Karnot's profession. He was one of several people in the Warner story department to whom agents, budding screenwriters, and others sent all manner of material either proposed or already purchased as source material for Warner Brothers films. His reports, pro or con, were then passed on to the Warner producers for further consideration.

When he finished the manuscript, Karnot liked what he had read. He quickly sent his report to Jack Warner and the W.B. producers, including Hal Wallis. In light of the unusual success of *Casablanca,* it is worthwhile to study the reader's report of *Everybody Comes to Rick's.* The report was headed by the notations that the play had been received from the New York office on December 8 and the report had been written by Karnot on December 11. It was given to Hal Wallis the same day.

Karnot felt that the central character in the play was a man named Rick Blaine who owned Rick's Café in Casablanca, French Morocco. Rick was something of a man of mystery to his patrons who were refugees, wealthy French expatriots, and officers of the Vichy French, German, and Italian military forces. An American citizen, Rick seemed cynically indifferent to the swirling political tides around him and maintained a policy of strict neutrality within his Café. His only intimates were Sam, his devoted Negro entertainer, and Captain Rinaldo, the French prefect of police. Rinaldo knew of Rick's background as a famous criminal lawyer in Paris who had taken up a life of exile in Casablanca after being divorced from his wife and children in 1939. Only Sam knew that Rick's bitterness was actually the result of another broken love affair.

The play opened with a scene between Rick and a character named Ugarte who made a living by selling stolen exit visas. Ugarte asked Rick to help him in his own plan to escape Casablanca. He urged Rick to take temporary custody of two priceless letters of transit which had been signed by General Weygand. Rick reluctantly agreed to do so and Ugarte exited just before the arrival of Rinaldo who was accompanied by a Gestapo agent named Strasser. Strasser had come to Casablanca in an attempt to stop the escape of a wealthy Czech underground leader named Victor Laszlo. Strasser was especially fearful that Laszlo would get his hands on the stolen letters of transit. As Ugarte was leaving Rick, he was arrested for being in secret possession of the letters and was led away.

Karnot did not go into great detail on the rest of the play's plot in his short report, but he did stress that the scene following Ugarte's arrest was an important one. Victor Laszlo arrived at the Café accompanied by a beautiful woman named Lois Meredith. Karnot wrote that Rick was visibly shaken by the arrival of the woman and that their casual greeting did little to betray an apparently close relationship sometime in the past. Strasser told Laszlo that unless he were to sign over his fortune to the Nazis, he would never be allowed to leave Casablanca.

In the next scene, as described by Karnot, the audience was told of the former love affair between Rick and Lois Meredith. Sam warned Rick that he could not allow himself to get involved with Lois again, but Rick ignored him and Lois returned to the Café to spend the night with Rick. The following morning, the still-bitter Rick confronted Lois about her relationship with Laszlo. Lois said she admired Laszlo and owed him her loyalty but still desperately loved Rick. She almost persuaded Rick to help Laszlo until Rinaldo arrived and convinced Rick that Lois was only playing him for a sucker, whereupon Rick exploded and violently rejected her.

Writing tersely, Karnot skipped over much of the detail of the Rick-Lois love affair as he continued to outline the plot of the play. Rick was told by Rinaldo that Ugarte had committed suicide. Rinaldo suspected that Rick had the letters of transit, but Rick was able to distract him.

Two new characters, young refugees Jan and Annina Viereck, were introduced. The young woman confided in Rick that Rinaldo had agreed to provide Jan with an exit visa if Annina would go to bed with Rinaldo. Annina's willingness to sacrifice herself for the safety of her husband pierced Rick's cynicism, and he began to understand Lois' feeling of loyalty for Laszlo. Jan physically attacked Rinaldo when the Frenchman made a pass at Annina, and the lights went off when Rinaldo attempted to arrest Jan. The Vierecks had disappeared when the lights came on again and Rinaldo ordered the Café closed on the suspicion that Rick had hidden the refugees.

Karnot concluded with a brief description of the play's denouement. Rick had hidden the Vierecks and insisted that they remain in his Café until Sam could get tickets for them to leave Casablanca the next morning. Rinaldo returned in the morning with another warning that he would keep the Café closed until the Vierecks were turned over to him. Upon his departure, Lois arrived to tell Rick that she was leaving Laszlo because she wanted to stay with Rick. Rick enlisted her aid in a plan to outsmart Rinaldo and Strasser. He called Rinaldo and asked him to come to the Café to pick up the Vierecks. The Frenchman arrived, interrupting a torrid love scene between Rick and Lois. Rick told Rinaldo that Lois' decision to stay with him had caused him to change his mind about the Vierecks. If Rinaldo would allow the Vierecks to leave with one of the letters of transit, he would use the other one to trap Victor Laszlo. Rinaldo agreed to the new plan and permitted the Vierecks to depart. Rick persuaded Laszlo to come to the Café to receive the other letter, and Rinaldo emerged from hiding to arrest the freedom fighter when he took possession of it.

Rick pulled a gun on Rinaldo and announced that Laszlo and Lois would use the letter of transit to escape Casablanca together. Lois, hitherto unaware of Rick's decision, begged him to reconsider. Aiding them would mean his certain death. But Rick insisted that she accompany Laszlo to freedom. The couple left for the airport while Rick held Rinaldo as hostage. At the end of the play, Rick surrendered to Rinaldo and Strasser as the Laszlo plane was heard taking off for neutral Portugal.

Stephen Karnot's brief synopsis hardly does justice to the intricate characters or sophisticated dialogue of the play script, but his enthusiasm for *Everybody Comes to Rick's* was obvious.

Hastily written and full of typeovers and errors in grammar, the one-page reader's report seemed to Wallis something of a birth announcement. The characters, setting, and story line had definite potential. He immediately asked to read the entire script, and it delighted him even more than the reader's synopsis. He didn't care for the title, but that could be fixed easily. New scenes would be needed to make the play suitable for film and the characters needed fleshing out. But the basic plot was excellent.

Everybody Comes to Rick's, or whatever he decided to call it, had most of the elements Wallis wanted in a movie.

The romantic angle was strong enough to appeal to women, and the political intrigue and action should prove a strong attraction for the potential male audience. More important, it was timely. It dealt with the problems of the world at the moment. With proper handling, it would stress some of the things he wanted to say as a contribution to the war effort.

Stephen Karnot had included some interesting suggestions along with his report, and Wallis kept them in mind as he read the entire script. The reader had added the notation that he considered the play an excellent, timely melodrama with plenty of suspense, psychological and physical conflict, and tight plotting. Karnot felt the role of Rick would be a box office natural for Humphrey Bogart, James Cagney, or George Raft as the offbeat café owner. He also wrote that Mary Astor might be suitable for the role of Lois Meredith.

Wallis couldn't see Cagney in the role of Rick, but he felt he could probably sell Jack Warner on the idea of doing the film with George Raft. Wallis could envision Warner getting excited about the possibilities of another movie with the appeal of *Algiers,* a colorful film which had done great business with Charles Boyer as its star. Before long one of the hottest rumors in Hollywood had Raft and Hedy Lamarr being considered for the leads in a new Wallis production which would be set in North Africa.

Karnot's suggestion of the possible casting of Cagney, Raft, or Mary Astor did not move Wallis, although he saw the reasoning behind a part of the reader's thinking. Wallis and his director had recently teamed Bogart and Astor, with surprising success, in *The Maltese Falcon.* Astor wasn't right for the female lead in *Everybody Comes to Rick's* but Bogart might do very well as the lead male.

There were still many questions in Wallis' mind about the play, and he was eager to hear some other opinions. At the same time he knew that Karnot's synopsis had made the rounds of the other producers' offices. His contract gave him first option on both stars and properties, but he wanted to take no chances on losing this interesting play. It could be transformed into an exciting film property. His message to the Warner story department was brief and to the point—"I want it."

Four

On January 12, 1942, playwrights Murray Burnett and Joan Alison made a happy trip from their New York apartments to the main headquarters of Warner Brothers Pictures on Ninth Avenue on Manhattan's West Side. After many years of devoted work, Burnett and Alison were about to realize some financial reward.

Inside the building they were ushered into a conference room and presented with a sheet of paper headed by the Warner Brothers logo and the legal phrase "Assignment of All Rights." With their agent, the Warner attorneys, and a justice of the peace looking on, the writers scanned the paper quickly. The Warner representative explained that it was a standard contract used in all such negotiations and apologized for the fact that some alterations had been made in the copy, explaining that the appropriate printed form could not be found in the New York office. He had scratched out the printed words "City and County of Los Angeles" and had typed in the correct location—"City and County of New York." Reassured, Burnett and Alison affixed their signatures to the document, which had already been signed by a Warner executive. They watched as the justice signed and notarized the contract, accepted a check for $20,000 from the Warner representative, shook hands, and left the building. From that moment, *Everybody Comes to Rick's* had ceased to exist for all practical purposes. Their work, with additions and revisions, would find its niche in the history of film as *Casablanca.*

It was a most satisfying moment for Murray Burnett and Joan Alison. They were proud of what they had written and, while a bit saddened that it wouldn't debut on Broadway, they were heartened that their faith in it had been justified. It had been purchased by the top people of a major motion-picture studio who had assured them it would get an expert film treatment. They had been further advised that their $20,000 check represented the highest price ever paid for an unproduced play. Burnett and Alison considered it a good beginning on a career that might take them on to the riches of California. Some time later they showed their copy of the contract to a theatrical friend who was far more experienced in the wheeling-and-dealing ways of the movie industry.

"Why in heaven's name would you sign something like this?" the friend asked. "This kind of contract went out with D. W. Griffith. You haven't left yourself any rights at all."

Considering the number of people who loved *Casablanca* when it was originally released and the countless millions who have elevated it to a special status since that time, it is incredible that so few know about the contribution of Murray Burnett and Joan Alison to it. The screen credits read "Play—Murray Burnett and Joan Alison." But screen credits are seldom studied by moviegoers. Many articles have been written through the years concerning the writing problems encountered on *Casablanca,* and they have tended to inspire a legend that the screenwriters created the plot from scratch. But Stephen Karnot's 1941 synopsis of *Everybody Comes to Rick's* clearly reveals that the plot of that play is the sound foundation on which the motion picture *Casablanca* was built.

During the summer of 1938 the play that became *Casablanca* began to form in the romantic mind of Murray Burnett on a trip he and his first wife made to Europe. Still in his twenties, Burnett was always on the lookout for ideas which he could turn into legitimate plays. A devotee of the theater, he hoped to make his mark in it. He had graduated from Cornell University with a degree which gave him the right to teach school in the State of New York and an ambition to win fame as a first-rate Broadway playwright.

For several years Burnett taught at Central Commercial High School in New York City, and he spent much of his free time writing. His vocation and avocation coincided to bring him his first recognition. Steadily employed, Burnett could afford the uncommon New York luxury of owning an automobile, which he used during the summer months to drive out to the Atlantic Beach Club on Long Island. Nearly every day of his vacation was spent soaking up the sun and pondering the involved plotting of what he hoped would be a masterpiece—a play he was writing about his experiences in a vocational high school.

During the course of the summer he struck up a friendship with another member of the beach club, an attractive young lady named Joan Alison who also had a great love for the theater. Alison moved in glamorous social circles far beyond the reach of the young school teacher. The chance meeting proved to be a fortuitous one for both of them. In time, Burnett confided in her that he wanted to become a playwright and that he had nearly finished a play about a vocational school such as the one at which he was employed. He hoped it had Broadway potential, he said, and he planned to call it *An Apple for the Teacher.*

Alison was enthusiastic about Burnett's idea and volunteered some immediate help. One of her longtime friends was a well-known Broadway producer named Delos Chappell. She was certain she could talk him into reading the play and, at the least, giving her friend an honest, professional critique. Burnett wasn't confident the play was ready to be seen by a producer, but at Alison's insistence he hurriedly polished it and gave it to her. Burnett was astonished when Chappell said he liked it and proceeded to option it for a Broadway production.

But the producer warned the two that the play was not yet ready for Broadway and sent them to one of his associates who would help them prepare it for its formal debut. Unfortunately, the three-way collaboration didn't work, the option was dropped, and the play wouldn't reach Broadway for a number of years. Still, Burnett was not depressed. He found strong support in his friend Joan Alison, who had nurtured his ambition and given him his first taste of success. They agreed to continue their collaboration on future projects.

The responsibilities of Burnett's marriage kept him at his teaching job despite his reinforced dream of life as a Broadway playwright. Like most Americans, he kept a wary eye on the worrisome developments in Europe. Adolf Hitler threatened and thundered while the British and French seemed to be trying their best to ignore him. On March 11, 1938, Hitler proclaimed his infamous *Anschluss* and sent his troops and panzer divisions across the border into Austria in a virtually bloodless coup.

Mrs. Burnett's stepfather lived in Antwerp, Belgium, and she became increasingly anxious about him and his family. Since a wider war seemed inevitable, she wondered if she would ever see them again. Burnett's steady employment made a vacation in Europe financially feasible before the entire continent went up in flames. The school term ended in June, and the Burnetts decided to spend part of the summer of 1938 in Europe. After a short visit with their Belgian relatives, they would head for the south of France and its fabled fun and games—while they were still available. That trip to Europe would provide the stimulus for many of the colorful events and characters preserved on the film reels of *Casablanca.*

Burnett was shocked to find his wife's Belgian relatives almost totally unconcerned about the prospect of war in their part of Europe. Although in less than eighteen months they would be forced to walk from Antwerp to the Mediterranean in their attempt to flee from the Nazi *Blitzkreig,* in the early summer of 1938 they were only concerned about other family members who lived in Vienna. Knowing that the Burnetts were heading for the south of France, they begged them to reroute their trip to check on the welfare of relatives living under the Nazi regime in Austria. The Burnetts agreed to delay their holiday on the Riviera.

The stay in Vienna proved to be one of the most profound experiences of Murray Burnett's life. Conditions were even worse than he had expected. Jews, Christian ministers, intellectuals, artists—anyone with any reason to oppose Nazi policy—found themselves face-to-face with the grim realities of the "New Order." Burnett met a new breed of people in Vienna—ordinary men and women who were about to become "stateless individuals"—refugees. They were no longer welcome in their homeland and were faced with the choice of imprisonment and death or voluntary exile. The latter option would require large measures of courage, luck, and money to make it better than the first. Burnett heard talk about the "refugee trail," a dangerous route that inched its way through the areas controlled by the Nazis and their Italian counterparts, across the Alps and into France. It led from Marseilles to Morocco, back across the Mediterranean to Lisbon and—with luck—to eventual safety and freedom in the United States.

As a writer, Burnett had always followed the dictum "Write about what you know!" That advice had prompted his first play about teaching in a vocational school. In Vienna, getting an up-close look at the Nazis and the refugees, he became emotionally saturated with the drama of the situation. Fate had brought him into contact with a powerful subject for a play, and he made a silent vow to put it down on paper when he got back to the States.

Satisfied that they had done the little in their power to aid and comfort their new friends in Vienna, Burnett and his wife traveled on to France to begin the vacation that had brought them to Europe. They were stunned again by the complacency evident in western Europe. The French seemed utterly confident in the strength of their vaunted Maginot Line. They evinced little worry, let alone fear, about the ranting Nazi leader who had arrogantly annexed Austria to his German empire.

In the south of France it was business as usual. The Riviera was still the playground of all nationalities. War seemed the least likely thought in the minds of the pleasure-seeking international set. Murray was deeply disturbed by the dichotomy of time and place, but he was also determined to make his vacation as pleasant as possible after the sobering trip to Vienna. The Burnetts were ready for days of sunshine and nights of romance.

An enthusiastic fan of popular music, Burnett was

delighted when a fellow vacationer told him of a small café on a back street of the resort town overlooking the Mediterranean. It was described as a different sort of place because it featured a black entertainer who played piano and sang popular American songs. The café proved to be even more interesting than Burnett had expected. The ambience was intriguing with its mixture of nationalities and personalities, and the black performer and his music were enjoyable.

With his writer's mind, Burnett drank in the entire scene. He realized that he and his fellow revelers were sitting on the edge of the abyss. Yet, inside the café, all seemed normal. All around him people were drinking and laughing and chattering away in a variety of tongues, while all of Europe was in imminent danger of being overrun by the Nazis. Even the entertainment seemed unreal. He found himself speculating on the possible reasons why an American Negro would be entertaining in such a place. How had he found his way from the States to this bar on the shore of the Mediterranean?

Burnett turned to his wife and said, "You know, this would make a really terrific setting for a play!" He filed the thought away for future use. It didn't particularly fit in with the play he was already beginning to formulate in his mind.

When he returned to New York, he quickly contacted Joan Alison and told her of his experiences in Europe and his determination to write a play on the Nazi menace. Deciding that a spy-thriller would be the suitable form for a play that would strongly condemn the Nazis and entertain the audience at the same time, they began work that focused on a million-dollar collection taken up by the pro-Nazi German-American Bund. They included the mysterious death of a female courier, a beautiful and heroic look-alike to replace her, and a frantic counter-intelligence effort to keep the money out of Nazi hands. When they took the play to Otto Preminger, he immediately optioned it on the condition that they follow his suggestions in their rewrite.

Preminger, who would later achieve fame as the sadistic bully wearing the black Gestapo uniform in a number of World War II films, was strongly anti-Nazi and eager to produce the Burnett–Alison play. Never known for an overabundance of patience, the director would grow angry when his playwrights began to stray from the point in their story conferences. The writers became increasingly interested in telling him about the idea they had for another play about romance and refugees, set in an interesting bar somewhere in Europe. Burnett had finally found a way to use that "terrific setting" he had discovered in the south of France.

"Don't tell me about a play I don't own!" Preminger would shout. "I want to hear about the play I own!"

The Preminger play, called *A Million to One,* was never produced, its strong anti-Nazi stance contributing to its downfall as a Broadway production. Burton K. Wheeler was a powerful figure in the U.S. Congress immediately prior to this country's entry into World War II and a leading spokesman for a conservative movement which operated under the slogan "America First." The Wheeler Committee of Congress exerted a strong influence over all areas of the media. With the country officially neutral, the committee served as a watchdog group to prevent any militant anti-Nazi propaganda from possibly drawing the United States into armed conflict with the military forces of Hitler and Mussolini. Burnett claims that Preminger shelved *A Million to One* in the face of pressure from the Wheeler Committee.

Burnett and Alison had no time to be upset by their second failure to get a Broadway production of their work. They were eager to begin work on a new play dealing directly with the problems of refugees, centered in a café such as the one Burnett had visited in the south of France. France had already fallen to the Germans, and Burnett decided to move the action elsewhere. Casablanca had been one of the major stops on the refugee trail he had heard about in Vienna. That city was now controlled by the so-called "Vichy French," who had agreed to an enforced alliance with Germany. It was the last stop on the way to Lisbon and eventual escape from the Nazis. Burnett knew Casablanca would be crowded with refugees. Although officially a port of unoccupied France, the city was likely to have plenty of Germans and Italians paying calls on officials of their French puppet-state. It had to be boiling with intrigue. Casablanca was the perfect setting.

The playwrights had already settled on the idea of an expatriate American—mysterious and cynical—as the owner of the bar. His closest friend would be a black American entertainer, modeled on the one Burnett had seen in the south of France. The American, Rick Blaine, would be in Casablanca because he was running away from a broken love affair and any other intriguing secrets they could work into the story. Perhaps Rick's long-lost love could show up at the bar seeking a way to escape to Lisbon. That would furnish the romantic angle of the plot and also bring in the plight of the refugees and the eventual reformation of the hero.

With this idea in mind, Burnett and Alison started work on the play they wanted to call *Everybody Comes to Rick's* in the summer of 1940 at the Alison apartment on West 54th Street in Manhattan. It had been two years since Burnett's European trip, but the sights he had seen and the things he had learned were fresh in his mind. Having worked out the basic plot, they began the actual writing with Burnett manning the typewriter. He had written only a few pages when he discovered that he had worked himself into a corner. He had been working on a scene in which a character named Ugarte tells Rick that he's in the business of peddling illegal exit visas. Burnett and Alison had invented the "exit visa" and had no idea that any such document even existed. If it did exist, Burnett realized it might be as easy for a minor Vichy official to cancel as an ordinary visa. A much more important kind of document was needed which Ugarte could leave in Rick's care.

One of Joan Alison's favorite ploys to combat writer's block was an exuberant "Let's go shopping!" On the occasion of the "exit visa block," Alison shepherded Burnett to Fifth Avenue and the swank salons of Bergdorf Goodman, one of the most exclusive stores in the nation. Neither of them could afford to purchase any of the high-priced merchandise on display, but that fact didn't deter Alison. Burnett was dumbfounded when Joan swept into the place with the air of an old and favored customer and began trying on expensive coats with solicitous aid from a senior saleswoman. When Alison eventually modeled an outrageously expensive camel's-hair number, Murray, determined to see how far she would go with her charade, said, "I think it's beautiful and you should buy it."

Without missing a beat, Alison said she would take the coat in a turquoise color. The clerk apologized because

40

she didn't have that exact shade in stock. Could she try to order it for her? Alison, with a voice filled with sorrow, said she needed the coat for that evening and would be forced to try another store. The incident lifted their spirits. If they could improvise such an elaborately successful scene in Bergdorf's, they should be able to solve the problem of the mythical "exit visas."

By the time they reached Joan's apartment, Burnett and Alison had invented the device which was to become the focal point of their play and the motion picture that would be adapted from it. Ugarte would steal two "letters of transit," personally signed by General Weygand—they would fall into the possession of their hero—and he would spend the rest of the play trying to decide what to do with them. The "exit visas" and the "letters of transit" were strictly products of the fertile imaginations of Burnett and Alison, and nobody in New York or Hollywood ever challenged them about the existence of such documents in Casablanca or any other Axis-controlled territory.

Burnett's trip to Europe had inspired the theme and setting for the play, and he went even farther back in his memory to produce something which would become the eventual trademark of the motion picture *Casablanca*. While still an undergraduate at Cornell, Burnett bought a recording of a song which had been introduced by a performer named Frances Williams in a Broadway revue called *Everybody's Welcome*. Burnett never saw the show, but he fell madly in love with the song, whose poignant melody and lyrics seemed to him an appropriate and timeless philosophy on the mysteries of love. Written by Herman Hupfeld back in 1931, it had never become a popular hit, but Murray felt "As Time Goes By" deserved another hearing in his new play. It could be sung by the hero's black friend to set the mood for the bittersweet reunion of Rick and his former paramour. It could be "their song." Murray wrote it into the first act of *Everybody Comes to Rick's*.

Burnett and Alison finished the play in six weeks of daily labor during Burnett's annual vacation from his teaching chores in the summer of 1940. Pleased with the play and convinced it would become a Broadway hit, they soon found

41

an agent who believed in it and who began looking for a buyer. The agent, Anne Watkins, found one in a relatively short time, and the play was optioned for Broadway by the producing firm of Martin Gabel and Carly Wharton.

Wharton and Gabel liked the play, but were concerned because the young playwrights had no real Broadway credits. They asked Burnett and Alison for permission to show it to some better-established writers who might be willing to offer constructive suggestions. If they could persuade a "name" author to come in on the collaboration, the producers felt the play would be an assured hit when it opened. Alison and Burnett agreed to the arrangement. A number of well-known playwrights, including Ben Hecht and Robert Sherwood, were approached. All delivered the same opinion: "The play doesn't really need a major rewrite."

The indecision about a Broadway production went on for months and reached a crisis when Carly Wharton spelled out another serious reservation she had about the play. She did not consider herself in any way narrow-minded or prudish, but she could not believe that a theater audience was ready to accept the contention that the heroine would be willing to sleep with the hero to gain possession of the letters of transit. When Burnett and Alison were unwilling to make such an important change in their plot, the option was dropped.

For the third time the playwrights' attempt to get a Broadway production of one of their plays had come a cropper—but they refused to give up. They knew the play had style and substance. Burnett and Alison were willing to listen when their agent came up with an entirely new suggestion. Anne Watkins told them, "The play is excellent movie material. Why not try to sell it to Hollywood where the real money is?" The playwrights agreed.

Joan Alison called Murray Burnett in early January 1942 to tell him that Anne Watkins had told her that Warner Brothers was prepared to pay $20,000 for *Everybody Comes to Rick's*. Burnett had grown weary of the constant squabbling about a possible Broadway production and told his partner, "Take it!"

Although he was busy with the filming of *Now, Voyager* at Warners, Hal Wallis was deeply committed to the production of *Casablanca* well before Burnett and Alison signed their contract on January 12. He had sought the opinion of many people on the lot concerning the pros and cons of *Everybody Comes to Rick's.* Several of them simply dismissed it as so much sentimental, romantic junk. But the romanticism of the piece, its colorful background and characters, and the timeliness of its theme were the very elements that Wallis liked. With careful planning, those elements would make it a fine commercial movie.

Everybody Comes to Rick's had been a one-set play with all the action taking place in Rick's Café. The director would have to take the camera out into "the streets of Casablanca" to show the audience the colorful bazaars, the crowds of refugees, and the ominous presence of the Vichy and German troops. The play could do little more than hint at such things. He felt the basic plot—the love interest, the struggle of the refugees to get from Casablanca to Lisbon, and most of the other intrigue—was fine, as far as it went, but it had to be expanded and heightened.

Wallis also liked most of the characters written by Burnett and Alison. Many of the roles in the play could have been written with Warner Brothers' actors in mind, especially the character parts. His confidence grew as he began casting the film in his mind. With the director he wanted, his new project could be transformed into an entertaining motion picture. But first it would have to be rewritten for film.

The style of *Everybody Comes to Rick's* was unusually sophisticated for an unproduced play. The original dialogue contrasted nicely with the somber background of the plot, and Wallis felt that style should be retained and improved. The brother team of Julius and Philip Epstein were respected writers on the Warner Brothers lot. Their dialogue had brightened the three big Warner successes which began with *Four Daughters* in 1938 and carried on into *Daughters Courageous* and *Four Wives* in 1939. Among their other credits were *The Big Broadcast of 1936, The Man Who Came to Dinner,* and *The Strawberry Blonde.*

Wallis felt the Epsteins' witty writing style would go well with *Rick's,* and he sent them a copy of Karnot's reader's report soon after he had received it. The brothers echoed

Wallis' enthusiasm about the play synopsis and asked to see the full script as soon as Wallis had finished reading it. The Epsteins became more excited about the play's potential when Wallis told them he wanted it written to encompass the styles of Humphrey Bogart and Ingrid Bergman in the leading roles.

Wallis wanted the Epsteins to write the *Casablanca* screenplay, but a major problem stood in the way. The brothers had already made a committment to begin work on another project outside of the studio, and they were obliged to honor the earlier agreement for patriotic as well as professional reasons. It was imperative that they leave for Washington, D.C., in mid-January to begin work on the film series *Why We Fight.* The War Department had asked Frank Capra to do the series as an important part of the motion-picture industry's contribution to the war effort, and the Epsteins had agreed to write it.

Wallis' persuasive powers and their own desire to work on *Casablanca* caused them to reach a compromise solution. The picture couldn't go into production for many months; if Wallis would assign them to the project, they would take a copy of the play script with them to Washington and work on it in every spare moment they had away from *Why We Fight.* Wallis agreed to the unusual arrangement and moved on to other areas of pre-production planning.

The producer knew that his next step could be the most important one he would make in transforming the play he had bought into a successful motion picture. It was absolutely vital to secure the services of the best possible director.

Five

Michael Curtiz was Hal Wallis' first and only choice as director of the forthcoming film which he had decided to call *Casablanca.* Wallis and Curtiz were close friends, and neither of them had a wide circle of intimates. They shared a passion for their work, and even the workaholic Wallis viewed Curtiz as "tireless." He was continuously awed by Curtiz' first question when he had worked himself to the point of exhaustion to finish a picture—"When do we start shooting the new one?"

The Wallis-Curtiz friendship was based on several other shared interests, particularly their love of art. Both were voracious readers who believed that devouring knowledge about all forms of art could only improve their expertise as filmmakers. And each shared the belief that motion pictures were not the "bastard children" of the legitimate stage. The producer and the director were firm in their convictions that the still-young film medium, with its bigger canvas and more modern technology, was capable of surpassing the legitimate theater in its ability to elevate the dramatic arts.

Still conscious of the dangers inherent in his role as an independent producer at Warners, Hal Wallis wanted Curtiz to direct his new project for another important reason. Wallis knew, as did Jack L. Warner and every producer on the lot, that Curtiz was a perfectionist who would go to any length to make the best picture possible while staying within the budget and "bringing it in on time." It is quite possible that Curtiz had the most secure position in the Warner organization. Less competent Warner employees liked to explain Curtiz' enviable status by quoting one of the widely circulated inside jokes of the time: "He's the only man on the lot who never makes sarcastic remarks about Jack Warner." Curtiz enjoyed his unusual job security because Jack Warner was well aware of the value of the dollar. Warner had the Curtiz autograph on a long-term contract, and he knew that every studio head in Hollywood would be knocking on Curtiz' door if the director ever broke away. Curtiz was the living embodiment of the ultimate line of show business praise: "He's a *pro!*"

The Curtiz route to the glitter of Hollywood was a circuitous one, like that of many of his directorial peers. He was born in Budapest, Hungary, on Christmas Eve, 1892. His father (a carpenter) and his mother ("She had operatic ambitions") produced a family of four girls and three sons in addition to young Mihaly Kertesz. The family's poverty during his childhood, which prompted them to move to Vienna when he was fourteen, held lifelong memories for Curtiz.

Still a boy, Michael Curtiz made his entry into show business by appearing as a supernumerary in mob scenes on stage in a number of theaters in Vienna. He would later admit to a "terrific ambition to overcome poverty," and it was the coins he earned rather than the glory that interested him. However, his early introduction to the business prompted him at the age of sixteen to join a traveling circus, where he mastered the trampoline. He toured Europe with the circus for nearly three years before deciding that his real future was destined for a higher level in the business of performing and performances. He invested a large part of his circus savings into study courses at the Austro-Hungarian Royal Academy of Theatre and Art and eventually was able to find jobs as an actor in both classical and contemporary dramas in companies in Budapest and other major European cities.

Curtiz' introduction to the world of movies came with the fledgling film industry of his native Hungary. The job paid him the equivalent of less than fifty dollars a week, and the young Curtiz found the new acting medium less satisfying than his work in front of a live audience. The film company gave the arrogant young actor another challenge. Curtiz told an interviewer in the late 1940s, "I go with primitive company. This time for me motion picture was sideshow. Also, is not here in studio man who tells actors the geography. So, I help out so actor shouldn't bump to each other."

In his garbled English, which became as legendary as that of Sam Goldwyn, Curtiz was attempting to tell the interviewer about his very first job as a film director. By Curtiz' reckoning, the time was somewhere around 1912 or 1913. While his dramatic soul longed for acting roles on the stage, economic necessity and his insatiable intellectual curiosity caused him to become more and more "intrigued from this new business."

He decided to expand his knowledge of movie making. Film acting didn't appease his artistic thirst, but the process of "telling the actors the geography" had been stimulating. He learned that directing good moving pictures could be a satisfying and lucrative profession. From all he had heard, the finest director in all of Europe was Sweden's Joseph Sistrom, who was employed by the Swenska Biograph Studio, and Curtiz traveled from Hungary to Sweden to confront him. The pioneer filmmaker was taken with the energetic young man and made him an assistant before promoting him to the status of full director by mid-1914.

World War I broke out in Middle Europe, Curtiz' home territory, just as he was beginning to achieve some stature in the Swedish film industry. Curtiz hurried home and enlisted in the mounted Austro-Hungarian artillery. A powerfully built young man and a daring horseman, Curtiz served gallantly for three years on the Russian front until he was relieved from combat duty because of serious battle wounds. He was then assigned to a unit which became one of the first in history to make war propaganda films. The Communist revolution ended his military service, and he returned to his pre-war interest in films.

He worked for two years at the famous UFA Studios in Berlin, where he met two other directors, Ernst Lubitsch and Fritz Lang. All three men would later follow the greenback trail for illustrious careers in Hollywood. Curtiz continued to develop as a director at studios all over Europe, including Sascha Films in Budapest, Cinema Eclair in Paris, and the Torino facilities in Italy. He returned for a period to UFA and also directed pictures for Gaumont British in London.

It was the era of the silent picture, and Curtiz became a master of the visual. He was particularly adept at managing the huge crowds of extras in action and Biblical epics. That talent would bring him to the attention of Warner Brothers. The specific film that interested his future employers was never released in America, according to Jack Warner. Warner accused Famous Players Lasky of buying the Curtiz picture and locking it away in the Paramount vaults to keep it from competing with Cecil B. De Mille's silent production built around the story of the Ten Commandments. The Curtiz film, titled *Moon of Israel,* was based on the same theme.

Harry Warner, the president of Warner Brothers, had taken a trip to Europe in 1926 and visited the set where Curtiz was completing *Moon of Israel.* He had never heard of the Hungarian director, but he was mightily impressed with his work. He advised brother Jack to find a copy of the film to see if he agreed that Curtiz would be a worthy addition to the growing Warner stable of talent. Jack Warner liked what he saw and signed Curtiz to a long-term Warner contract with a starting salary of $180 per week. The money was more than Curtiz was making in Europe, and it was a bargain for the Warners. Needless to say, they held onto all the inevitable options.

In his autobiography, *My First Hundred Years in Hollywood,* published by Random House in 1964, Warner wrote,

Harry promised Curtiz press conferences and a gala reception in New York, and instructed him to memorize a short speech in English. As the steamer slid up the Hudson River to the dock there were fireboats hurling spears of water high above the ship, there was a band playing martial music on shore, and the sky was on fire with Roman candles and bursting rockets. Mike was so overcome that he wept.

"Ah, thees America!" he cried. "Vot a vunderful velcome for the great Michael Curtiz. Und these Varner Brothers! I luff all five at vunce!"

Warner went on to write that Harry corrected Mike on the proper number of brothers in the Warner family but never had the heart to tell the recent immigrant that the reception wasn't entirely in his honor. Curtiz' arrival in America had accidentally happened to coincide with his new country's annual birthday celebration, the Fourth of July.

Nearly everyone who knew the late Michael Curtiz agrees that enthusiasm, unlimited energy, and an uncompromising desire for perfection were the key ingredients in his directorial greatness. He had arrived with very little knowledge of American society and would never be completely comfortable with the language. Yet, he managed to overcome these disadvantages through his drive and dedication. He was incapable of approaching any task in a half-hearted manner. He had to *know!* His description of the director's rights and responsibilities was pure: "He shouldn't interfere with the work of others, but he should be the final judge of rightness."

To ensure that he was fit to be "the final judge of rightness," Curtiz sometimes went to extreme lengths to do his homework. One of his earliest assignments at Warner Brothers was one of that studio's gangster films. Curtiz had little knowledge of the true nature of his subject matter, and he was not content to simply ask for a technical adviser to help him on the film. Long before the scheduled shooting date, the director began spending a great deal of time in the courtrooms and the office of the Los Angeles district attorney. He also got permission to pose as a common criminal and serve a week behind bars in order to get the real feel of the experience he hoped to depict accurately on the big screen.

Similarly, the boy from Budapest became an expert on the history of Texas. To prepare himself to direct a Western film set in the Lone Star State, he read every book he could find on the Texas of the period. By the time the cameras were ready to roll, he knew more than most Texans about the customs, costumes, and details of everyday life in the frontier era of that state. His critics would decry his brusque manner and his occasional inability to communicate with his stars, but his grasp of the filmed subject matter was second to none.

Michael Curtiz wasn't afforded the luxury of a "breaking-in period." The Warners had paid for his talent, and they expected him to go to work immediately. They showed little concern about the possibility of any "culture shock" he might suffer. Curtiz' passion for learning helped to ease the way.

The Warner investment in Michael Curtiz paid off quickly with the 1928 release of *Noah's Ark.* Curtiz immediately demonstrated his imagination and screen sophistication in the story which utilized parallel plots between World War I and Biblical times. *Noah's Ark* also used the new Warner Vitaphone sound system in several scenes of dialogue. The Warners were so impressed they decided to assign their imported director to a full-length talking picture with Al Jolson, star of the first talkie. The picture was *Mammy,* made in 1930, and it became Curtiz' first box-office hit. One of the first films shot with sound and color, several of its production numbers, set in a touring minstrel show, were filmed in two-tone Technicolor.

Curtiz proved to be the perfect director for the brothers Warner. He was talented, and he loved to work. Jack Warner and his brothers kept him in that joyous state by assigning him to direct the incredible total of forty-four Warner features between 1930 and 1939. Many of the forty-four were important only because they kept the WB cash registers jingling, but others have withstood the test of time and remain entertaining, well-made films.

The versatility of Michael Curtiz proved to be a valuable asset within the framework of the old studio system. There seemed to be no subject matter that he wasn't capable of tackling. He loved to work at a frantic pace and turned out feature after feature in as little time as possible. Curtiz seemed equally at home with musicals, comedies, domestic films, melodramas, and even Westerns. He was the first director to shoot an all-color horror film, *The Mystery of the Wax Museum,* in1933, and in the same year he directed Spencer Tracy and Bette Davis in *20,000 Years in Sing Sing.* A year earlier he had introduced Davis in her first notable portrayal of a sweet-talking, evil-minded Southern belle in *Cabin in the Cotton.*

Much of Curtiz' output in the early 1930s, consistent with Warner Brothers' policy, was second-rate because of time-and-budget limitations. Still, his directorial filmology illustrates his startling versatility. In 1933, he did films concerned with a husband who suspects his wife of infidelity *(The Keyhole)*, a government agent who falls in love with the woman he is supposed to investigate *(Private Detective 62)*, an amusing romantic triangle in literary circles *(Goodbye Again)*, a Philo Vance mystery *(The Kennel Murder Case)*, and even an early career-woman story called *Female*.

In 1934, with America still deep in economic depression, Warner Brothers decided to direct the public's attention away from their monetary problems by sending Mike Curtiz on an "international" journey. Never leaving the Burbank sound stages, Curtiz directed *Mandalay, British Agent,* and a film called *The Key*. In *The Key* William Powell played a member of the infamous British Black and Tans who used terror tactics in attempting to quell the Irish quest for freedom following World War I. It was also in 1934 that Curtiz directed James Cagney in a memorable farce called *Jimmy the Gent.*

By the mid-1930s, products directed by Michael Curtiz were very successful at the box office, and he was moved to a special status on the Warner lot. Other directors were assigned the tasks of grinding out the standard, seven-reel melodramas of the period, while Curtiz was saved for more important projects. His films would feature the biggest names on the studio's roster of stars. Curtiz had been in the country less than ten years when he was handed the directorial reins for a 1935 film called *Black Fury*. One of the early Warner films which attempted to point out evils in the current American social system, *Black Fury* starred Paul Muni as a coal miner fighting the strong-armed hoodlums the companies imported to break up justifiable strikes over labor grievances. Jack Warner, who considered Muni to be possibly America's best actor, was proud of his role in casting Muni in the picture.

Curtiz, the perfectionist, did not necessarily agree with Muni's style of acting. To him, Muni was larger than life—passable on the stage but not compatible with the super-realism Curtiz wanted for the film. Again and again the director tried to persuade the star to hold himself in check—

but Muni had a mind of his own. Finally, Curtiz exploded in anger and accused the actor of being a "ham." Muni reminded the director that he undoubtedly knew as much about performing as Curtiz did since Muni had already spent thirty years on the stage. The Curtiz comeback was simple and beautifully articulated. "That," he said, "is the trouble, Mr. Muni."

In 1935 the first of a number of films was produced that came close to labeling Michael Curtiz an "action director." Jack Warner had made a trip to London where he met an extremely handsome, debonair young extra on an English film. Having no idea if the man had any acting ability, Warner signed him to a long-term contract because, "He was one of the most handsome men I had ever seen." The good-looking unknown came to America, where he eventually became the box-office king of Warner Brothers Pictures. The unknown was Errol Flynn.

Flynn made his first Warner appearance as a corpse in a Michael Curtiz film and made his actual debut under Curtiz' guidance in *Captain Blood* in 1935. Robert Donat, the British star, had already signed to play the title role but was forced to bow out because of ill health. The cameras were ready to roll and a replacement had to be found in a hurry. Warner, eager to prove he had a fine eye for talent, urged Curtiz to test Flynn for the role. The screen test was phenomenal, Flynn got the part, and the movie became a box-office smash.

Flynn's love interest in the Raphael Sabatini story was played by a young Hal Wallis discovery named Olivia De Havilland. It was the beginning of a legendary and long-lived Hollywood romance—in the purely filmatic sense. Jack Warner would later write that Flynn and De Havilland made so many pictures together that a large portion of the public thought they were actually married. The man greatly responsible for the teaming and the high quality of their work on screen was Michael Curtiz.

Curtiz directed Flynn and De Havilland in a string of big-budget pictures which became huge Warner grossers during the 1930s and early 1940s. The pair drew in the crowds in *The Charge of the Light Brigade* (1936), *Gold Is Where You Find It, The Adventures of Robin Hood,* and

Four's a Crowd (all in 1938). Curtiz was at the helm again when Flynn and De Havilland made *Dodge City* and *The Private Lives of Elizabeth and Essex* in 1939. Bette Davis gave one of her finest performances as Elizabeth I of England in the latter film. Curtiz also teamed Flynn and De Havilland in the successful *Santa Fe Trail* of 1940. During the same period Curtiz' expertise at the action film was furthering Flynn's career, without De Havilland, in the movies *Virginia City, The Sea Hawk,* and *Dive Bomber.*

Curtiz was fast making a name for himself as a director of epics alongside such long-established giants as John Ford and Raoul Walsh. But he was never content to stay in one *milieu.* In between the Flynn adventure films, Curtiz directed such diverse fare as *The Walking Dead* with Boris Karloff in 1936, and in 1938 he directed *Four Daughters* with Claude Rains and the Lane Sisters as well as *Angels with Dirty Faces.* The stars of that picture were Jimmy Cagney and Pat O'Brien, with standout performances by Humphrey Bogart and a collection of young New Yorkers who are known to today's TV addicts as "The Bowery Boys."

Ironically, as time went by, Curtiz would have his most bitter feuds on the Warner lot with the actor he had directed to the pinnacle of popularity. Errol Flynn, a carefree man and a devout individualist, found it more and more difficult to work with the driving Curtiz, who seemed to be totally without a sense of humor. Olivia De Havilland, like Paul Muni before her, also found Curtiz a stern taskmaster and eventually expressed her distaste at the prospect of working with him. Years later she would say that she always thought of him as "an angry man." Bette Davis also complained about his arrogant attitude.

On the set, Curtiz expected his word to be obeyed without argument unless he had great respect for an actor. The finished product, rather than the sensitivity of the actors, mattered most to him. His goals in life, as expressed in his own words, were beautifully simple: "To make the best pictures I can that will give audiences their money's worth; to please myself as much as I can without forgetting that the pleasure of my audiences comes first. Thus only do I think I can make any substantial contribution to the art of motion pictures."

Those goals didn't make working for Curtiz a necessarily comfortable experience for his actors. The director often became so wrapped up in his work that he would forget to call for a lunch break. Those who found it necessary to remind him that they were growing weak from hunger were considered "lunch bums." When reminded of this in later years, he said he deliberately preferred to film important love scenes in the late morning or early afternoon "because when actor is hungry, he is big lover."

When Claude Rains was doing *Four Daughters* with Curtiz, he became so infuriated with the director's constant violation of the prescribed lunch break that he made up his mind to cure him of the abuse in a dramatic fashion. Rains secreted an alarm clock onto the "hot set" and rigged the timer to go off at the standard lunch hour. As Rains had expected, Curtiz ran overtime and the ringing alarm threw a "take" into chaos as cast and crew frantically searched for the source of the noise. In typical dry fashion, Rains finally produced the hidden clock, studied it in mock surprise, and said, "Good Lord, it must be lunch time."

Michael Curtiz' problems with the English language also proved to be a source of confusion to the actors he was trying to direct. He once attempted to persuade Olivia De Havilland to use a more American accent in delivering her lines. Failing to make himself clear, he finally burst out with, "You speak too much from afternoon tea!" On another film he found it impossible to explain to two actors the way he wanted them to play a scene. In desperation he instructed them to watch him and then proceeded to ad-lib their lines in the best grammar at his command. The cast and crew were so befuddled at his reading of the supposed "lines" that they broke into spontaneous laughter, further infuriating the director.

The widely circulated stories about his misuse of the language were a constant source of irritation to him—so much so that he asked a writer, "What are they trying to make from me, a jingle bells?" When another newspaperman once called out to him, "Say something funny, Mr. Curtiz!" the director growled back, "I say something funny all right. I say a three-letter word beginning with 'f.'"

When they were still on friendly terms, Errol Flynn liked to tell his friends about one of Curtiz' amusing language gaffes. Curtiz instructed Flynn, "You are thrilled, excited. Let me see the *tinkle* in your eye!" Incidentally, to Mike Curtiz, Errol Flynn was always "Earl Flint." Jimmy Cagney, flippantly trying to re-create a Curtiz acting demonstration in the Curtiz style, was told, "Don't do it the way I showed you! Do it the way I mean!"

Many years after Curtiz' death, David Niven immortalized one of Curtiz' most famous language errors by using it as the title for his book of anecdotes about his early years in Hollywood. While directing *The Charge of the Light Brigade,* Curtiz decided a dramatic effect in the aftermath of a battle scene would be the appearance of a riderless horse galloping across the frame. His command was the classic "Bring me an empty horse!"

Curtiz' passion for perfection caused him to create other cries of misguided anguish such as, "The next time I send a dumb sum of a beetch, I go myself," and on a noisy set, "Anybody who has any talking to do, please shut up." He once told the trainer of a dog with an important scene in one of his pictures, "No, No! Dog should bark from left to right." And he attempted to calm actors who misunderstood his gruff manner with the line, "Don't be nerwous. I am loud but never wicious."

Despite his gruffness and problems with the language, Curtiz generally got on well with his actors when things were going smoothly. But, to him, they were essentially only figures in the moving landscape he was trying to paint. In times of stress he was not above venting his frustration on the acting company. He found it nearly impossible to relax when he was shooting a picture and deeply resented any off-duty carousing of the cast, especially during location shooting. On one mountain location he arrived ready for work only to find impossible weather conditions. There was a minimum of light, and only a miracle could make it possible for him to shoot any of the scheduled outdoor scenes. He looked at the assembled cast and snarled, "Sums of beetches, you drink and raise hell all night and now God take it out on me."

Curtiz found nearly everything except the business of

filmmaking boring and pointless. He did enjoy skeet shooting and polo, but he seldom set aside much time for the pursuit of either sport. He survived for years on a daily regimen of five hours sleep followed by at least an hour in an icy cold shower. Before going to sleep, he always took a copy of a film script to bed with him.

Hal Wallis liked to tell the story of a dinner party he attended at the Curtiz ranch. Midway through the meal, Curtiz ended the idle conversation by jumping to his feet and demanding that the guests follow suit. He then began rearranging the company and the food on the table. Forming an imaginary viewfinder with his hands, he said triumphantly, "That is from how you should seat!" Bored with the idle chatter, he had been working out a mental picture of a dinner-party scene he was scheduled to shoot the next day. There was a studio rumor that he had once done the same thing to a startled group of strangers on the dining car of the Super Chief on one of his trips back East.

Because of his success as a "workhorse studio director," Curtiz' role as a film innovator was generally overlooked until *Casablanca*. Jack Warner would later credit him with the introduction of the glycerine dissolve—at least at Warner Brothers. That technique involved the spreading of a coat of glycerine over a glass slide in front of the lens to produce, in one example, the point-of-view shot that the subject was seeing the scene through tears. Curtiz' love for film movement also prompted him to pioneer the use of the camera dolly and the zoom shot.

Warner was not always a supporter of Curtiz' use of trick shots with the camera. Curtiz was in the middle of filming his tenth picture for Warner Brothers late in 1929 when Warner made one of his periodic visits to the set. The movie was called *The Gamblers* and concerned the timely topic of unwise financial plunging in the stock market. Frustrated by the locked-in position of a camera on a permanent mount, Curtiz was continually looking for ways to make it become a more integral part of the action. Warner was shocked to see Curtiz, camera, and cameraman all on a moving treadmill-like contraption as the scene was being shot. He angrily demanded that Curtiz cease and desist. Curtiz ignored him. Warner was surprised and happy when he viewed the interesting results of Curtiz' experiment. He ordered all his other directors to study the Curtiz camera technique.

Curtiz' last film before *Casablanca* was the colorful *Yankee Doodle Dandy.* It had almost nothing in common with his next endeavor. *Yankee Doodle Dandy* was a boisterous musical about one of America's most outspoken patriots, while the upcoming *Casablanca* would be a low-key black-and-white film about an American who was not at all sure about the values of patriotism, among other things. The mood, the feel, the entire process of filming *Casablanca* would be different. But Hal Wallis had learned that those differences would pose no unsolvable problems for a man of Michael Curtiz' stature.

There was another reason Hal Wallis wanted Michael Curtiz to direct his new project. With his imaginative film technique, Curtiz would be able to project the plight of the refugees trapped inside the teeming Moroccan port in realistic terms. Curtiz had never lived in Casablanca, but he had been a refugee. In 1919, he had abandoned production on his film version of Ferenc Molnar's *Liliom* (a story Americans would love decades later as the musical *Carousel*) in order to flee his native Hungary during the oppressive Béla Kun regime. Curtiz would have a special affinity for the homeless characters who peopled the plot of *Casablanca.*

A Middle European himself, Curtiz had recognized the probability of all-out war on the continent long before it came. Learning that Jack Warner was planning a trip to Europe in 1938, the director asked him for a favor. Curtiz' family in Budapest had written him about their fears of the pro-Nazi feeling that was growing inside Hungary, and he became more and more worried about their safety. Curtiz had done well in his new country, and he wanted his mother and two brothers to leave Hungary and share in his success.

He gave Warner the money for plane fare for his family and asked the studio chief to call on them at the family home just outside of Budapest. Curtiz had been unable to stir them—perhaps the important American movie mogul could convince them how vital it was to get out of Europe before it was too late. Warner agreed to do the errand, met with the

Kertesz family, and did persuade them to join their famous kinsman in America. Although they had made their escape before Hitler's armored juggernaut rolled into their homeland, now Curtiz' own mother and two brothers were European refugees. He would have no problems empathizing with the refugees in *Casablanca.*

Wallis had talked to Curtiz about *Everybody Comes to Rick's* and his first interest in it shortly after he had finished the script. Curtiz trusted the producer's judgment and was always interested in doing a Wallis project. When copies of the script were reproduced and sent to the various offices at the studio, Curtiz eagerly took his back to "The Grove," his ranch in the Valley, for a good read before going to sleep.

He found it would need additions to make it suitable for the screen, but it would be a good challenge. He liked the character of Rick Blaine—he was tough and complicated and in no way a "standard hero"—and that would strengthen the love story. Curtiz was no romanticist, but he approved of this romance because it was "different." Most of all he loved the setting, the intrigue, and the interesting minor characters. He would like to see more of those refugees.

Curtiz jotted down some ideas to pass on to Wallis. The play, as written, was much too static for film—the mood, the action outside the café, must first be established. In a sense, the play was dated. With America now in the war, the brutality of the Nazis and their Vichy allies should not be soft-pedaled in any way. He would like to use some newsreel footage somewhere to show the real situation the refugees had fled. He thought the menace, the suspense, and the love story offered him an opportunity to create a real mood piece. With some strengthening of the script and careful casting, he could make it a fine motion picture.

Many days later, when discussing the project with Jack Warner, Curtiz told him,"Vell, Jock, the scenario isn't the exact truth—but we have the facts to prove it." Coming from a director who had once said on an earlier picture, "I'm vorried because I'm so optimistic," this was "left-handed" but high praise, indeed.

Six

When Hal Wallis told Jack L. Warner that he wanted to cast Humphrey Bogart opposite Ingrid Bergman in *Casablanca,* Warner was more than a little worried. Warner is supposed to have yelled, "Who the hell would ever want to kiss Bogart?" In his opinion, beautiful young Bergman would be frightened by Bogart rather than attracted to him.

Considering the enduring romantic appeal of *Casablanca* and Bogart's compellingly honest portrayal of its hero, Warner's attitude now seems ludicrous. Of course, that wasn't Warner's first mistake: He also refused to pick up an option on Clark Gable, early in his career, because he thought the actor's ears were too big. Gable escaped the Warner typecasting, but Bogart was mired in it for years. There had been no hint of a breakthrough until 1941, and the frustrating years of "shrugging it off" made him the perfect choice to play Rick Blaine.

Humphrey Bogart had been a "square peg in a round hole" since he arrived in Hollywood in 1936. He was grateful that the studio kept him solvent and allowed him to work at his chosen profession, but he hadn't expected to play the same, one-dimensional role in film after film. He was a serious actor and an intelligent man, and he had no intention of giving up his fight for better roles. He was even more irritated by the role he was expected to play off the screen. Hollywood expected its actors to be model citizens incapable, to the public, of thought, statement, or deed unworthy of the average cloistered nun. There was no way he would agree to that sham.

Bogie liked nothing better than needling the system and all those who took it seriously. He had been a rebel all his life, and he had no intention of ever "going Hollywood." Like the character he would play in *Casablanca,* Bogart had become something of a loner. He had a good-sized circle of intimate friends whose intelligence and talent he respected, but he had no time for the general Hollywood social scene. He had been made a gangster on the screen, but he would be his own kind of outlaw when he wasn't working. The instincts of Hal Wallis told him those qualities would make Bogie very right for the role in *Casablanca.* Jack Warner gave his grudging approval.

The man the movie fans would refer to as "Bogie— the one who plays all the bad guys in the movies" was born with the elegant name of Humphrey DeForest Bogart in New York City on December 25, 1899. There was little in his family background to suggest that he would ever become an actor, especially one who would gain fame by portraying a number of scurrilous gunmen. Humphrey Bogart was the firstborn of Dr. Belmont DeForest Bogart and Maude Humphrey, a socially prominent young married couple with an affluent lifestyle. The Bogarts would be listed in the New York Blue Book of Society from its first edition in 1907 until it ceased publication in the 1930s. Dr. Bogart was a respected physician who had inherited money from his father, and his wife was a successful career woman who earned as much as $40,000 a year as a commercial artist.

Shortly after their marriage, Dr. Bogart and his wife bought an elegant four-story limestone townhouse in what was then one of the most exclusive neighborhoods in Manhattan, 103rd Street off Riverside Drive. The Bogarts also owned a country home in the Finger Lakes area of upstate New York. Each summer they would journey to Canandaigua Lake to escape the heat and humidity of the city. Young

Humphrey's early years would be filled with fine houses, servants, and parties, and he would eventually be joined by two baby sisters.

Dr. Bogart delighted in telling his colleagues that young Humphrey was going to grow up to be a surgeon. He would attend the best prep schools and then matriculate to either Columbia or Yale for his higher education. But fate would seem to push Humphrey Bogart toward a public rather than a private career from the beginning. He got his first taste of wide public adulation long before he was old enough to realize it. His mother did a sketch of him as a baby and sent it off to an advertising agency which sold it to the Mellins Baby Food Company. The sketch was used as the company trademark, and the future actor quickly became the most famous infant in the country as the "Original Maude Humphrey Baby."

Humphrey Bogart's childhood was not a particularly happy one. Outward displays of affection between his parents and their children were rare, and because Dr. Bogart and his wife were both busy with their careers, the task of raising the children was left largely to the domestic help. In time, Mrs. Bogart became the dominant force in the family finances as well as in the marriage itself, and new problems arose. The Bogart children lived in dread of the increasing domestic battles between their parents. Humphrey's happiest moments came when his father closed his office to take him on hunting and fishing outings. When Dr. Bogart's interest in his practice waned, he began to indulge his love for sailing and taught his young son how to handle a sloop by himself by the time he was eight. A passion for sailing would stay with Bogie for the rest of his life.

Although Bogart would earn a deserved reputation in Hollywood as a man who liked nothing better than a no-holds-barred intellectual conversation, he showed little interest in intellectual pursuits as a boy. When he was nearly fourteen, his parents enrolled him in the very proper Trinity School for young gentlemen on 91st Street in Manhattan. The staid Episcopal institution held no attraction for the young Bogart, and he became known as a bored student who was only concerned with the tilt of his black derby hat, playing it "cool," and flaunting authority. With the outbreak of World War I in Europe, the adventures of the moment were far more important to him than the history of the past.

His best friend at the time was William A. Brady, Jr., who lived next door to the Bogart home on 103rd Street. Brady's father was a respected theatrical producer, and one of the few of that breed who were accepted into polite society. Humphrey's fast friendship with the younger Brady gave him an opportunity to investigate the fascinating world of the stage on free passes. Young Bill Brady also shared his love of adventure. The two boys became involved in a series of youthful pranks, sparked by their fascination with the European war, which ended with Bogart being shot in the wrist with a .22 caliber pistol. That dangerous incident prompted Mrs. Bogart to view her young son in a stern new light—a general disapproval that would continue to disturb Humphrey Bogart for years.

Dr. Bogart felt it was high time that young Humphrey was sent away to Phillips Academy at Andover, Massachusetts, in preparation for entrance to Yale and a career in medicine. But the doctor was informed that his son would first be required to repeat his final term at Trinity because of bad grades. When he finally arrived at the academy in 1917, Humphrey Bogart hated it. He found his classmates too bookish and the faculty much too strict. After the fun and freedom of New York, he felt stifled and found it almost impossible to concentrate on his studies. His first report card, which he tried to hide from his parents when he came home at Christmas vacation, showed that he had flatly failed three of the five courses he was taking.

Dr. Bogart was relatively philosophical about the matter and assured his wife that it would simply take time for Humphrey to grow accustomed to the new routine at boarding school. But Mrs. Bogart would tolerate no excuses and heatedly told her son that he must improve his grades immediately. If he didn't, he would be taken out of school and sent to earn his own living.

Neither his father's understanding nor his mother's cold warning produced the desired effect. By February 1918, Humphrey was placed on scholastic probation, and in May he was asked to leave the academy. His faculty advisers saw him as a young man who lacked "serious purpose"—no matter what his other good qualities might be. To Bogart, formal schooling as practiced at Trinity and Andover was a boring waste of time. The world outside was too full of exciting possibilities.

Dr. Bogart quietly put away his long-held dreams for his son, but Mrs. Bogart was livid with anger over Humphrey's "lack of character." She wasted no time in telling him that "from this moment on, you're on your own!" Although he was barely old enough, when Humphrey Bogart enlisted in the United States Navy his parents and his former headmaster at Andover concluded that the military might succeed in teaching the boy responsibility and respect for authority.

The navy succeeded only in strengthening Bogart's distaste for authority. He was in trouble from the beginning to the end of his naval career. While still in boot camp, eager to get "at those French girls" across the Atlantic, Bogart was caught trying to add his name to embarkation orders for sea duty. He weathered that storm and was assigned, after training, as a common seaman on the ship *Leviathan,* which carried troops between Hoboken, Liverpool, and Brest. In a continuing attempt to make contact with the storied girls of France, Bogart was accused of taking an unofficial leave and was sentenced to ten days in the brig. When he insisted on arguing with his captain, the officer extended the sentence to twenty and then thirty days of confinement.

His navy service did have a lasting effect on his physical person and his eventual career. In 1918, shortly before the war came to an end, the *Leviathan* was shelled by a German U-boat during one of its Atlantic crossings. Bogart was at his battle station when a shell burst shattered the wooden deck. A long splinter from the deck flew through the air and pierced his upper lip, leaving a bloody but not dangerous wound. The ship's doctor removed the splinter and stitched the gash closed. It wasn't until later, as the wound was nearly healed, that Bogart realized his upper lip was going to continue to be numb and partially paralyzed. The war wound would give him the grim lipline and speech impediment which caused Jack Warner to decide that Bogie was not "the stuff of which leading men are made."

Bogart was given an honorable discharge after two

years of service and was immediately faced with the same problems he had had before enlisting. Now he was twenty years old, with no constructive ideas of what to do with his future. His father had retreated farther into the background of family life, and his mother began to harangue Bogart anew about his lack of education and training. Bogart took a variety of jobs in the business world, including a stint as a runner for a Wall Street brokerage firm, but the money he earned, little as it was, only served to whet his appetite for the postwar high life in New York.

His return to civilian life coincided with the beginning of the Jazz Age. The Roaring Twenties were coming in on the impetus of the newly enfranchised American woman who was eager to kick off the shackles of Victorianism and kick up her heels. Humphrey Bogart was happy to join the crowd that liked to thumb the nose at the crazy Prohibition law which decreed that "Thou shalt not drink." The boys were home again, the world was at peace, business was booming, and those who could afford it felt they had earned the right to have a good time.

The Bogart family fortune had dwindled seriously and the heir to it was barely able to keep his head above the waters of insolvency during this period. Bogart was determined to enjoy his current freedom, but his strict upbringing eventually forced its way into his consciousness. His mother was right— he had no future. He expressed his worry to his constant companions, William Brady, Jr., and William's half-sister, Alice, who advised him to look for a career in the theater and offered to talk their producer father into starting him on the way. William A. Brady, Sr., was expanding his business, and his son and daughter were sure he would welcome help from the likes of an eager young Humphrey Bogart.

World Films, an independent motion-picture production company, was the latest Brady venture. The Broadway producer had seen the "handwriting on the wall" and decided to buy the company and get in on the ground floor of an exciting new branch of the entertainment industry. He agreed to hire Bogart as an office boy with the promise that he could work himself into a better position if he applied himself. True to his word, the senior Brady gave his son's best friend an incredible promotion in record time.

64

Brady became unhappy with the director he had hired for a picture called *Life.* He fired the man and told Bogart to finish the picture as its director. The jump from office boy to director proved to be too much for the inexperienced Bogart, and Brady finished the film himself. Nonetheless, the lost opportunity was a stimulating experience for Bogart, and it convinced him that he might have a future as a writer for the movies. His first attempt in that capacity also ended in failure, and he went back on the Brady payroll as a $50-per-week stage manager for a Broadway play. He was certain his brief career in the movie business was a mistaken notion that would never trouble him again.

The always unpredictable and sometimes explosive Irish temperament of William A. Brady, Sr., kept Bogart amused, interested, and on his toes. Friendship with Brady's wife, son, and daughter kept the non-conformist employed. Mrs. Brady, actress Grace George, helped him get the job as stage manager for her next play, *The Ruined Lady.* During the run of that play, Humphrey Bogart nearly made his acting debut as a fill-in for a sick actor. His eventual debut came about in a play called *Drifting,* which starred Alice Brady.

The senior Brady was also obviously fond of Bogart. He had watched his young neighbor grow to manhood and was as aware of his weak points as his strong ones. Working together, they developed a love-hate relationship that endured many stormy sessions before Brady was able to point Bogie toward a straight-and-narrow path. During the Atlantic City tryout of *Drifting,* Brady lost his temper and actually gave Bogart a boot in the stomach. Bogie got his revenge by raising the curtain early and embarrassing his boss in front of a full house while he was still on stage giving instructions to the cast. Bogart was summarily fired. It wasn't the first of such blow-ups, but Bogart was quickly forgiven and rehired the next day.

Brady's way of getting even with his cocky employee was even more subtle. Knowing that Bogart delighted in teasing actors about the simple-mindedness of their work, he gave his stage manager one line as a Japanese houseboy and insisted that he appear on stage in full makeup when the play opened at the Fulton Theatre in Brooklyn.

Badly frightened at the idea of appearing on stage "in

front of all those people," Bogart was also determined to show Brady that he couldn't be intimidated. His one-line debut went off without incident. Brady then astounded Bogart by casting him as the juvenile lead in a play titled *Swifty,* starring Neil Hamilton and Frances Howard. Without consciously planning it, Humphrey Bogart was suddenly beginning to earn a living as an actor.

The loud Bogart-Brady war continued throughout the rehearsals of *Swifty.* Brady was an old-fashioned director who didn't believe in pampering actors. Bogart found that Brady's discipline was far tougher than anything he had encountered at Andover or in the Navy. Forced to learn under shouted orders, he became a tangle of nerves as the rehearsals dragged on and finally lost his cool during a run-through of his biggest scene. Brady had him repeat the scene again and again and continued to voice his unhappiness with the results. Bogart, who wanted to do well, tried to calm his nerves and called upon all his reserve energy to play the scene in a feverish display of emotion. He was positive he had finally given a performance that would please his tormentor and looked out into the darkened house to see Brady's reaction. The director was sprawled in his seat, head back, eyes closed, and mouth open—seemingly fast asleep.

That was the final straw! Shouting obscenities, Bogart began rushing toward the auditorium, and Brady jumped to his feet and headed for Bogart. Neil Hamilton and William Brady, Jr., had to physically restrain the actor to keep him from hurling himself at the director. The younger Brady led his friend outside the theater where he could regain his composure. There was no further trouble, but Bogart was so nervous on opening night that he could hardly talk. He actually walked off the stage at one point to get a drink of water, forcing the play's star to try and carry on alone in the important scene.

The reviews, caustically recited to him by his mother the next morning, were disastrous. The play closed shortly after its opening, and Bogart's debut was less than spectacular. The acid-tongued Alexander Woollcott wrote, "The young man who embodies the aforesaid sprig [Bogart] was what might mercifully be described as inadequate."

Early photographs of Bogie bear little resemblance to the world-weary, tough Bogart of *Casablanca* fame. He was an attractive juvenile in the early 1920s, with a ready smile, boyish exuberance, and the slicked down "Valentino" hairdo that was popular at the time. The Broadway stage was flourishing with as many as fifty-one shows in production at one time and there was a need for new faces. Rather than hurting him, Bogart's disappointing introduction as a juvenile actually led to his first success. Producer Rosalie Stewart had seen *Swifty* and thought the young juvenile showed promise except for a bad case of nerves. She contacted Bogart and offered him a role as a newspaperman in her play *Meet the Wife,* which was to star Mary Boland and Clifton Webb. The play became an instant hit and enjoyed a run of thirty weeks.

Under the stormy guidance of William A. Brady, Sr., Humphrey Bogart had finally been steered into a career that offered him the recognition he sought and the wherewithal to revel in the lifestyle he found attractive. He and his friend William Brady, Jr., made it a nightly ritual to visit the best speakeasies and show clubs between Greenwich Village and Harlem. After *Meet the Wife* closed, he continued to work steadily, alternating between acting and stage managing. None of his acting roles were plums, and Bogart would later dismiss them as "tennis anyone" parts—his way of saying they were lightweight characters who only spouted a few lines of innocuous dialogue to fill the gaps between the important scenes of a play.

A play called *Nerves* was the most significant in Bogart's early career. It starred Kenneth MacKenna, Paul Kelly, and Mary Phillips, and was a war play which had the misfortune of showing up at the same time as *What Price Glory?* It closed after a few weeks, but it provided Bogart with his first excellent notices. It also enabled him to meet a girl who would eventually become his wife. The rave reviews convinced Bogart that he had a real future as an actor, but the play's brief run forced him to swallow his pride and return to stage managing a touring production of *Drifting* under William A. Brady, Sr.

Alice Brady was to have played the lead in the road show despite her pregnancy. But her baby threatened to arrive ahead of schedule, and the stage manager was given the added responsibility of preparing another leading lady to take over the role. He enjoyed the work because the new star was a beautiful, red-haired actress named Helen Mencken, who was a few years older than Humphrey and fast on her way to becoming a top-ranking Broadway personality after a life in the theater as child-actress and ingenue. Bogart had more fun cueing her than worrying about maneuvering the intricate eight sets of the play with inadequate rehearsal.

On opening night, the play was a technical disaster. The stage machinery refused to operate properly for Bogie, and some of the sets actually came crashing down during Miss Mencken's biggest scenes. The star marched angrily off stage after the curtain call and furiously lashed into the frustrated stage manager. Bogart quietly gave her a boot in the bottom. Miss Mencken clouted Bogart in return and fled to her dressing room to cry.

That was the beginning of a romantic pattern which was to follow Humphrey Bogart through much of his life. Fascinated by beautiful women who loved a fight, especially if they were actresses, Bogart began a whirlwind courtship of Mencken that saw them taking out a marriage license within a few short weeks. But Bogart, who decided to delay the wedding until he could afford to support her, watched Mencken's career continue to outstrip his. Helen Mencken's star exploded over Broadway when she played the heroine of *Seventh Heaven,* and she became the special darling of public and critics alike.

Still desperately eager to marry Bogart in spite of his so-so success, she encouraged him to give up stage managing in order to concentrate on his career as an actor. Bogart worked for fifteen weeks with Shirley Booth in *Hell's Bells* and found himself out of work again. Attempting to keep up with Mencken's pace only heightened his frustration.

Even at that time his closest friends, other than the Bradys and Helen Mencken, were members of the writing fraternity who shared his passion for witty banter at cozy speakeasies. His writer friends often made him the target of their most pointed barbs, casting amusing aspersions on his apparent incompetency in a thoroughly worthless profession.

He understood the needling—he had dished out his share of it to other actors before he became one—but it inwardly angered him to the point that he became obsessed with a desire to develop better skills and prove his friends wrong.

Mary Boland, furious because a debilitating hangover had caused Bogart to blow some lines in a scene with her in an earlier play, had told him that she would never work with him again. However, she changed her mind and invited him to appear in her new play *The Cradle Snatchers.* It became the longest-running hit of the 1925-26 Broadway season, and Humphrey Bogart's reviews were exceptionally good. One critic wrote: "He is as young and handsome as Valentino and elegant in comedy as E. H. Sothern, as graceful as any of our best actors."

Helen Mencken continued to press him to utilize the marriage license that was collecting dust in her dresser drawer. She was certain that marriage to her would also help his career, and his friends agreed with that appraisal. Though deeply in love, Bogart was still concerned about the problems inherent in marrying an older woman who was also one of the top stars in the business. He gave in on the strength of his long run in *Cradle Snatchers,* and they were married in New York City on May 20, 1926. *Cradle Snatchers* closed a few months later.

The marital problems he had foreseen began quickly. Bogie accepted an opportunity to replace Roger Pryor in the Chicago company of *Saturday's Children,* and because his wife's play had already closed, he expected her to accompany him to the Windy City. She refused, saying she had to remain in New York to prepare for a new play. They tried to patch things up, but the marriage was doomed. At the time Miss Mencken filed for a divorce, they had shared quarters for only a fraction of the year-and-a-half length of their union. She cited his decision to put career ahead of marriage as the reason for the split.

Bogart didn't contest the divorce and refused to talk about his first attempt at marriage. When he came to Broadway with *Saturday's Children,* he found that his writer friends took him a bit more seriously. With Bill Brady, Jr., as his constant companion, he poured himself into one bar after another in an attempt to drown the sorrows of his personal life. Only his closest friends understood that he would be willing to try marriage again, if he could find a girl who would be content to stay at home and be a wife.

His introduction to the wonders of Warner Brothers Pictures coincided with the beginning of his next serious romance. He bought a ticket and watched Al Jolson in Warners' first talkie, *The Jazz Singer,* and afterwards decided to visit some actor friends backstage in a nearby theater. He hadn't expected to meet Mary Phillips, also a member of the cast, with whom he had worked and feuded in *Nerves* a few years earlier. He found her attractive and friendly and invited her to join him for a drink at Sardi's. Bogie felt that Mary seemed far more settled than Helen Mencken, if not quite as beautiful, and their chance meeting quickly turned into a steady relationship. She had a burning ambition to be a better actress and admired Bogart's resolve to improve his own stage technique. He found her sweet and supportive, and she thought of him as "charming and old-fashioned." They were married a year after his divorce became final.

The 28-year-old actor's second marriage seemed perfect. Miss Phillips was in a hit play at the time of the wedding, and Bogart went into the short-lived *Skyrocket* when *Saturday's Children* closed. After *Skyrocket* folded, his old friend Alice Brady helped him land a featured role in her new starring vehicle called *A Most Immoral Lady.* That play enjoyed a run of several months, and when it ended Bogart went into David Belasco's comedy, *It's a Wise Child,* which became the most popular play of the year.

The year 1929 was a productive one for Humphrey Bogart, personally and professionally. It wasn't so rosy for others. *It's a Wise Child* was doing fine business on Broadway, but in lower Manhattan the stock market began to tip perilously. It fell with a thunderous crash in November, prompting *Variety* to headline: "WALL STREET LAYS AN EGG." The stock market crash and the advent of "talking pictures" would combine to change the entertainment industry and the career of Humphrey Bogart.

The crash of the stock market quickly began to affect ticket sales on Broadway and at the local movie theaters.

Already panicked by the sudden rush to switch to sound films, the entire motion-picture industry decided to launch a concerted drive to end the financial drought and lure customers back into the theaters. It was obvious that new blood was needed—on the performing end. The day of the exaggerated leer and the grandiloquent gesture was over. Now movie stars had to be able to act—to talk! Agents of the Warners, the Mayers, the Zukors, and the rest began invading the Broadway hunting ground of those interesting stage actors.

Fox Studios let it be known that its talent scouts were looking for a stage actor to play the lead in a movie called *The Man Who Came Back.* Mary Phillips detested the idea of movie acting, and Bogart preferred the stage, but the New York financial picture was changing rapidly. Bogart asked his brother-in-law, who worked for Fox in New York, to line him up a shot at the part. After several refusals, the Fox people finally agreed to let Bogart test for the film. The results were much better than anyone had expected, and Bogart was offered a contract and train tickets to Hollywood.

Bogart had mixed emotions about this opportunity. It was a decision he had never seriously expected to face. He preferred to stay in New York where he and his wife were both happy, but he had to consider the money Fox was offering. For the first time he would truly be able to support a wife on his income alone. It had been difficult to make ends meet as a stage actor—Fox was offering him $750. With the bleak financial picture in New York, he decided to be practical. Bogart headed home hoping that Mary would agree that their best interests lay in boarding the train for Hollywood.

Mary Phillips was of a different mind. She was in the middle of a long run in a hit play and could get out of it only by breaking her contract. Hollywood might be all right for her husband, but her future was on the Broadway stage. She encouraged Bogart to go ahead with his plans and assured him it would not adversely affect their marriage. They struck a "modern" bargain that he could date other girls during her absence and she would be allowed to be seen in the company of other men. Saddened by his wife's decision, Bogart boarded the westbound train alone, hopeful that all would work out for the best.

His dream was shattered shortly after he arrived in Los Angeles. Several of his New York friends told him they also had been given contracts and brought to California with the idea that they would be playing the lead in *The Man Who Came Back*. The role was finally handed over to silent star Charles Farrell. The whole process didn't make sense to Bogart, and he was further infuriated when he was told he would earn his $750 weekly salary as Farrell's voice coach. Dutifully he did his best to teach Farrell the art of reading lines, but fired off a bitter note to the Fox executives when the film was completed. He told them he hadn't signed their contract with the idea of spending the rest of his life as a vocal coach for stars who couldn't act.

The angry note brought results of a sort, and Bogart was allowed to start his career as a screen actor. Between 1930 and early 1934 he appeared in eleven films, but the roles were primarily small and insignificant juvenile parts that gave him little chance to display his talents or further his career. The two most interesting were in *A Holy Terror* (1931), for which the costume department provided him with shoulder pads and high heels to make him appear bigger for his first cowboy role, and *Three on a Match* (1932), in which he portrayed the first of his many gangsters.

Hollywood couldn't decide what to do with Humphrey Bogart. In their eyes he wasn't handsome enough to be a regular leading man and a box-office draw, and he also wasn't big or "outdoorsy" enough to make it as a standout in cowboy movies. When his option wasn't picked up, Bogart headed east again. The entire Hollywood experience had been unpleasant, and he only hoped he would be able to pick up the threads of his once successful career on the stage.

Back in New York, he discovered that his sojourn in Hollywood had hurt his personal life as well as his professional prospects. His wife confessed to him that she had had an affair with one of her leading men on tour. Bogie appreciated her honesty and blamed himself as much as he blamed her. He forgave her, and they attempted to put their relationship back on the rosy level it had been on before his departure. But things would never quite be the same.

The Broadway depression was artistic as well as financial. Neither Mary Phillips nor Bogart was able to land in long-run shows. Bogie appeared in five Broadway plays during the 1933-34 season, and only one of them ran for more than one week. In desperation, they played summer stock together in Massachusetts. On their return after a summer of heavy drinking, they found the Broadway scene gloomier than ever. Bogart, to earn "eating money," turned a hobby into a paying job. He began playing chess at fifty cents a game, winner take all, at the seedy entertainment parlors along Sixth Avenue.

To add to his sorrow, his father died in early September 1934. Years later Bogart would say it was possible that Dr. Bogart, who had allowed his practice to fade away along with the money he had in the bank, had become addicted to narcotics. Bogart's once-promising inheritance proved to be only his father's ring, which he wore for the rest of his life. He also assumed the responsibility of paying off his father's debts which amounted to nearly $10,000.

In 1934 the future "bad man of Warner Brothers" made a movie in New York called *Midnight* that attracted little attention outside the city. But the movie again gave Bogart a chance to portray a gangster, and he did it so well that it propelled him into another villain's role in a successful Broadway play called *Invitation to a Murder.* He found that "heavies" offered him better acting opportunities than his earlier "tennis anyone" parts, and he was determined to look for more such roles. Shortly before *Invitation* was due to close, he heard about a gangster role that really fit the bill.

Robert E. Sherwood, one of Bogie's longtime speak-easy detractors, had written a melodrama called *The Petrified Forest.* The pivotal role in the play was that of a cold-blooded killer, Duke Mantee, cut in the mold of the infamous John Dillinger. The role hadn't been cast yet, and Bogie immediately called producer Arthur Hopkins and scheduled an audition. Sherwood told Hopkins that Bogart was a friend who had become a fine actor. He might be suitable for another role in the play, Sherwood said, but he was entirely wrong for the part of Duke Mantee. Hopkins decided to let Bogart read despite the playwright's warning. The producer and his director were joined at the Bogart audition by Leslie Howard, who had

73

already been cast for the lead in the play. Hopkins and the director were impressed; Howard was absolutely thrilled. Howard had cast approval and made his decision then and there—nobody except Humphrey Bogart could play the role of Duke Mantee.

The Petrified Forest became an instant Broadway hit, and "Bogart, the gangster" became the talk of the town. People were fascinated at the way the former lightweight juvenile had so completely transformed himself. Their attention was riveted on the snarling, staccato-voiced killer with the three-day growth of beard who dominated the stage with his submachine gun at the ready. The play enjoyed a healthy run, and Bogart was able to pay off his father's debts and stash some money away into what he called his "F.Y. Fund"—a bank account that he would keep to give him the independence to live on his own terms. The role of Duke Mantee not only brought Bogart the artistic recognition he had always sought in New York, it also opened the door for a possible triumphant return to Hollywood.

Warner Brothers bought the rights to *The Petrified Forest* and signed Leslie Howard to re-create his role for the screen. They also optioned the services of Humphrey Bogart as Duke Mantee. When the play closed, Bogart made excited plans to travel to California. This time things would be better in every way because Mary Phillips had agreed to go with him. His $400 per week contract was only a little better than half of what he made the last time out, but that didn't matter. Now he would have an opportunity to make a real impact as an actor.

The long, cross-country train trip had been relaxing and fun, and when he arrived in Los Angeles he was ready to go to work. But he found that lightning can "strike twice in the same place." This time the news was unthinkable. The Warner hierarchy had decided to cast Edward G. Robinson in the role of Duke Mantee. They knew that Bogart had done a fine job in the part on Broadway, but Robinson was already a well-established screen actor. His name, coupled with that of Leslie Howard, would ensure the financial success of the film version of *The Petrified Forest.*

Bogart was stunned. Duke Mantee was *his* role. He had created it, and nobody was going to take it away from

74

him! His portrayal of Duke Mantee had contributed to the very success of the play, and Leslie Howard knew that as well as he did. Howard had helped him get the part on Broadway—would Leslie go to bat for him again? Bogart fired off a cable to his friend, who was vacationing in Scotland. Howard had promised Bogie that they would do the screen version of the play together, and he acted quickly. The next day Jack L. Warner received a cablegram from Howard saying that he refused to do the film unless Bogart played Duke Mantee.

Jack Warner guarded his supreme authority on the lot just as closely as he guarded his money. He wasn't about to bow to an ultimatum from any actor. He assured Howard that Bogart would be treated fairly and would have every opportunity to prove himself, however, he doubted that the young actor was experienced enough to handle such a demanding role in an important motion picture. It now became a matter of saving face. Warner insisted that Bogart test for the role again and again before giving his reluctant approval. In *l'affaire Bogart,* Leslie Howard became one of the first actors to win a dispute with Jack Warner. Bogie never forgot the favor, and many years later he honored his friend in a very personal way, naming his daughter Leslie.

Bogart's performance in *The Petrified Forest* proved to be as electrifying on the screen as it had been on the stage. Jack Warner was well-satisfied with the work of his "new discovery" and pleased that he had signed the actor to a long-term contract at a low salary that would bring happiness to his brother Albert in New York. Gangster movies were the bread-and-butter product of Warners at the time, and Bogart would be a most useful addition to the Warner stock company.

Sobered by his earlier stay in Hollywood, Bogart was determined that he would approach his new status in the film capital with a wary eye. He and Mary rented a bungalow at The Garden of Allah on the Sunset Strip. The Garden was a hangout for Robert Benchley and other rebel types and a self-sustained Hollywood version of a miniature Greenwich Village. It was a place where a neighbor's knock on the door usually preceded the request, "May I borrow a cup of whiskey?" It was the perfect place for nourishing the cynical wit and wisdom of Humphrey Bogart.

Bogart was thirty-five and had endured too much to take his acting career lightly. On the set he would be thoroughly professional and give the best performance he had in him. But experience had taught him that a serious view of the other aspects of Hollywood life was a sure road to eventual madness. When he wasn't acting, he would play.

Before *Petrified Forest* was ready to be released, he discovered a game that gave him much pleasure. The studio publicity writers continually plagued him for information about his background, and he found that truth wasn't important to them; it was color that counted. Bogart obliged the flacks by inventing outlandish stories, and he was delighted when the newspapers and fan magazines gobbled them up. To this day many believe Bogie only made up the story that he was born on Christmas Day so he could voice the poignant complaint, "I've been cheated out of birthday presents all my life."

His success in *The Petrified Forest* ensured his long association with Warner Brothers and freed him forever from the hated "tennis anyone" parts. But the Bogart sense of humor would be essential in the preservation of his equilibrium as he was thrown into an even longer string of similar "Get your hands up" roles. He went from *The Petrified Forest* in 1935 into four more Warner films in which he donned a dark suit and snap-brim hat and played gangsters. The only role that had much dimension was the one in *Bullets and Ballots.* He made seven pictures in 1937, always cast as a bad guy, and only one of them retains much lasting value. He came across very well that year when Warners loaned him to Sam Goldwyn for the film version of Sidney Kingsley's stage hit *Dead End.*

In the Warner Brothers set-up, Bogart was near the bottom of the list of established names who populated that studio's gangster films. He was never able to land the choice roles handed to the other Warner heavies like Robinson, Cagney, Raft, and Muni. Even the young John Garfield got a better variety of parts. Bogart was almost always the crazed, second-fiddle baddie who was kicked around by the heroes of his films and made to look foolish by the lead heavy. The Motion Picture Code demanded that he be punished for his evil screen deeds, and he endured electrocution or hanging in eight of his early Warner films. His face became readily recognizable to fans of crime movies, but he had been locked into a screen image that would be almost impossible to change.

The hopeless creative stagnation was terrible for a man of Bogart's intelligence and potential. He let off the steam at anyone who would listen. Jack Warner, the one person who could change things, listened but only mollified him to the point of raising his pay. Bogart hated public hypocrisy, and the press found his views "hot copy" in contrast to the sweetness-and-light statements issued by his contemporaries.

He told a reporter for the *New York Telegraph* in 1936 that he had no intention of going Hollywood. With tongue in cheek, Bogie said he had made a study of the subject and discovered that 47 percent of all New York actors "went Hollywood" by the time they had been in town for six months. In another interview in 1937, he declared his intention of stating his honest opinion no matter what anybody else thought of it. He acknowledged that everyone in Hollywood was continually advising him to watch what he said, but it seemed to him it would be impossible to have an honest discussion without *somebody* expressing an opinion.

One of the most powerful Hollywood columnists of the time wrote scoldingly that "Bogart refuses to conform to Hollywood standards of behavior." In reply to the criticism of that columnist and many others, Bogart gave a lengthy interview in 1937 which spelled out his attitude. It would have been a clear-eyed, thoughtful interview coming from any number of actors of grander box-office stature. It was an incredible statement for a man known for the kind of roles Bogie was handed.

In part it said:

Why can't you be yourself, do your job, be your role at the studio and yourself at home, and not have to belong to the glitter-and-glamour group? Actors are always publicized as having a beautiful courtesy. I haven't. I'm the most impolite person in the world. It's thoughtlessness. If I start to be polite you can hear it for forty miles. . . . It's an effort for me to do things people believe should "be done." . . . I'm a human being with a pattern of my own and the right to work out my pattern in my own way. . . . I really can't understand why actors can't have human frailties like other people; why they can't make the same mistakes, guess wrong now and then; why they must be presented to the world as of a uniform and unassailable virtue. . . . I take my work seriously, but none of this art for art's sake. Any art or any job of work that's any good at all sells. If it's worth selling, it's worth buying. I have no sentimentality about such matters.

He went on to state his honest opinions on love and marriage in an unusually candid soul-baring by a Hollywood actor. Bogart made it clear to Jack Warner and all the other powers in town that he intended to be his own man in his spare time. His growing coterie of fans across the country loved it, although they had trouble connecting it with the one-dimensional character they saw on the screen.

Bogart's time away from the studio was spent largely at the bungalow he shared with Mary at The Garden of Allah. A collection of bungalows with a communal swimming pool, the place had gained a reputation as the liveliest spot in the oversized, small town, which had a livelier nightlife scene in the 1930s than it has today. Bogie was stimulated by the drinking company of the writers and other industry individualists who visited The Garden of Allah. For a time, Mary Phillips also seemed to be happy with the countless rounds of parties. After more than a year in California, she began to fret about her own lack of work. She wanted to get back on the legitimate stage where she belonged.

When Mary was offered the lead in a new play on Broadway, she told her husband she intended to accept it. Bogart, who tried to talk her out of it with calm logic, read the script and told her he was not impressed with it. More important, he honestly didn't think that she was right for the part—it would be a mistake to do the play. But his wife was adamant in her decision to accept the role.

Then Bogart exploded. He was financially able to support her, and he could see no sane reason for her to desert him. In the end she ignored his pleas and left for New York. It wasn't a formal or legal separation, and the marriage wasn't officially ended, but Bogart was alone again.

Bogart's appraisal of the play and his wife's role in it proved to be correct. However, although the show closed after a short run, Mary Phillips decided to stay in New York until she found something more suitable. Bogart was left to his own devices away from the studio. He sought solace in his old friends, the bottle, and the barb. He became, for him, almost a "social butterfly," spending much of his free time in the better bars and nightclubs, though many found his behavior less than socially acceptable. His marriage seemed doomed but he was determined to survive its downfall as best he could.

With Mary in New York and out of his life, Bogie began to cast an eye about for suitable female companionship. He was a man who believed in fidelity within marriage, but his marriage was obviously on the rocks. He settled on a woman who attracted him physically and impressed him with her lively sense of humor and her ability to drink. Her name was Mayo Methot, and she was destined to play the leading role in the most turbulent period of his life. An actress who had achieved recognition opposite George M. Cohan in his New York show *Song and Dance Man,* Mayo later won kudos for her work in another Broadway play titled *Great Day.*

Mayo and Bogie had first met in New York, and their unexpected second meeting at a formal industry dinner in Los Angeles quickly turned into a torrid affair. Bitter over Mary's absence and the apparent failure of his second marriage, Bogart had been drinking heavily. He found Mayo Methot a drinking companion who offered considerably more in the way of comfort than his male friends, and before long, he was asking her to join him for weekends on his newly-purchased boat that he kept at Newport Beach. The relationship thrived, and it was decided that she should move into The Garden of Allah bungalow he had shared with Mary Phillips. When Mary found Mayo there following an unannounced trip back to Hollywood, she immediately filed for divorce.

Bogart's views on marriage were basically conventional. Earlier, when he was pleading with Mary not to return to New York, Bogart told her he had hoped they could start a family. He once told an interviewer, "If you're not married or in love, you're on the loose and that's not comfortable." Now he felt comfortable with Mayo Methot. She was a "drinking buddy," sexually attractive, and enjoyed a good fight as much as he did, and Mayo wouldn't allow him to be bored. Neither of them had any illusions about marriage because both had experienced earlier failures. He could afford a wife—so why not have one? Humphrey Bogart and Mayo Methot were married in Beverly Hills on August 20, 1938. He was thirty-eight, she was three years younger.

Mayo had agreed beforehand to give up her career in order to be Mrs. Humphrey Bogart. That gave the actor a sense of security he had never known, but his third wife's other traits would create bigger problems. Inside movie circles, their marriage was thought of as a continuous round of booze and brawls. The Bogarts bought a house in West Hollywood (he still frowned on the pretentiousness of Beverly Hills), and Bogie put up a sign in front naming the homestead "Sluggy Hollow" in honor of the occupants' favorite pastime. His boat was also rechristened *Sluggy* in honor of his bride.

His home life did little to aid Bogie in preparation for his work at the studio. Bogart had told reporters before their marriage that he had nothing but admiration for Mayo's capacity for alcohol and her well-known inclination toward extreme jealousy. Always an enthusiastic drinker, Bogart had gained a reputation for handling it well, but now with Mayo, his drinking and his frustrations increased until they boiled over into occasional fist fights in the parking lots of Hollywood's most famous nightclubs. Mayo's jealousy of other women, real and imagined, became an increasing problem. She also became jealous of his success and expressed it by belittling his acting and the parts he played, assuring him he would never rise any higher in the popularity polls. This criticism was doubly painful because he recognized the truth behind it.

He made twenty-four pictures between 1937 and 1940 in which the Bogart screen requirements were clearly defined: 1) He will be a despicable human being with only occasional, flickering undertones of basic decency; 2) he will forever get his comeuppance before the final reel; and 3) he will never, ever get the girl! Of those twenty-four films, only *Dead End* and *San Quentin* (1937); *Crime School, The Amazing Dr. Clitterhouse, Racket Busters,* and *Angels with Dirty Faces* (1938); *The Roaring Twenties* and *Dark Victory* (1939); and *They Drive by Night, Virginia City,* and *Brother Orchid* of 1940 could be considered top-notch films of the period.

The Bogart-Methot marriage did little to help his professional status. In her calmer moments, Mayo encouraged him to fight for better parts. Her encouragement and her criticism made him even more bitter with "Papa Jack" Warner's brand of paternalism. Bogart was looking for a solution to his problems at the bottom of a bottle and would often report for a long day of work at the studio without any sleep after a full night of drinking and domestic travail.

By 1940, Bogart knew that he had to make some major advances if his career was to continue. War had already exploded in Europe and Asia, and the appeal of the gangster movie began to pale in the face of the more violent action taking place outside the United States. He had no luck in trying to convince Jack Warner that he should be offered different types of roles. In a feeble experiment he was cast as a Western badman in *Virginia City.* He looked totally out of place in his black cowboy suit and mustache, according to his wife.

The public at large was not informed of the seamier episodes in the stormy marriage of the "Battling Bogarts." However, the stories became the whispered topics of conversation in the homes of many in the movie colony. The strong influence of the studio and the concern of close friends kept the press uninformed when Mayo stabbed Bogie in the back with a butcher knife. Fans never learned of Mayo's feigned suicide when she fired several shots through the ceiling of her bedroom. Still, Bogart recognized that his wife had mental problems and continued to care deeply for her. He managed to survive the worst moments and seemed to thrive on their minor squabbles. Mayo's goading served to prod him into arguing more vehemently with Warner for a chance to play better roles in better pictures with better directors.

In 1941 Bogart finally got his chance. Even then, his

casting in two good roles were more accidental than calcu-
lated. The studio had decided to film a story called *High
Sierra*. The piece had a finely tuned plot and the challenging
role of a man gone bad who unjustly gets the label "Mad Dog"
hung on him and dies in a fusillade of gunfire from the
lawmen who surround him in the California mountains. Ida
Lupino had been set for the female lead, and the scenario had
been written to suit the talents of George Raft in the role of
"Mad Dog" Earle. Raft, in spite of his professional beginnings
as a tango dancer, had become enormously popular through
a series of "tough guy" roles at Warners. Embued with self-
importance, Raft told Jack Warner he could never agree to do
a film in which he was forced to die. Other Warner stars
suitable for the role refused to accept one that Raft had turned
down. Warner was faced with a delicate decision: borrow a
star from another studio at great expense or assign the part to
another "gangster type" already under contract. Bogart got
the role by default.

It was the opportunity Bogart had been fighting for
since 1936. Roy Earle would be another character on the
wrong side of the law, but the role was not at all like the other
parts Bogart had been playing. This character had dimension.
The audience would be allowed to sympathize with him, and a
bit of tenderness could be displayed with the woman in the
plot. Bogart wouldn't get the girl, but he would be permitted
to act as if he had considered the possibility.

High Sierra proved to be one of the strong films of
the year, and Bogie won both popular and critical acclaim for
his playing of Roy Earle. One New York critic called him the
perfect choice to play the role and emphasized that Bogart
had always been a fine actor whose performance in *High
Sierra* lifted the film out of the category of just another exciting gangster picture.

Jack Warner was still not overly impressed. Bogie
had, after all, only played another "tough guy"—his versatility
was still in doubt. The actor had to put his trust in luck and the
help of a friend, John Huston, to land the role which would
expand his horizon. Huston, son of the famed actor Walter
Huston, was intent on making a name for himself as a director.
He had a writer's contract with Warner Brothers but was still

regarded as something of a misfit. Huston came up with an unusual treatment for a film version of a Dashiell Hammett novel called *The Maltese Falcon*. He told Bogart about it and suggested that he would be perfect for the leading role.

Bogart was delighted about the prospects of working with his friend on a picture which sounded exciting. Sam Spade was a hell of a part, and he was eager to play it for a number of reasons. For one thing the guy was tough as nails, but he wasn't a criminal. He was a private detective trying to track down the bad guys. He would even have a little love interest. The two schemed to get the project approved with Bogart in the starring role. Two earlier productions of the Hammett story had failed, but Jack Warner and Hal Wallis liked Huston's scenario. It would be a moody, low-key kind of film which would be exciting and different. Huston was given the go-ahead to direct the film, but Warner couldn't buy Bogart as the hero. Sam Spade had to be tough but still handsome enough to attract the woman in the story. Bogart didn't fit that description, and he had never done anything like that in pictures. The public wouldn't buy it. The proper actor for this role was George Raft!

Mary Astor was cast in the female lead of *The Maltese Falcon,* and Raft was asked to star opposite her as Sam Spade. Raft read the scenario and thought the part was decent enough, but he had one very serious reservation. What had Warner and Wallis been thinking of when they assigned the director? They couldn't have expected George Raft to work with a neophyte like John Huston! He would consider taking on the role only if they got an experienced director. *The Maltese Falcon* had been Huston's idea from the beginning, and Warner, a man of his word, had already signed him to direct it. When Warner found that he couldn't replace Huston, and that he couldn't persuade Raft to change his mind, he realized that Bogart would have to do. Raft and Bogart may have disliked each other, but Raft's stubbornness was becoming a positive force in Bogart's career. Happily donning a trench coat as Sam Spade, Bogie helped build *The Maltese Falcon* into an enormously popular film.

Hal Wallis produced the movie, and he and John Huston cast it with such strong supporting players as Sydney

Greenstreet and Peter Lorre. Under Huston's brilliant direction, a new kind of Warner Brothers picture was born. The role fit Bogart like the proverbial glove, and he delivered a memorable understated performance. Even his drinking bouts with Mayo Methot proved to be a help; they reflected realistically in the sad, battered face that brought life to the tough character born of the pen of Dashiell Hammett. Playing Sam Spade enabled Bogart to transfer his long pent-up emotions to the screen while still controlling them with all the knowledge he had gained in his forty-three films.

In keeping with the mood of the plot, the romantic angle in *The Maltese Falcon* was deliberately downplayed by Huston. But it was believable and a perfect introduction for Bogart into the once-impossible realm of screen romance. This was a side of Bogart the public had never expected to see, and the box-office receipts proved, despite the fears of Jack Warner, that they had bought it. Bogart's reviews in *The Maltese Falcon* were the best he had ever received.

Bogart felt like a new man. He was finally being allowed to prove that he was an actor who could handle anything that Jack Warner or anyone else cared to throw at him. In the meantime his wife was throwing other things at him—glasses, plates, and bitter invective. Though she was pleased with his success in *The Maltese Falcon,* her drinking and fits of depression had increased at the same pace that her ability to handle them had decreased. The Bogarts continued their noisy public battles on a vacation in New York after the release of *Falcon.*

In the aftermath of one of their New York fights, Bogie was so depressed he told a reporter that Jack Warner was a "creep" for not giving him a decent opportunity earlier. The reporter broke the story, and Warner phoned Bogart and demanded an explanation. Bogart could only say, "I meant creep with a 'k,' not a 'c.'" When he returned to Burbank, he sought out the studio chief and formally apologized. Despite their many feuds, the two men had an underlying respect for each other, and Bogart didn't want Warner to feel he had "gone Hollywood" or become a total ingrate. Warner accepted the apology, and the relationship between the actor and his employer began to move to a new level. Bogart was now a bona fide star.

As a favor to the friends, Warner assigned Bogart to John Huston's next picture. The film was to be called *Across the Pacific* and was one of Warner's first attempts at a picture with a World War II theme, but it was in no way comparable to *The Maltese Falcon*. Midway through the picture, with the United States officially involved in the war, Huston was called to active service in the military and another director was recruited to complete the film. Mary Astor was Bogie's love interest again in *Across the Pacific* and his prospects were looking up!

While Hal Wallis was making plans for *Casablanca*, Bogart's agents were negotiating a new contract for their client. On the strength of his showing in 1941, especially his box-office impact in *The Maltese Falcon*, the agents were able to convince Warner Brothers to give Bogie a huge jump in his weekly salary. The contract covered the standard period of seven years, but it was unusual because it did not include many of the usual Jack Warner options. Bogart was guaranteed $3,500 a week for forty weeks in each of seven successive years, and he would get paid even if he wasn't able to work.

Bogart was surprised at his longtime adversary's generosity. He was a contract player who had long experience with Warner's skillful use of his treasured options. He felt compelled to ask his boss what had prompted him to give away such an important point in the negotiations. Warner grinned and managed to make Bogie feel a bit uneasy about his future choice of roles by replying, "Nothing can happen to your face that will hurt it a bit!"

But Hal Wallis had a different feeling about the Bogart face. He desperately wanted Bogie as the leading man in his new romantic thriller, *Casablanca*. During the filming of *The Maltese Falcon*, Wallis had discovered that Bogart's personality and rugged features were attractive to women—and the success of the picture proved it. Bogart's quality would add a special shading to the role of Rick Blaine that would strengthen it. When Wallis made a trip to the set of *Across the Pacific* to tell the actor he wanted him to star in his next film, the producer told him a bit about the plot and the character he wanted him to play. Bogart was interested.

The actor asked for a copy of the script, and Wallis

was forced to tell him that a complete scenario was not available. He had assigned the Epsteins to revise the original three-act play called *Everybody Comes to Rick's,* but they hadn't managed to finish it. Wallis agreed to send Bogart a rough copy of the play script with notations about prospective changes. He also confided to Bogart that he had every hope of landing Ingrid Bergman to play opposite him.

Bogart was impressed by that news. He had enjoyed playing opposite lovely Mary Astor in *The Maltese Falcon,* and he was pleased that their "romantic" teaming had worked. But she was an older actress who was making something of a comeback in *Falcon.* Bergman was something else again. She was young, beautiful, and definitely on her way up. The whole idea amused him. He had fought for years to play anything other than mindless mobsters, and Hal Wallis was now eager to cast him as the screen lover for a gorgeous and talented Swedish actress. Good ol' Bogie was about to become a romantic leading man—at the age of forty-one.

When Bogart received the script, he gave it a quick scan and realized that Wallis hadn't exaggerated in telling him he would be the central figure in the piece. The role of Rick Blaine was a big one. However, his enthusiasm waned as he began to read it. All the stuff of a good movie was there, but it had to be made a lot stronger. The play had evidently been written before the United States got into the war, and now that the Americans were in it, there was no point in so much pussyfooting around with the Nazis.

Bogart had mixed feelings about the role of Rick Blaine. The guy was complex, all right. He was basically a loner with a good relationship with his black buddy. Bogie liked that. Rick obviously had a sense of humor, and Bogart was sure the Epsteins would improve on that area. But the romance bothered him. The way the script had been written, Rick seemed like too much of a "whiner" for Bogart's taste. The Epsteins would have to build up the character's background. The guy had to be tougher than he seemed in the script. He didn't like the idea of Rick as only a one-time lawyer who felt sorry for himself because of a broken love affair. His "F.Y." attitude about everyone had to have come from more than just the woman who ran out on him. He needed more substance.

Still, Bogart could see why Wallis had thought of him for the part. Rick's cynicism and "look out for number one" point of view had been his own public pose for a long time. In many ways the character was already as close to his own nature as anything he had ever played. He could act the hell out of that—if they shaped it up. Playing a lover didn't make him too nervous, even if it would be new territory for him on the screen. He knew all about sour love affairs. He had already had two and a half of them—inside the bounds of legal matrimony.

Bogart told Wallis about his worries, and the producer was sympathetic. Wallis was certain the Epsteins would improve things, but to be on the safe side he would add another writer. Howard Koch was a young fellow out of New York who was politically aware and who wrote realistic, tough dialogue. Wallis would tell Koch about Bogart's problems and have him concentrate on them in particular.

Reassured that the role of Rick Blaine would be rewritten to his specifications, Bogart looked forward to doing *Casablanca*. It would certainly be different. Bogart, the lover! If Wallis talked Ingrid Bergman into playing opposite him, it could be the start of a whole new career. He had a better contract, a damned good part to look forward to, a beautiful leading lady, and a wife waiting at home for him.

All of this gave him reason for sombre reflection. If Mayo had gone into fits of jealous rage when he just looked at another woman, how was she going to react when he started smooching it up with a dazzling dame like Ingrid Bergman?

Seven

Signing Ingrid Bergman as the female star of *Casablanca* would prove to be Hal Wallis' most difficult task during the pre-production phase of the film. From the moment he first read *Everybody Comes to Rick's,* Wallis had never seriously considered any other actress for the role. Bergman wasn't right for the part as it was written in the play, but that didn't disturb Wallis. She would be worth the effort necessary to rework the role to suit her. The Epsteins' first task was to transform the American Lois Meredith into the Norwegian Ilsa Lund.

Wallis, like many others, had been first attracted to Bergman when he saw her American debut in the David O. Selznick film *Intermezzo.* She was different. She exuded a vulnerable freshness that no other actress on the Warner lot could duplicate. She had none of the well-lacquered veneer that Hollywood applied to its beautiful women. Even more important to Wallis, she could act!

Bergman had been brought to Hollywood by Selznick and signed to an exclusive long-term contract. Wallis would have to deal with David O. Selznick if he wanted the services of Ingrid Bergman. Selznick, an independent producer with his own studios in Culver City, had attained magnificent stature in the industry with his epic *Gone With the Wind,* and he wasn't a particularly easy man with whom to deal. He guarded the stars in his control with a super-protective zeal. The entire industry knew that Bergman was on the threshold of becoming a major star, and Wallis understood that he would have to approach Selznick with the utmost tact if Ingrid Bergman was ever going to become his Ilsa Lund.

Wallis started courting Selznick as subtly as possible. The two men came into contact frequently at movie premieres and other industry functions, and Wallis began to arouse Selznick's curiosity by telling him about the wonderful property he had bought that had a perfect starring role for Ingrid Bergman. When Selznick showed interest in the idea and even asked to see a script, he was assured that the completed script was not yet ready because Warner Brothers had a team of writers especially tailoring the leading lady's role for the superb talents of Ingrid Bergman. However, despite his stated interest, Wallis sensed that Selznick was in no hurry to commit himself.

What Wallis didn't know was that Ingrid Bergman was very eager to work—but the actress and her producer had set their sights on another very specific project. Selznick had been working for a long time to negotiate a deal for Bergman's services with another studio which was preparing an important film with a role that the actress was aching to play. The role that Wallis talked about in his little picture was nothing to get excited about. But Selznick didn't want to give Wallis a flat refusal on his proposal. If the bigger deal fell through, *Casablanca* sounded like a suitable substitute. It was just that Selznick's eyes were on greater goals.

In Bergman's mind, her Hollywood career was in a slump at the time Wallis first approached Selznick about borrowing her for *Casablanca.* The actress admired and trusted David O. Selznick, who had brought her to the United States from Sweden in spring 1939. She admired his handling of her debut in *Intermezzo* and believed that her decision to leave her native land to gamble on success in far-off California had been the correct one. But then, after a splendid beginning, everything seemed to be going wrong. Her career was not progressing.

To Bergman, Selznick's greatest flaw was that he was too cautious in finding work for her. She was certain that he had her best interests in mind, but he hadn't had much success in placing her in good roles. She had completed only four films in nearly three years in Hollywood, and they hadn't advanced her career at all. She was so desperate to work, she probably would have snapped up the part in *Casablanca* immediately if Selznick had mentioned it to her. He told her he was prepared to go to any lengths to get her a role that would make her a major star. The waiting would be frustrating, but she would abide by Selznick's decision. Still, it would be lovely to *work*.

Ingrid Bergman found the whole giddy world of Hollywood far different from that in which she had been raised. She was born in Stockholm, Sweden, on August 29, 1915. Her father, Justus Bergman, was a man who appreciated the arts and practiced them as a painter and a photographer. He conducted his business in a shop on the ground floor of the apartment building where he lived with his wife and baby daughter. Friedel Adler Bergman, Ingrid's mother, had been born in Hamburg, Germany. Her marriage had been a solid, happy one until her death two years after Ingrid was born.

Justus Bergman was a doting father who became even closer to his little daughter following the death of his wife. He was a talented man with a camera and became interested in motion-picture photography as soon as it became available to him. His favorite moving-picture subject was his daughter, Ingrid. Bergman would tell a national American television audience in the winter of 1979 that her father probably had an indirect influence on her eventual career as an actress. She proved her point by showing his home movies of her as a toddler through her early adolescence. It was her father who also took her to see her first stage play when she was eleven years old, a year before his death.

The young Bergman, a lonely child, had to invent many of her own playmates. She found solace by acting out adventure and love stories in her imagination. On seeing her first play, she was astounded, to learn that some grownups did that for a living. She was certain she would always be too shy to expose herself that way in public, but she never forgot the experience. After her father's death, Ingrid stayed in the family home under the care of his spinster sister. Just six months later, her aunt also died and Ingrid was very much alone.

Ingrid was sent to live with her uncle and his wife who had five children. None of her cousins were her own age, but it was a lively household, and the young orphan gradually began to come out of her shell of shyness. Her uncle treated her as one of his own and even sent her to the Stockholm Lyceum for Girls, an exclusive private school, where she found she had a talent for pleasing people by performing. She became a class favorite in the art of reading dramatic poems aloud. Her uncle was encouraged by her development and often urged her to demonstrate her talents before the guests in his home, never dreaming that she would decide to become an actress by her seventeenth birthday.

A career on the stage was still not considered by most Swedish families a proper ambition for decent young ladies. Without asking for or receiving any encouragement from her uncle, she auditioned for the School of the Royal Dramatic Theater, acting scenes from plays by Strindberg and Rostand, and was enthusiastically received. She was invited to enroll in the school, and so began a happy time for her. Her natural talents were shaped and enhanced by the formal classes and the discipline stressed, and she was given leading roles in several school productions during the season of 1933-34.

Bergman's first year at the Royal Dramatic Theater School would prove to be a spectacular one for the young actress. By the end of it, she would be thrilled by two events which would change the course of her personal and professional life. She had met a young man named Peter Lindstrom on a blind date during the year, and they had grown close. He was ten years older than she, already established as a dentist, and determined to continue his studies until he earned a degree as a medical doctor. In the meantime her school performances had so impressed the executives of Svenskfilm-industri, Sweden's top motion picture company of 1934, that they offered her a contract. It would mean leaving her formal education, but it was a wonderful opportunity. Peter Lindstrom, who approved of her acting ambitions and encouraged them, agreed that she should accept the offer.

Her first film role, as a hotel maid in the contemporary Swedish comedy *Munkbrogreven,* was relatively insignificant. But the critics did take note of her "statuesque beauty," and she was proud of her status as a working actress at the age of nineteen. That would be the first and only small role she would play in films. In 1935 she was upgraded to the leads in three pictures at the studio: *Branningar, Swedenheilms,* and *Valborgsnassoafton.* Each part called for different styles and emotions, and the young actress carried the roles off beautifully. During the year she had worked with distinguished director Gustaf Molander, and she had been honored with a chance to play opposite Sweden's most popular romantic star, Lars Hanson, in her final film of the year.

By the end of 1935, critics and fans throughout Europe began to look for the vibrant Swedish actress. Her film with Hanson played the Venice film festival, and a German critic took pains to single out Bergman's performance in it. The success of *Valborgsnassoafton* prompted the Swedish film company to cast Bergman opposite Hanson again in 1936 in *Pa Solsidan,* directed by Gustaf Molander. The plot of the picture was anything but intricate or original, dealing with Hanson's petty jealousy over his wife, but the critics raved about the bright female star who played the wife. Ingrid Bergman was called "blindingly beautiful," an actress who had suddenly matured to a point that her stunning beauty and talent were *indescribable.*

When the picture reached Manhattan, the reviewers of *The New York Times* and *Variety* also fell in line to praise her. *The Times* critic became infatuated with "the natural charm of Ingrid Bergman, the young Stockholm actress whose star has risen so rapidly in the Scandinavian film firmament." The *Variety* man, in a more pragmatic vein, stated flatly that the Swedish beauty should "rate a Hollywood berth."

But the best was yet to come for Ingrid Bergman. Her next film, *Intermezzo,* would start her on the road to international stardom. The film was essentially the work of her favorite director, Gustaf Molander. Molander was also the coauthor of the screenplay, adapted from his own original story. Bergman's sensitive performance in the role of a pianist who falls desperately in love with a famous married violinist was her best to that point. The picture teamed Hanson and Bergman again, but it was the actress who stole the film. The love affair between Ingrid and the Swedish press reached even greater heights, and the thunderous acclaim began to echo louder and with new urgency across the Atlantic. This time the *Variety* reviewer predicted, "Ingrid Bergman's star is destined for Hollywood."

In the 1930s foreign films were not as widely distributed in the United States as they would be in the years after World War II. British films found some success because of the "similarity" in language, but dubbing was seldom practiced and most American distributors had little inclination to go to the bother of adding English subtitles to imported movies. Foreign-language films, by and large, were confined to showings in the appropriate ethnic neighborhoods. Bergman's American notices were significant because every major studio was on the lookout for important European talent.

No Bergman films were released in 1937, but it became a memorable year in the life of the Swedish star. Peter Lindstrom, who had completed his medical studies and earned his license to practice, was now confident about his future and asked Ingrid to marry him. She had lost her mother at the age of two and she was only twelve when her father died. She longed for the warmth of a real home of her own, but she also wondered if it would be possible to combine a career with marriage. The actress and the doctor decided they loved each other enough to risk it, and they were married on July 10, 1937.

In many ways 1938 was a banner year for Ingrid Bergman. She played drastically different roles with great success in three films: *Dollar, En Kvinnas Ansikte,* and *Die Vier Gesellen. Dollar,* a bedroom farce, introduced an entirely new Bergman. She was lavishly dressed in the movie and appeared completely at ease in her first sophisticated comedy role. In *En Kvinnas Ansikte* she played a woman with a badly scarred face which enabled her to give a bravura performance encompassing the entire range of emotions. Joan Crawford

93

would play the role a few years later in the American version of the story retitled *A Woman's Face.* Bergman's third film of the year was made at the UFA studios in Germany. With relatives in that country, Bergman, quickly mastered the language. The movie was an unimpressive bit of fluff about career girls and their search for suitable husbands, ironic because it came from Nazi Germany a year before the start of World War II.

Other developments in 1938 were far more important to Ingrid Bergman. She gave birth to a daughter, Friedel Pia Lindstrom, on September 20 of that year and immediately squashed any curiosity about a possible retirement. Her statement to the Swedish press: "Why shouldn't an actress have babies? It's perfectly natural."

Shortly before Pia's birth, Bergman's name was being called to the attention of David O. Selznick in Hollywood. Kay Brown, Selznick's chief story editor in New York, would call on the actess in Stockholm with an offer to come to America before the year was out.

Kay Brown and Ingrid Bergman established an immediate rapport. The Selznick offer was tempting and troubling at the same time. Ingrid felt a strong duty to stay close to her husband and newborn daughter. She was happy as a wife and mother, and she could continue to build her career in Europe without sacrificing her personal life. The Selznick offer would require a great deal of thought.

Kay Brown, who would become Bergman's personal agent and lifelong confidante, sympathized with her dilemma and came up with an alternative. Perhaps Selznick would consider a short-term deal covering only the time it would take to film his version of *Intermezzo.* That way, Ingrid's separation from her family would not be a long one. She would be able to see how she like working in Hollywood, and then make a knowledgeable decision about returning to Sweden to stay or bringing her baby and husband over to join her. The idea seemed like a sensible one to Bergman, but she would not be able to leave for several months. She had made commitments for two more European films: another sophisticated comedy with Gustaf Molander and a heavy dramatic film for Per Lindberg. Kay Brown went home empty-handed, but she advised David Selznick that he would be wise to continue his efforts to sign the beautiful Swedish actress—even to a simple, one-picture contract.

The Molander film was called *En Enda Natt,* and Bergman again wowed the critics with her portrayal of a proper lady with erotic fires smoldering beneath the surface. The second picture, *Juninatten,* starred Bergman in a highly dramatic role of little originality which was not released until 1940, long after the star had gone to Hollywood.

Bergman's rave reviews in Europe and in New York, coupled with the glowing personal report delivered by Kay Brown, caused Selznick to consider relinquishing his preference for long-term contracts. His conviction that the gamble might be a good one was reinforced when he saw her performance in the Swedish version of *Intermezzo.* The actress projected a kind of radiance on the screen, and he was also impressed by the unaffected way she performed in front of the camera.

Work on *Gone With the Wind* was progressing nicely, and Selznick felt sure he could take *Intermezzo,* revise it for American tastes, and make it a hit. He had Leslie Howard signed for another film after he completed *GWTW* and felt the English actor would be well cast as the violinist. Bergman would be the perfect choice to play the pianist in his film. Selznick decided he would try to convince her during the filming that her real future would be found in Hollywood, as so many had predicted.

After a family discussion in which the Lindstroms agreed the Selznick offer would enhance her career, Bergman agreed to his terms and arrived in Hollywood in spring 1939. Selznick immediately assigned her to Ruth Roberts, a language coach at MGM. Bergman had a fair knowledge of English as well as a natural gift at picking up languages. She was a quick study and felt comfortable with the new dialogue in a very short time.

With Gregory Ratoff as director, *Intermezzo* began filming in early summer. Selznick instructed Ratoff to duplicate most of the filming techniques Molander had used in his Swedish version of the screenplay as well as utilize the music of the Swedish film. However, Bergman was made aware of some subtle nuances in the approach to her character. In the film she was having an affair with a married man and, under the Hollywood code of morality, that made her a bad woman. That political point made little difference in her playing. Bergman thrived on the work, and everyone at the studio, Selznick included, were impressed by her intensity and thoroughly professional behavior on the set. Before the film was released, Selznick changed the title to *Intermezzo: A Love Story.* He wanted to hedge his bet on the American movie public's ability to comprehend the original title.

After watching her work, Selznick was convinced that Bergman was destined to be a major star. Long before the film was released, he began encouraging her to sign a long-term contract with his company. Ingrid had enjoyed working at the Selznick studio and had learned that Selznick was one of the most respected figures in the American film industry. When the picture was completed, she agreed to sign with the Selznick organization for seven years and booked passage back to Sweden. She was anxious to return to her husband and baby.

Intermezzo: A Love Story never became a huge financial success, but the film was a critical triumph. In her American debut Ingrid Bergman had appeared with two experienced actors in roles at least the equal of hers. Still, she literally stole the picture away from Leslie Howard and Edna Best. They seemed to be *acting* while Ingrid Bergman appeared to be *living* the part. *The New York Times* review of October 1939 said, "There is that incandescence about Miss Bergman, that spiritual spark which makes us believe that Selznick has found another great lady of the screen." Other major critics were equally impressed. The American career of the young Swedish actress had been well-launched.

Bergman had become "a hot property." She and David Selznick both knew it was essential that her talents be showcased in another vehicle as quickly as possible. It was doubly important in her case because she was a newcomer in the eyes of America's movie fans. But Selznick was completely stumped for what he considered an appropriate property. Bergman suggested that he have his writers work up a story on Joan of Arc. She had always wanted to portray the

96

French saint on stage or film. But Selznick didn't think the timing was right and told her that he would find something for her that would be equally good.

Bergman had agreed to report back for work in January 1940. She had hoped her husband and baby would take up residence with her in California, but Dr. Lindstrom was unable to leave Sweden. He was of military age and, although Sweden had been able to maintain its neutrality to that point, the government wanted its eligible manpower at the ready. Dr. Lindstrom had to continue his duties as a professor at Sweden's Royal Academy of Medicine, but he agreed that Ingrid should take their daughter with her to America.

Selznick had no work for her when she returned to the States, and so Bergman decided to spend some time in New York. She liked the city and was somewhat surprised to find that she was already considered a celebrity on the strength of her one American film. That realization only increased her anxiety. She knew she should be working if she hoped to build her career. Her next opportunity came from a rather surprising quarter—the Broadway theater. Producer Vinton Freedley, who had seen her performance in *Intermezzo* and knew she would be right for his next production, sent her a script.

The play was *Liliom,* by Ferenc Molnar. Ironically, it was the same story that Michael Curtiz had been directing for film when he was forced to flee his native Hungary many years earlier. Burgess Meredith had signed to play the male lead, and Bergman knew his work and respected it. She loved the role of Julie and hoped that David O. Selznick would give her permission to do the play. Selznick might have had strong objections, but the revival was scheduled for a limited run of only three months. He had no suitable film role for her. At least the play would keep her name in front of the public and relieve some of her impatience. Selznick gave his approval, assuring his star that he had grand plans for her after the play closed.

Liliom was a success, and Bergman's talents drew praise from those who still considered most movie stars unworthy practitioners of the art of acting. Ingrid gloried in her return to the stage and thoroughly enjoyed her friendship with

97

Burgess Meredith who had affectionately dubbed her the "Big Swede." *New York Times* critic Brooks Atkinson, never known to be reckless with his praise, wrote, "Miss Bergman keeps the part wholly alive and lightens it from within with luminous beauty." Atkinson joined the growing list of admirers who took note of her unusual radiance, a quality she projected even more mysteriously on the motion-picture screen.

It had been more than a year since her last appearance in front of a camera, and Bergman began to doubt her wisdom in accepting Selznick's offer of a long-term contract. She was convinced the following she had built with *Intermezzo* would surely forget her if she didn't find another picture soon. Gregory Ratoff, the director of *Intermezzo,* let it be known that he wanted her in his new film which he would be doing for Columbia Pictures. She begged Selznick to loan her to Columbia for *Adam Had Four Sons.*

Selznick read the scenario and was not at all impressed. The role proposed for his star was the central one, but the story appeared to be nothing more than a creaky melodrama. He advised her against accepting the film, but she pleaded for him to reconsider. She needed to work to keep from growing rusty. He agreed to the deal only after insisting that Columbia pay dearly for her services.

Bergman learned that Selznick's appraisal of *Adam Had Four Sons* was accurate. Her part as the long-suffering governess offered less opportunity for dramatic fireworks than the minor role played by Susan Hayward. It was as unchallenging as anything she had played in her early days in Sweden. She was now concerned with another possibility. Her own impatience might have caused her to lose whatever acting stature she had gained from *Intermezzo* and the Broadway play. Selznick told her not to worry, he had finally negotiated a deal with MGM Studios for her to star in the film version of a successful James Hilton novel. She reported to MGM shortly after she had completed *Adam Had Four Sons.*

James Hilton was one of America's best-selling authors. The screen versions of his books *Goodbye, Mr. Chips* and *Lost Horizon* had been box-office smashes. His *Rage in Heaven* (1932) had been a big seller, and Bergman and Selznick felt her appearance as its heroine should undo any harm the Columbia picture might have on her budding career. Robert Montgomery would be her co-star, and MGM had signed George Sanders and Lucille Watson in strong supporting roles.

Unfortunately, MGM had decided to film *Rage in Heaven* on a tight budget, and the finished product reflected it. To her sorrow, Bergman again found herself cast in the role of a faithful family retainer who marries above her station and is forced to nobly endure the sins of her husband. W. S. Van Dyke II directed the film in his usual speedy style, and Bergman had little opportunity to shine.

The speed of Van Dyke and the MGM editors was such that *Rage in Heaven* actually premiered in New York a week before the opening of *Adam Had Four Sons,* which Bergman had completed first. The overall reviews were not good, and both films were box-office disappointments. The critics who had loved Bergman in *Intermezzo* could not understand her inability to find comparably good roles since that time. They publicly sympathized with her while soft-pedaling her own possible complicity in the making of *Rage in Heaven* and *Adam Had Four Sons.* In a rare bit of editorializing, the reviewer for the New York *Herald-Tribune* wrote, "If our screen keeps overlooking her great talent much longer, it will be a really black mark against it."

Bergman's gnawing doubts about her work future were eased somewhat by one improvement in her personal life. Dr. Lindstrom had been allowed to leave Sweden in fall 1940 and had taken up residency in Rochester, New York. He studied neurosurgery at the University of Rochester while Ingrid was kept busy on the West Coast. There had been little time for personal contact, but the young marrieds were able to feel close to each other via the long-distance telephone. Their baby daughter was happy and healthy, and Ingrid hoped the family would be reunited soon. The progress of her career was less promising.

Bergman had been in the United States less than two years, made three movies, and played one role on the Broadway stage. But only the play and her first film had given her any real satisfaction. She had been given far better parts in Sweden, where she was allowed to prove that she was an actress. She felt that she was already becoming a victim of the notorious Hollywood practice of "typecasting." She could not let that happen.

Heeding his star's advice that she must keep working, David Selznick had been negotiating with MGM for another role for Ingrid as she was completing *Rage in Heaven*. Victor Fleming, who had directed Selznick's *Gone With the Wind*, had talked MGM into a big-budget remake of *Dr. Jekyll and Mr. Hyde*. Against his better instincts, Spencer Tracy had agreed to play the "dual roles" which had earned Fredric March an Oscar for his dazzling portrayal in 1932. Fleming had decided that Ingrid Bergman would be perfect as Dr. Jekyll's chaste financee, and Selznick assured Bergman that MGM was prepared to spend millions of dollars on lavish sets, costumes, and advertising. *Dr. Jekyll and Mr. Hyde* would be the most suitable showcase for her beauty and talent since *Intermezzo*. Bergman read the script and made a decision. Her intuition told her it was time to put her foot down.

Her decision dumbfounded Selznick, Victor Fleming, and the MGM brass. She was certain *Dr. Jekyll and Mr. Hyde* would be a fine movie, and she was flattered to be asked to participate in it, but she absolutely would not play Jekyll's fiancee. Could she offer a suggestion? She would be delighted to play the role of Ivy Peterson, the barmaid-prostitute who becomes the victim of the maniacal Mr. Hyde.

It was an astonishing idea. The studio had already penciled in the seductive Lana Turner for the role. Her status as a sex symbol made Turner perfect for that part just as Bergman's growing image as "the thinking man's girl next door" made her an exciting choice to play Dr. Jekyll's love interest. Bergman suggested that she and Turner exchange roles. That arrangement would make for a healthy change-of-pace for both actresses.

The idea was sheer madness to Selznick and the MGM people. Actors became stars only because the public took a fancy to them and went to see all their movies. Movie fans demanded to see their favorites in the kinds of roles they expected them to play. Only Spencer Tracy, already considered by many to be the finest actor in Hollywood, could empathize with Miss Bergman's idea. Tracy was instrumental in persuading Fleming to grant her plea that she be allowed to prove her point. She was willing to *test* for the role of Ivy Peterson. The Bergman screen test surprised everyone, except Tracy, and Selznick helped pressure MGM into giving her the part. Lana Turner obliged by readily agreeing to play Beatrix Emery, the role originally slated for Bergman.

MGM spared no expense in making *Dr. Jekyll and Mr. Hyde* a lavish production, but the memory of the earlier film with Fredric March was still too fresh in the minds of critics and fans alike. Only Ingrid Bergman came off positively. She had relied on a maxim considered reliable by actresses since the beginning of theatrical history—"If you are in a rut playing goody-goody parts, get yourself cast as a whore and play it for all it's worth!" She had gambled on an opportunity to display her versatility, and she had won. She was able to be coarse and vulgarly flirtatious and still gain sympathy in a display of sheer terror when the monstrous Mr. Hyde turns on her. It was a bravura performance, and most of the critics loved it.

Ivy Peterson wasn't a great role, but it had given Ingrid Bergman a chance to demonstrate that she had far more to offer than the "luminous" quality everyone had found so fascinating in her previous films. Again, the influential *New York Times* singled her out for its highest praise: "The young Swedish actress proves again that a shining talent can sometimes lift itself above an impossibly written role. . . . Of all the actors, only Miss Bergman has emerged with some measure of honor."

Ironically, her personal success in *Dr. Jekyll and Mr. Hyde* would thrust her into another frustrating period of inactivity about as long as the one she had endured following *Intermezzo*. Her work on the MGM film was completed in February 1941, and she wouldn't face a camera again until she moved to Warner Brothers and *Casablanca* in late spring 1942.

In the beginning she welcomed the chance to take Pia and set up housekeeping with Dr. Lindstrom in Rochester. She revelled in the warmth of her real-life role as a wife and mother in the comfort of her own home. Having completed three motion pictures in a little more than six months, she was tired and a reasonable vacation period would be therapeutic.

After many weeks away from work she began to grow weary of the domestic routine. She was, after all, an actress with a strong need to perform. Still, Selznick was unable to find a suitable follow-up vehicle. He was intent on bringing her career along carefully after the earlier disappointments caused by sheer impatience. Bergman begged him not to be overly protective. She didn't care about the size of a role or if it was specially tailored to her specifications—she only wanted good acting parts. Selznick came up with a compromise.

As part of a scheme to train and develop the talents of young performers he had marked for future stardom, Selznick had brought John Houseman out from New York to direct a season of plays at the Lobero Theater in Santa Barbara. Houseman had joined Orson Welles in founding the Mercury Theater in New York and was an ideal teacher for the new contract players at the Selznick Studio. One of the Houseman students was a Selznick protegee named Phyliss Isely Walker. She would later win acclaim as Jennifer Jones and eventually become Mrs. David O. Selznick.

Selznick realized that Ingrid Bergman had no partic-ular need for further stage experience, but a play at the Lobero might appease her taste for work. It occurred to him that the Swedish star would be a natural for the title role in a revival of Eugene O'Neill's *Anna Christie*. It would be a wonderful way of showcasing her talents until he could find an important film role for her. Bergman accepted the proposal.

The Bergman-Houseman collaboration worked well, and the play opened at the Lobero in July 1941 with all the prestige and fanfare that Selznick's industry power could provide. The theater was jammed with dignitaries from the motion-picture business who had made the long journey north to see Selznick's shining, imported star on stage. They were not disappointed. The play attracted so much attention that it was decided to continue it after Santa Barbara. Berg-man opened *Anna Christie* to good reviews at the Geary Theater in San Francisco in July and then moved on to a summer theater in Maplewood, New Jersey, where Margaret

Humphrey Bogart poses for a publicity shot in front of the ornate entrance to his nightclub in Casablanca. *An authentic model of the entrance has been duplicated for a popular jazz club in Chicago.*

Nazi Major Strasser (Conrad Veidt) is welcomed to Casablanca by Claude Rains as the Vichy French Captain Renault. Veidt, elegantly sinister as the Nazi menace, proved to be a very valuable and most expensive addition to Hal Wallis' cast of top-notch supporting actors.

Ugarte (Peter Lorre) begs Rick Blaine to do something to help him as he is taken into custody by the Vichy French gendarmes. Bogart (as Rick) dashes any hope that he is going to be a "good guy" by refusing for the reason that "I stick my neck out for nobody."

Sam (Dooley Wilson) tries to convince his friend Rick (Bogart) to stop drinking and go to bed in the aftermath of Rick's unexpected meeting with Ilsa Lund (Ingrid Bergman). The moody scene set the stage for the flashback to Rick and Ilsa's romantic, pre-war idyll in Paris.

Joan Alison and Murray Burnett celebrate the sale of their
stage play, Everybody Comes to Rick's, to Warner Brothers
Pictures in January 1942. The $20,000 they
received was reportedly the most money paid for an
unproduced play to that point.

Victor Laszlo (Paul Henreid) is wounded as he and Carl (S. Z. Sakall), a waiter at Rick's Café Americain, make their escape from an underground meeting in Casablanca. S. Z. Sakall's portrayal of Carl in Casablanca launched him on a major career as one of filmdom's most-beloved grandfather-types. His performances, endearingly funny, earned him the billing S. Z. "Cuddles" Sakall.

"Were you lonely when I was in the concentration camp?" asks Victor as he gently questions his wife, Ilsa, about her activities when he was away. Laszlo puts two and two together and surmises that his wife has had an affair with Rick Blaine. The tender conversation prompts her to threaten to kill Rick in order to obtain the letters of transit, understanding Laszlo tries to convince Rick to take his wife with him to freedom.

Rick tells Señor Ferrari (Sydney Greenstreet) that he is leaving Casablanca and will sell him Rick's Café Americain. He provides one proviso to the deal—his old friend Sam must have a permanent job as the café's resident entertainer.

"Round up the usual suspects!" That single line, drolly delivered by Claude Rains when the gendarmes discover that Nazi Major Heinrich Strasser (Conrad Veidt) has been shot, proved to be the key one in finding a solution to the troublesome ending of the filming of Casablanca. An automobile ride and "ESP" brought it about.

"Look, I'm no good at being noble, but it doesn't take much to see that the problems of three little people don't amount to a hill of beans in this crazy world. Someday you'll understand that. . . . Here's looking at you, kid." Those are the famous lines in the most poignant and romantic farewell scene ever filmed. Bogart and Bergman are magnificent as they share a last good-bye at the fog-shrouded Casablanca airport.

Webster redirected it for a run the following month. The play never reached New York, although the critics gave Bergman fine notices when they came out to New Jersey to review it.

With her run in *Anna Christie* completed, Bergman was again faced with the knowledge that Selznick had no film work for her. During one of her idle periods, she had read Ernest Hemingway's 1940 novel, *For Whom the Bell Tolls.* She had thought at the time that she would love to play the part of the rebel girl, Maria. When she heard that Paramount had bought the rights to the book, she immediately told David Selznick that she must have that role. After her work in *Dr. Jekyll and Mr. Hyde* and her stage portrayal of *Anna Christie,* Selznick didn't need much convincing. With dark makeup and her hair cropped close to her head, Bergman would be excellent in the part. It was exactly the kind of opportunity he had been seeking. He began an immediate campaign to convince the people at Paramount that Bergman and *For Whom the Bell Tolls* were meant for each other.

But the Paramount people were not easy to sell. They had already cast Gary Cooper as the male star of the film and had planned to use a page out of Selznick's own casting book to conduct "a wide talent hunt to find the perfect girl" to play opposite him. They agreed with Selznick that Bergman's still-unproven clout at the box office would not be a hindrance. Cooper would supply the drawing power. But Maria was a wild Spanish girl, a guerrilla fighter who tramped the mountains in men's clothing and fought side by side with them in their battles. Maria had to be Spanish and earthy. Bergman, despite her proven versatility, wasn't right physically. She seemed far too ladylike, and she was a Swede. They didn't give the hard-selling Selznick a flat turn-down, but they were not enthusiastic about Bergman's chances.

Bergman was nearly frantic in her desire to land the part. Selznick, caught up in the chase, equalled her determination. He continued to press Paramount to sign Bergman for the role while she was available. He could get no firm commitment. Meanwhile, Paramount's publicity department further irritated him with the heavy mileage it was beginning to get out of its "search for the perfect actress to play Maria." Selznick decided to fight fire with fire.

Learning that Ernest Hemingway was making a trip to China with a stopover in San Francisco, Selznick set up a meeting between the author and Ingrid Bergman. Bergman told Hemingway how much she loved the book and how eager she was to portray Maria on the screen. The actress and the author got along beautifully, and the meeting was a total success. Hemingway gallantly gifted Bergman with a copy of the book, personally autographed: "For Ingrid Bergman, who is the Maria of this story."

Selznick was convinced that the San Francisco rendezvous would clinch the role in *For Whom the Bell Tolls* for Bergman. How could the Paramount people resist after a personal endorsement from the man who had created the character? He instructed his publicity people to inform the press about Hemingway's selection of Bergman as the "real" Maria. Paramount appreciated the unsolicited publicity for its upcoming film but refused to bend before the challenge of Selznick and Hemingway. The war of nerves would continue for several months.

It was during the latter stages of this period that Hal Wallis began to press Selznick to loan Bergman to him for *Casablanca.* Selznick respected Wallis' integrity and his abilities as a producer. If Wallis said the *Casablanca* role would be a good one for his star, Selznick was inclined to believe him. But Selznick was convinced that Bergman would receive nothing less than an Academy Award nomination if she was given the opportunity to play Maria in *For Whom the Bell Tolls.* He wasn't prepared to throw away the Warner Brothers offer, but he also wasn't ready to put anything in the way of Ingrid Bergman accepting an offer from Paramount. He decided to stall Wallis as long as possible.

Hal Wallis would tell a film symposium in the 1970s, "I wanted Ingrid Bergman to play opposite Humphrey Bogart. I had to borrow her from Selznick. It was very difficult at that time to borrow anyone from him. I chased him from Malibu to New York and back and finally made a two-picture deal for her."

Actually, Wallis had worked himself into a corner over Bergman. The Epstein brothers had already begun changing the role to suit Bergman, and all his pre-production planning centered on a Bogart-Bergman teaming. Wallis was as determined to secure Bergman's services for *Casablanca* as Selznick was to peddle them to Paramount for the Hemingway picture. They had reached an impasse.

The breakthrough came when *Casablanca* was only weeks away from its production date. It came with an announcement from the Paramount publicity department that gave Ingrid Bergman her most crushing disappointment since leaving Sweden. Paramount announced that Vera Zorina had been signed to portray the role of Maria in Paramount's forthcoming production of *For Whom the Bell Tolls*. The news was doubly bitter for Selznick and his star because the actress chosen to play the role appeared to them even less "suited" for it than Bergman had been.

Paramount had claimed Bergman wasn't right for the role because she was too Scandinavian and ladylike for the earthy, Spanish Maria, and yet Vera Zorina had been born of Norwegian ancestry in Berlin. She was every bit as Nordic or Scandinavian as Bergman. Furthermore, Zorina had been a celebrated ballerina before deciding to become a dramatic actress. The personality she projected was as ladylike as Bergman's, only it was tinged with more sophistication and less vulnerability.

Selznick felt his counterparts at Paramount had made a huge mistake, and he minced no words in telling them so. He also assured Bergman that a "miracle" could still happen. He had a feeling that, somehow, she would still play Maria. To cheer her, he decided to tell her about the offer for *Casablanca*. It didn't excite her as *For Whom the Bell Tolls* had, but she had not acted in a film in more than a year, and she was anxious to learn more about the offer.

Hal Wallis was desperate. He told Jack Warner about his problems with Selznick, and Warner listened with a sympathetic ear. As far as Warner was concerned, Selznick owed him a favor. He had begged Warner to loan him Olivia De Havilland for *Gone With the Wind,* and Warner finally did so against his better judgment. De Havilland had won an Oscar nomination for Selznick on that picture. Warner suggested that Selznick might be interested in a De Havilland-for-Bergman deal. Wallis considered it a worthy idea since he had no finished script suitable to show to Selznick. In any event Selznick wouldn't be happy that the Bergman role would be secondary to Bogart's.

Warner and Wallis agreed on another idea and decided to put it into action. The Epsteins had been working on the screenplay and had the best grasp of the Ilsa Lund character and what it could do for the Selznick star. The Epsteins were extremely personable men who were liked and respected throughout the entire industry. Wallis told them he would set up an appointment for them with Selznick. They had *carte blanche* to be as inventive as they could—say whatever they liked about the proposed Bergman role and the story itself—so long as they got an okay for Bergman to appear in *Casablanca.*

Selznick agreed to the meeting with the Epsteins. He was interested in more details about this marvelous picture Hal Wallis had planned for Ingrid Bergman. The Epsteins were nervous about the responsibility Wallis and Warner had placed on their shoulders, but they were determined to carry it off. They arrived at Selznick's office and were surprised to find that Bergman would also attend the meeting. Her presence only spurred them on to greater efforts. They told Selznick that *Casablanca* would make Ingrid Bergman a major star. She would be magnificently costumed and filmed to her best advantage. Selznick seemed impressed with this, although Bergman had long proclaimed her boredom with the incidental trappings of stardom.

She was impressed when the Epsteins explained that she would be playing a complex role. She would be forced to make a romantic and dangerous decision between two men, one of whom was the rediscovered, passionate love of her youth and the other a brave and noble leader to whom she felt great loyalty. It would be an important picture dealing with the realities of the war in Europe. At the same time it would be a romantic melodrama with a sinister atmosphere, complete with dark lighting and plenty of smoke and fog. The Epsteins were amazed when Selznick suddenly slapped his hand on the desk and said, "That's all I need. You've got Bergman!"

The contract, in the form of a letter dated April 24, 1942, was delivered to the Warner Studios in Burbank and duly signed. Ingrid Bergman would co-star with Humphrey Bogart in the Hal Wallis production of *Casablanca.*

Point number one of the contract stated:

Concurrently herewith and as part of one transaction, we are entering into an agreement with you whereunder you agree to lend us the services of Olivia De Havilland on the terms and conditions herein set forth. Said agreement may hereinafter be referred to as the De Havilland agreement.

Point number two:

In consideration of your entering into and executing the De Havilland agreement, and if the agreements on your part be observed and performed hereunder, we agree to lend to you and you agree to borrow from us pursuant hereto, the services of Ingrid Bergman, hereinafter called artist, to portray the leading female role in the photoplay now entitled Casa Blanca *to be produced by you and directed by Michael Curtiz, and in which Humphrey Bogart will portray the leading male role. Said lending shall be, and you hereby accept such lending, on terms and conditions hereinafter set forth.*

The contract went on to state that the star must receive notice at least fifteen days prior to starting work, but the starting date could be no later than May 25, 1942. Selznick was obviously still hopeful that something would happen to cause Paramount to team Bergman with Gary Cooper. The contract also stated that Bergman's services would be available for only eight weeks unless Wallis got a written agreement from Selznick to extend it.

Selznick drove a hard bargain with Wallis in the paragraph concerning the compensation for his loan-out of Ingrid Bergman. Wallis was to pay Selznick $3,125 per week for the services of his star for a minimum of eight weeks work, whether or not her services were required for that long. Should she be required to work more than eight weeks, it would cost Wallis a minimum of $520.83 for each additional day.

This was considerably more than Selznick was paying Bergman, but it was standard practice at the time and a primary reason studios loved to get the signatures of capable performers at the bottom of a seven-year contract. After his long struggle to get Selznick's permission to use Bergman, Wallis was very happy to pay it. Jack Warner was also pleased. Selznick had agreed to pay Warners the exact same money for Olivia De Havilland that Warners would spend on the Bergman loan-out. He looked at it as an "even-Steven horse-swap."

The Bergman contract also stated that she must be provided with a "stand-in" and a "star's" dressing room both on and off the set. It also went to great pains to define the terms of her billing. Ingrid Bergman must receive credit on the "main credit title" of all positive prints of the photoplay and in all paid advertising and publicity used to promote the film. It specified that Bergman must receive star billing above the title along with Humphrey Bogart and Paul Henreid and that her name must precede that of Henreid. Furthermore, her name must be set in type at least as large as that used for the names of Bogart and Henreid, and it must also be as large as that used to spell out the title of the film. No other member of the cast, except for Bogart and Henreid, could have his or her name exhibited in type more than 75 percent as large as that used to display the Bergman name.

Losing the part in *For Whom the Bell Tolls* still rankled Ingrid Bergman, but she was grateful that she would be working again after nearly a year and a half away from the camera. She would have liked to know more about the role, but the Epsteins had made it sound interesting. The Warner people insisted that the story was a good one and that she would be working with a top-notch cast and an exceptional director in Michael Curtiz.

Bergman felt some concern about another aspect of *Casablanca*. She had looked forward to playing opposite Gary Cooper, an established star who was considered one of the real gentlemen of Hollywood. She had never met Humphrey Bogart, though she had watched him in some of his gangster films, and now she wondered if he was anything like the characters he played so well on the screen.

Bergman had heard the Hollywood gossip about his drinking, his fights with his wife, and his insulting attitude toward many of the people in the business. Since coming to America, she had worked opposite Leslie Howard, Warner Baxter, Robert Montgomery, and Spencer Tracy—all of whom had been professional and pleasant. Bogart seemed like a very different sort of man. She began to grow more apprehensive as the starting date approached.

Eight

Paul Henreid was about to make a tremendous impression on the collective libidos of American womanhood with his unique approach to lighting two cigarettes when Hal Wallis approached him about playing the part of Victor Laszlo in *Casablanca.* Wallis was convinced that Henreid would become an important star upon the release of *Now, Voyager.* He would be added box-office insurance as the other man in the Bogart-Bergman romance.

Now, Voyager had been the first Hal Wallis production under the producer's new contract at Warner Brothers, and Wallis had cast Henreid opposite Bette Davis in the actor's second Hollywood role. The newcomer's talent and imagination satisfied Wallis that he had made a good choice. During the shooting of *Voyager,* Henreid had approached him with an interesting suggestion.

"I'm supposed to offer Bette a cigarette in this scene," Henreid said. "I think I've found a way to make the business a bit more intimate. Instead of simply handing her a cigarette, I'll take out two cigarettes, put them close together between my lips, light them both at the same time, and then hand her one of them already lighted. It would be rather like a secret kiss."

110

Wallis was pleased with the inventiveness of the actor and gave him permission to use the business. Henreid's unusual manner of lighting a cigarette for himself and Bette Davis has become one of the most memorable pieces of romantic nonsense in film history. Even today, the audience responds with nostalgic guffaws when the business is occasionally trotted out by an unsophisticated "loser" during a comedy sketch. *Now, Voyager* made the top-ten list of popular pictures of 1942, and Paul Henreid was highly touted as a possible "new Charles Boyer" because of his good looks and continental charm.

Hal Wallis was eager to sign Paul Henreid for the role of Victor Laszlo. Henreid was a fine actor and a handsome man who, with his suave appeal, would be well-matched opposite Ingrid Bergman and an appropriate contrast to the off-beat looks and gruff personality of Humphrey Bogart. The natural contrast between the two leading men, coupled with their strengths and weaknesses in the plot, would make Bergman's decision of choosing between them all the more poignant and believable to the women in the audience.

One of the legends concerning *Casablanca* had Warner Brothers testing Henreid opposite Michelle Morgan to see if they would be suitable for the roles of Laszlo and Ilsa Lund. Henreid vehemently refuted the story in 1980, adding, "I never tested for *any* picture. I never even auditioned for any play in my life except one. The truth of the matter is, I didn't even want to do *Casablanca!*"

The circumstances of his birth and America's entry into World War II were the motivating forces which prompted Henreid to accept the role of Victor Laszlo. Henreid was born in Trieste, Austria-Hungary, in 1908. His father was Baron Von Henreid, head of a noble family. World War I greatly changed the political picture in that part of Europe, and the financial condition of the Von Henreid family changed with it. The Von Henreids settled in Vienna, and young Paul became devoted to the arts. In time, he decided to make a career for himself in the theater.

During the 1920s and 1930s Vienna was a serious rival to Paris as the most beautiful and cultured city in Europe. Many of Europe's greatest talents made their headquarters in Vienna, including the legendary Max Reinhardt, who had gained a reputation as a brilliant theatrical impressario and director. Paul Von Henreid set a goal for himself; he would study with Max Reinhardt.

Henreid was accepted as a student by Reinhardt, and the studies paid off. Before long, Paul Von Henreid was acting increasingly important roles in Reinhardt's professional theater in Vienna, and soon became a popular young leading man in a number of classical and contemporary plays in Vienna and many of the other major cities of Europe. In 1937 his success brought him to England, where his career would continue to prosper.

The English film industry was rapidly expanding in the years prior to the outbreak of World War II, and Von Henreid found no difficulty in getting work. But Adolf Hitler was making increasingly warlike noises, and Paul decided to drop the Germanic-sounding *Von* from his name. When Hitler proclaimed his *Anschluss* and marched into Austria in early 1938, Henreid found himself a man without a country. Strongly against Hitler's Nazi policies and with a legitimate reason to fear for his life should he return to Austria, Henreid elected to remain in England.

Henreid made a number of films there, and several of them were released in the United States. Henreid gave fine performances in both film and stage works, and he was not overlooked by American producers. He was especially well-received in two successful British offerings of the era, *Victoria the Great* and *Goodbye, Mr. Chips,* and became a bona fide London matinee idol during the run of the play *The Jersey Lily.*

Prime Minister Neville Chamberlain's policy of appeasement for peace failed in 1939 and Hitler's panzer divisions began their rapid roll across Europe. Britain entered the war, and Paul Henreid's career was vitally affected. He was an Austrian citizen, and Hitler had declared Austria a permanent part of "Greater Germany." To the British government, Henreid had become an enemy alien overnight. Fearful of an organized "Fifth Column" of spies and saboteurs in its midst, England began a roundup of suspected "enemy" foreigners. Within weeks, most of Europe had fallen to the Nazi blitzkreig, the British expeditionary force had been hurled off the continent, and only the narrow English Channel stood between Hitler and an invasion of the British homeland. Any alien suspected of even the smallest German sympathy was immediately locked up in English internment camps.

Only a valiant effort by his theatrical friends kept Henreid from suffering that fate. One of his best friends was the distinguished actor, Conrad Veidt, who had, himself, been born in Germany. Veidt had been an international star for years, had long detested Hitler and the Nazis, and was well-respected among the English. Along with other distinguished British actors, Veidt pleaded Henreid's case with the authorities, and Henreid was never interned. However, he was classified an "A Alien," which meant that he was kept under scrutiny with the knowledge that he could be interned at any time without warning. It was an uncertain position that was not at all conducive to his efforts to build a career.

Although the people of London gallantly "carried on" as best they could under the continuous bombardment by the *Luftwaffe,* the first year of World War II was not the most active in the history of the English theater. Henreid's acting career suffered more than most. He was overjoyed when he received an offer to do a play in New York, though he knew it would not be easy to get permission to leave England or to enter the United States. He had long harbored an ambition to try his luck in America, and the unexpected opportunity would be worth any effort it took to get there.

The play that brought Henreid to New York was the one he had starred in so successfully in London's West End. The famed American producer Gilbert Miller had tendered him the offer to play the male lead in the New York version of *The Jersey Lily.* It was a first-rate role for Henreid, and he was further excited by Miller's plan to co-star him with Katherine Cornell. Cornell, of course, was widely acclaimed as "The First Lady of the American Stage." Vestiges of his Austrian accent lingered, but that had not hindered his success in London and Henreid expected no problems from it in New York.

He was excited by the hustle and bustle of New York City after the blackouts and devastation of London. The

113

American people seemed to have little concern that Hitler's aircraft might eventually seek targets on their soil. America was still neutral, although decidedly in favor of the English in the "Battle of Britain." More importantly, Henreid felt free again. He was no longer an "enemy alien." He was simply an immigrant actor.

Unfortunately, he was unable to realize his plans for an immediate success in his new country. Gilbert Miller's production of *The Jersey Lily* never reached the Broadway stage. Still, Henreid's European credits impressed the American theatrical community and brought him quick representation by MCA Corporation. He was advised to set his sights on film work in Hollywood.

Although the United States was still officially at peace, the Roosevelt administration was preparing for possible war. The draft had been reinstated, and many of Hollywood's up-and-coming young leading men were leaving for military service. Henreid was not a citizen, and he was also just past draft age. With the proper handling, there was reason to hope that he could find a great deal of work in Hollywood in the years ahead. His personal agent at MCA was Lew Wasserman, a man who would guide the careers of many stars in films before taking over as head of Universal Studios.

Under Wasserman's guidance, Paul Henreid quickly won a most unusual contract with RKO Pictures which guaranteed him a fine base for the future. The deal called for Henreid's services for only one picture a year for seven years and specified that his one yearly picture for RKO must have a starting date between June 1 and August 31. For the rest of the year, Henreid was free to work anywhere as much as he liked. Under that contract, Henreid made his first American film in 1941—in an RKO picture called *Joan of Paris*.

Henreid's first U.S. movie broke no box-office records, but it did provide Lew Wasserman with a tool to use in the selling of his client. Jack Warner had a strong dislike of Wasserman and would eventually bar him from the lot because of what he considered the agent's undue influence over another client, Bette Davis. But Wasserman got along well with Hal Wallis, who was about to film his first picture under his own production banner at Warners. The film would star

Bette Davis, and Wasserman suggested that Paul Henreid would be perfect as the Davis love interest in *Now, Voyager.*

Wallis looked at the *Joan of Paris* footage and was impressed with Henreid's performance. The man was handsome, and he handled himself well in front of the camera. Although Henreid had an accent, it only made him more interesting. The role in *Now, Voyager* called only for a New York architect, and Wallis didn't think it was important that he be a native-born American. Bette Davis also thought Henreid would be fine for the part, and Wallis signed him to a one-picture contract.

With Henreid's success in his first Warner film, Wallis was convinced that he was the best possible choice for the role of the underground leader in *Casablanca.* The actor had been born in Middle Europe, not far from Victor Laszlo's Czechoslovakian homeland, and his accent would fit well in that role. On the screen, Henreid projected warmth, intelligence, and strength—all necessary qualities for Laszlo. Paul Henreid respected Wallis and was flattered when the producer offered him the part. He had enjoyed Wallis' association on *Now, Voyager* and, when Wallis told him that Michael Curtiz would be directing *Casablanca,* he was even more interested in the project. But he had made a fine beginning on his Hollywood career, and he knew it was important that he carefully consider the pluses and minuses of any future roles offered. He asked for a copy of the script.

Henreid's study of the script left him disappointed. He felt the role that had been offered would do little to further his career. The story was fine, and he was confident that Mike Curtiz' direction would make it an interesting movie. The idea of appearing opposite Ingrid Bergman had also appealed to him. But that was the rub. Would he actually be playing "opposite" Bergman? The role he had been offered was in no way as interesting as the one Humphrey Bogart would play. If the ending of *Everybody Comes to Rick's* was retained, Victor Laszlo would fly away with the heroine but her heart would remain in Casablanca with Rick Blaine.

One of the first things Henreid had learned at the acting academy was that secondary roles "should be avoided, if at all possible." William Shakespeare had written an excel-

115

lent actor's role with the character of the scheming Iago in *Othello.* But he had called the tragedy *Othello,* not *Iago.* Henreid felt that playing Victor Laszlo would slow, rather than increase, the momentum of his career. He told Hal Wallis that he did not think he should play Victor Laszlo in *Casablanca.*

Henreid's turn-down was a severe setback to Wallis' plans. Henreid had only a one-picture deal with Warner Brothers, and there was no way Wallis could coerce the actor into accepting the part. The producer talked to Lew Wasserman and asked the agent to join him in attempting to persuade the actor to change his mind. America's reaction to the Japanese attack on Pearl Harbor would create the pressure to influence Henreid's final decision.

In the aftermath of that attack, an urgency approaching panic seized the West Coast of the United States. The reason for the panic was quite logical. If the Japanese could hit the Hawaiian Islands with impunity, what would prevent them from moving their aircraft carriers off the coast of California to strike at the strategic defense industries scattered throughout that state? Jack Warner, as a gag, had his studio crew paint an arrow and a huge sign on the roof of one of his sound stages saying, "LOCKHEED THAT A-WAY!" Lockheed, correctly, didn't appreciate the gag and persuaded Warner to paint over his sign. Warner also sent his technicians to Lockheed to help in camouflaging the entire aircraft plant.

A further indication of the fear of a Japanese attack on Los Angeles was the cancellation of the Academy Award Dinner. The ceremony was finally rescheduled for February. Even more earthshaking was the cancellation of the 1942 Rose Bowl Football Game on New Year's Day. For the first and only time in its long history, the Rose Bowl Game was played outside of Pasadena, a long way outside the L.A. suburb in Durham, North Carolina. Security officials had no intention of collecting 100,000 people in a stadium on the West Coast as an inviting target for the marauding Japanese.

The strongest repercussion of Pearl Harbor and America's entry into World War II was the effect it had on the nation's Japanese population. California, in particular, had large numbers of people of Japanese descent. Most were full

American citizens, born and raised in the United States, but the Roosevelt administration felt sure that it was Japanese ethnic sympathizers in Hawaii who had advised Tojo's forces that Pearl Harbor and other military targets in the islands were vulnerable. Whether or not these assumptions were correct, the military men were determined to prevent an attack on the West Coast. The authorities began rounding up all Japanese-Americans, regardless of their backgrounds and sympathies. Their properties were confiscated, and men, women, and children were confined to internment camps.

To Paul Henreid, it was a repeat of the frightful experience he had managed to escape in England. America, like Britain, was now at war with Germany and Italy, as well as Japan. Hitler had annexed Austria, and Henreid was an Austrian in this country on a work permit. If the government had interned Japanese-American citizens, what chance did he have as an "enemy alien"? He told his worries to his agent.

Lew Wasserman recognized the potential seriousness of Henreid's plight and listened sympathetically as the actor told him of his earlier problems in England. It seemed reasonable to him that Henreid's background as a distinguished actor in Europe, plus the success he felt would come from *Now, Voyager,* should be able to offset any worries the American government might have about Henreid's loyalties. But Henreid wasn't at all confident. Many of the interned Japanese-Americans had been respected members of the community. Wasserman advised him again to accept the role of the Nazi fighter in *Casablanca.* That would certainly help his public reputation.

The actor repeated the objections he had to the role of Victor Laszlo. The agent could appreciate his professional thinking. But Wasserman assured him that Wallis would give *Casablanca* and all of its actors every production value at his command. Wallis would also be willing to give Henreid star billing behind only Bogart and Bergman. There was an even better possibility. Maybe Warner Brothers could be persuaded to sign Henreid to a long-term contract. If that could be arranged, the combined influence of RKO and Warner Brothers could be brought to bear on the authorities to keep Paul Henreid a free and properly employed resident alien. Certainly, with seven-year contracts from two major studios in his pocket, Henreid would be free from any financial worries.

Henreid was still not enthusiastic about the proposal. As far as he was concerned, he already had a secure and flexible working arrangement. He was being paid by RKO on a one-picture-per-year deal, and he was free the rest of the time to pursue acting parts at other studios as a freelancer. His set-up wasn't as good as Gregory Peck's contracts, which called for one picture a year for seven years with both Twentieth Century-Fox and Selznick, but Henreid had gotten off to a good start in his first year in California. However, the threat of possible internment with no chance to do anything forced him to consider Wasserman's idea.

Hal Wallis was delighted when Wasserman made his proposal for the services of Paul Henreid. He had been pleased with Henreid's work on *Now, Voyager,* and he knew the actor would be a fine addition to the cast of *Casablanca.* Jack Warner gave his okay, the financial and other aspects of the contract were negotiated, and Paul Henreid became an official member of the Warner stock company.

Henreid's first assignment under the new contract would be playing the role of Victor Laszlo in *Casablanca.* He would receive star billing following the names of Humphrey Bogart and Ingrid Bergman.

Things were beginning to fall into place nicely for Hal Wallis. He had gotten his three stars for the leading roles, and Jack Warner had been most cooperative. Wallis didn't have the luxury of a huge budget, but with careful manipulation he could make it adequate. Michael Curtiz was champing at the bit and eager to start filming. Wallis' next step would be taken in company with Curtiz—the casting of the smaller roles. Painstaking care in this chore could truly make *Casablanca* a quality motion picture.

Nine

Everybody Comes to Rick's was written with a cast of sixteen speaking parts plus extras. Hal Wallis and Michael Curtiz had encouraged the screenwriters to revise the play and write additional scenes which would give *Casablanca* twenty-two speaking roles and hundreds of extras for atmosphere. The Epstein brothers and Howard Koch would retain most of the dialogue written by Murray Burnett and Joan Alison, but they enlarged and also renamed some of the roles and created new ones to better establish the overall feel of wartime Casablanca.

An examination of the cast list quickly disproves the old myth that *Casablanca* began as little more than a "B melodrama." Wallis and Curtiz peopled their cast with some of the finest character actors in Hollywood history. The movie colony was swollen with an influx of actors attempting to escape the war in Europe. It was a perfect opportunity to utilize an international cast, because many of those European actors were already well-established members of the Warner stock company. That would simplify some of the casting, but Wallis had no intention of cutting corners. He was willing to spend whatever money was necessary to bring in specific actors from elsewhere to fill the many small but important roles in his film.

Perhaps the second best acting part in *Casablanca,* as well as in the original play, was that of the amoral Vichy French Prefect of Police. Burnett and Alison had written him as a handsome, charming womanizer whose cynicism equalled Rick's. But the captain was a man with power second only to that of his Nazi bosses and an ability to use it ruthlessly. The curse was taken off the part by the Frenchman's charm and sardonic sense of humor. The Epstein brothers had immediately been fascinated by the role and decided to expand it. The character had been called Luis Rinaldo in the original play, but the Epsteins decided Louis Renault sounded decidedly more French. They also thought the role would be perfect for the underplayed style of Claude Rains. Hal Wallis agreed and told them to shape the part for Rains. The Epsteins enjoyed rewriting the Renault role, and the scenes between Rick and Renault contain some of the wittiest, most memorable lines in any motion picture.

Although no longer bound by a long-term contract, Claude Rains had long been a mainstay of Warner Brothers movies. An unusual Hollywood actor because he had become a star without being blessed with faultless good looks, he had portrayed a wide variety of roles, usually reflecting whimsy or villainy, in a number of successful films. Rains had managed to climb to an enviable position in the acting profession strictly on the merits of his acting ability.

Claude Rains was born in London, England, on November 10, 1890. His acting talent was such that his pronounced English accent would seldom have any effect on the roles he played in one way or another. His portrayal of the title role in the 1933 film *The Invisible Man* brought him almost immediate stardom in the United States. That unlikely story remains something of a minor classic today. His star continued to rise during the 1930s, and the respect for his versatility became so strong that he would be cast in a ballyhooed remake of the silent screen classic, *The Phantom of the Opera,* in the role made famous by Lon Chaney.

Like Humphrey Bogart, Rains signed an early contract with Warner Brothers and began a long string of pictures for that studio. Unlike Bogart, Rains was generally given meaty roles which made him a major force at the studio. Because of his stature in the industry, many of Rains' movies were directed by Warners' top director, Michael Curtiz. Between 1936 and 1942, Rains completed eight Warner films with Curtiz. Hal Wallis was the producer on most of them.

Some of the Claude Rains pictures were standouts in which he had ample opportunity to display his talents at portraying wily villains. He was Fredric March's antagonist in *Anthony Adverse* (1936), the scheming Prince John in *Robin Hood* (1938), and Errol Flynn's Spanish enemy (Don José Alvarez de Cordoba) in *The Sea Hawk* (1940). He also came off well in such popular films as *Mr. Smith Goes to Washington* and *Juarez* (both in 1939), and *Here Comes Mr. Jordan* and *Kings Row* (1941).

Rains became a special favorite of Jack L. Warner because of his huge success in a 1938 Hal Wallis–Michael Curtiz picture called *Four Daughters*. The picture was light-weight stuff on a par with a radio soap opera, but Rains added his British charm to good effect as the irresponsible father of the Lane sisters, Rosemary, Lola, and Priscilla. Gail Page played the fourth daughter. The picture became such a box-office smash that Warners made two follow-ups in 1939. Rains, Page, and the Lane sisters again starred in the sequels called *Daughters Courageous* and *Four Wives.*

Hal Wallis had cast Rains in *Now, Voyager,* and when Rains read the unfinished master script of *Casablanca,* he liked it and readily agreed to portray Captain Louis Renault. Rains, the man, had the same sort of ironic sense of humor he displayed on the screen. Working with Curtiz always caused him minor irritations, but he enjoyed plotting ways to overcome them.

Wallis, Curtiz, and the screenwriters had decided to upgrade the role of the Nazi officer in *Everybody Comes to Rick's.* To make Rick Blaine's motivation plausible, it would be necessary to keep the time of the screen action before December 7, 1941. Since America was actually already in the war against Germany, the part of Major Strasser could be emphasized as the arch-villain of the picture. Deciding there was no actor on the Warner lot with all the proper credentials for the role, Wallis and Curtiz began to consider actors from other studios. Their eventual choice would cost Jack Warner more than he had paid for the services of Ingrid Bergman.

Because it was being adapted from a work of the stage, *Casablanca* would be a film of ideas and dialogue rather than one of action. Scenes were being added to bring needed action into the picture, but the main story line would be motivated by implied threats rather than actual violence. For that reason, Wallis wanted Strasser to be played by an actor who could bring a large degree of subtlety to the role. Strasser had been a captain in the play, but he was being "promoted" to major for the film. He was no ranting, bestial Nazi on the surface, but a man who could chill his potential victims with Teutonic charm. Wallis and Curtiz knew the perfect man to play the part, but he was under contract to MGM. They began a campaign to sign Conrad Veidt, Paul Henreid's old friend from London.

Veidt was born in Germany in 1903. Like so many of his contemporaries, Veidt's pursuit of an acting career on the stage was interrupted by a detour into silent films. He became an international star after the release in 1919 of *The Cabinet of Dr. Caligari,* a German film which continues to show up on the "best" lists of many serious film students and was voted the twelfth-best film of all time in the film survey at the Brussels World Fair in 1958. The movie was so successful that Conrad Veidt, as its leading actor, was assured of a ready reception wherever he chose to work. He came to Hollywood during the 1920s and made a number of silent films before moving on to England in the 1930s.

Veidt starred in a number of highly successful films in Britain during the 1930s, including *The Thief of Baghdad, Storm Over Asia,* and *The Passing of the Third Floor Back.* Although in a more secure position than his friend Paul Henreid, Veidt, who was in England at the outbreak of World War II, also decided to escape the pressure of the Nazi blitz on the British capital and returned to Hollywood, where his agents signed him to a contract with MGM. Veidt's good looks and talent quickly landed him a number of fine roles in films such as *Escape, Above Suspicion,* and *A Woman's Face.* In the latter film, a remake of one of Ingrid Bergman's Swedish hits,

Veidt co-starred with Joan Crawford as the actress's cruel, nobleman lover.

The *Casablanca* script called for Major Strasser to be grandly decked-out in his dress uniform for his appearances at Rick's. He would order only the best wines and caviar, and Veidt's manner, bearing, and Prussian features made him perfect for the role. Wallis began negotiating for his services with MGM and found that they came very high. Conrad Veidt was finally signed for the role of Major Strasser only after Warner Brothers agreed to pay MGM $5,000 a week for his services.

The studio was paying Bogart $3,500 weekly, and the services of Ingrid Bergman had cost only $3,125 per week. Veidt, in a relatively minor role, would cost Warner Brothers more than any of the three stars of *Casablanca*.

Much of the success of *The Maltese Falcon* was due to the work of Sydney Greenstreet and Peter Lorre in support of Humphrey Bogart. Wallis was well aware of this. Both character actors were signed to Warner contracts, they were available, and Wallis felt sure that another Bogart-Greenstreet-Lorre teaming in *Casablanca* would have a positive effect at the box office. Bogie's first outing as a hero in the John Huston film had been more clearly defined by the menace and treachery of Greenstreet as the "Fat Man" and Lorre as his "Weasel" henchman. There was an excellent small part in *Casablanca* that would be a natural for Lorre. But casting Greenstreet would be more difficult.

Sydney Greenstreet was born in Kent, England, in 1879 and spent decades building a reputation as a fine actor on the English stage since his debut performance in 1902. Ironically, he had no interest in becoming a movie actor. His first film role would come in 1941 in *The Maltese Falcon*. Although he was a novice movie actor, Greenstreet's *Falcon* performance established him as a memorable figure in American films and earned him an Academy Award nomination as best supporting actor. There was no comparable role for him in *Everybody Comes to Rick's*, but Wallis wanted him in *Casablanca* even if the writers had to create a part for him.

The Epstein-Koch writing team had to do a juggling act in coming up with the Greenstreet role. The original play had a character named Señor Martinez who owned a rival café called The Blue Parrot, but Martinez had only one scene in *Everybody Comes to Rick's*. He came to Rick's Café in an attempt to buy it or, at the very least, purchase the services of Rick's friend and entertainer, Sam. Greenstreet would be fine for that role if it were big enough.

One of Wallis' specific instructions to his writers was to expand the role of Martinez until it was more worthy of Greenstreet's talents. With an unexplained penchant for naming characters after foreign automobiles (Luis Rinaldo was renamed after the French Renault car), the writers decided to call the Martinez character Señor Ferrari. (They neglected, however, to switch the Spanish *Señor* to the Italian *Signor*.) The Epsteins and Koch added a few more scenes for Greenstreet, making him the most powerful dealer in the Casablanca black market as well as the owner of The Blue Parrot. Greenstreet would still be pretty much wasted in the small role, even after it had been lengthened, but his appearance and villainous charm would add much to the strength of the supporting cast.

Greenstreet's film sidekick, Peter Lorre, was delighted with the opportunity to do *Casablanca*. His role of Guillermo Ugarte was not big, but it was of great importance in the story line. It is Ugarte who kills the German couriers and steals the two letters of transit which become the chief motivating factor in the plot. Ugarte was given a highly emotional scene in which he is captured by the authorities and taken off to jail. Ugarte also has good scenes with Humphrey Bogart's Rick Blaine. It was the latter situation which appealed to Lorre most, because he and Bogie were good friends on and off the Warner lot.

Born in Rosenberg, Hungary, on June 26, 1904, Peter Lorre seemed an unlikely candidate for future fame in motion pictures. His father was a businessman and his grandfather had been a rabbi. The young Lorre was destined for a career in medicine, specializing in the new field of psychiatry. He studied with pioneer psychoanalysts Sigmund Freud and Alfred Adler in Vienna, and later worked as an assistant to both men. Unfortunately, Lorre had also been gifted with a wild sense of humor. He soon discovered that his inner

124

feelings were more irreverent than analytical as he listened to the neurotic stories of his patients. He would later compare the experience with "looking at rectums all day."

However, it was his study of psychiatry which eventually led him into an acting career. Lorre and a fellow student in Vienna began an experiment in what has come to be called psychodrama. The actors were required to improvise scenes and lines on the spot. Lorre, the exhibitionist, eagerly took a part in the dramas, and found the work enjoyable and challenging. When the theater failed as a profitable business, Lorre was penniless. Upon deciding he had no future in the medical profession, he had burned all his bridges behind him. But fate came galloping to the rescue. A theatrical producer had seen one of Lorre's performances in the defunct experimental theater and was impressed enough to offer him a job in a professional company in Breslau, Poland. The ex-psychoanalyst jumped at the chance, and the job gave him valuable experience. Lorre became a fine actor in a number of shows in Breslau, Zurich, Vienna, and elsewhere, and the stage work led to his first motion-picture role.

German director Fritz Lang saw Lorre in a play and asked him to play the lead in a new movie, *M* (1931), based on a series of actual murders which had terrorized the city of Dusseldorf, Germany. The film became a sensation and continues to rank high on the lists of many critics' all-time favorites. Lorre's portrayal of the murderer brought him not only profit, but unexpected suffering. Shortly after the film's release, Lorre was attacked by a mob of rock-throwing Berliners who had been convinced that he was an actual murderer.

M made Lorre a great star in Germany and the rest of Europe. Anxious for a change of pace after *M*, he tried to talk the Berlin studio into giving him a comedy role for his next film, but his request was denied. Lorre flatly refused to play another villain and decided to return to the stage where he would be allowed to do comedy. But the fast-moving political events inside Germany brought an early end to his Berlin acting career. The Nazis were becoming increasingly powerful, and Lorre was one of the first to make a public prediction about the insanity that lay ahead.

Peter Lorre was a bright, outspoken young man. He disliked the Nazis' announced intention of limiting intellectual freedom as much as he detested their blatant anti-Semitism. His wild sense of humor, which would later make him a notorious Hollywood practical joker, prompted him to accept an invitation to appear at a Berlin festival sponsored by the Nazi party. He decided to demonstrate his comedic talents along with his loathing of Nazi ideas. The festival sponsors announced that the famous movie star would speak on the subject of poison gas in warfare as advocated by a cele-brated Nazi professor, but instead of upholding the ideas ad-vanced in the professor's booklet, Lorre burlesqued them out-rageously. His virtuoso performance was greeted by rousing boos and threatened violence from the surprised audience. It was later reported that Peter Lorre's name was third on Hitler's infamous list of those to be exterminated.

Long after the war Lorre was adamant in his stand that he wasn't forced to flee Germany—he knew he had no future in Hitler's country and simply left. "I didn't sneak away," he said. "I just went down to the station and got on a train to Vienna."

Lorre eventually traveled from Vienna to Paris and on to London. He arrived in the British capital with no knowledge of English and no means of supporting himself. However, he had a friend there who gave him shelter, and Lorre quickly learned that his reputation as an actor had preceded him across the English Channel. In less than a month he met British film director Alfred Hitchcock, who was looking for someone to play the lead in his new film, *The Man Who Knew Too Much*. Lorre was in the unfortunate position of not knowing enough—of the English language. He managed to fool Hitchcock about his lack of English by nodding, smiling, and saying "yes" to everything and anything the director said. Given the lead in the film, Lorre managed to play the part beautifully with the help of English friends who translated the script for him and helped him memorize the lines phonetically. Fortunately, Lorre was quickly able to pick up a working command of the language. He established a good relation-ship with Hitchcock, and the film became a success. He began to investigate a number of offers he was receiving from

American studios and decided to sign a contract with Harry Cohn at Columbia Pictures.

His term at Columbia did not go at all as he had hoped. Cohn had promised to star him in an important picture but tried to back out of the strictly verbal agreement when Lorre arrived in Hollywood. After a stubborn battle, Cohn agreed to make *Crime and Punishment* with Lorre in one of the lead parts. The picture broke no box-office records, and Lorre was happy to return to England after a year and a half to make another picture for Alfred Hitchcock. That film, *Secret Agent,* was well-received when Lorre returned to the United States.

Lorre freelanced for a time and then agreed to play an Oriental character in a Twentieth Century-Fox picture called *Mr. Moto.* His huge, hypnotic eyes and his convincing portrayal of Moto caused many people to believe for years that he was at least part Oriental. The Moto pictures caught on, and Fox made ten of them with Lorre in the title role. Lorre hated the work but was able to build up a sizable bank account by the time he decided to sign a seven-year contract with Warner Brothers on the promise of better roles.

At Warners, Lorre found that he was to be typecast as a minor heavy. His success as the Oriental Moto made it even more difficult for the studio to find roles for him. His big break coincided with that of Bogart and Greenstreet in *The Maltese Falcon.* The teaming of the three actors in that picture so delighted the audience that Warners would repeat it in a number of pictures beginning with *Casablanca.* Lorre and Bogart struck up a friendship on *Falcon* that would endure until Bogie's death. Both men had a genuine love for acting and a passionate loathing for the overblown pomposity of some of their higher-placed contemporaries. Lorre surpassed even Bogart in the disdain he felt for the roles he was forced to play. He referred to his profession as "making faces."

The two friends were delighted to be working together again and immediately began plotting the practical jokes they could pull off during filming. They often toured Hollywood's more famous watering holes together, and even Bogart had to take a back seat to Lorre's needling of his coworkers and superiors.

One famous Lorre practical joke was pulled on one of his directors, Herman Shumlin. During the filming of *Confidential Agent,* Lorre decided that not only was Shumlin risking his health by smoking cigarettes, but he also was taking himself entirely too seriously. Deciding to leaven the occasion with an elaborate gag involving Shumlin's habit of chain-smoking, Lorre obtained an eye dropper which he filled with water and eagerly waited for Shumlin to approach him. When Shumlin rested his lighted cigarette in an ash tray, Lorre would squirt it. Every time the director would try to take a puff, he would find that it had gone out. Shumlin gave vent to his famous temper and began to complain loudly about the quality of his tobacco, not knowing that no glowing cigarettes could survive the delighted and deadly aim of Peter Lorre and his hidden eye dropper.

Lorre had pulled an even bigger practical joke on the late Alfred Hitchcock after they had completed *Secret Agent.* Before boarding the ship to return to the United States, Lorre had bought out the entire stock of a London canary shop and paid to have the birds delivered to Hitchcock. The "aviary" was accompanied by an elaborate note explaining the canaries were only a small token of the gratitude Lorre felt he owed the director. But Hitchcock was no easy prey. He kept Lorre awake on the entire trip to New York by sending him repeated cablegrams with thoughtful comments on the health and welfare of each and every canary Lorre had given him.

Now Lorre and Bogart were together again, and the set of *Casablanca* promised to be anything but dull.

With Lorre, Greenstreet, Veidt, and Claude Rains already signed, Wallis and Curtiz were prepared to begin the search for an actor to play another of the central roles in *Casablanca.* They knew the part wouldn't be easy to cast because it would require the talents of an especially gifted black actor who could also sing and play the piano. Hattie McDaniel had made a smashing breakthrough for black performers when she won the Academy Award for best supporting actress in 1939 for her work in *Gone With the Wind,* but Hollywood, by and large, was not a place where black Americans could easily win fame for their acting talents.

The Hollywood moguls of the thirties and forties believed that "art reflects life." With few of the educational and employment opportunities available today, most black Americans of that period were forced to find employment in menial jobs. The roles offered well-known movie actors like Eddie "Rochester" Anderson, Mantan Moreland, and Willie Best reflected this situation. Murray Burnett and Joan Alison, in their play, had created a character who was an entertainer (not an unusual role for a black player) and also the only close friend of the hero. The character created by Burnett and Alison was retained almost totally for the screen. Both the play and the film would emphasize that Sam was no standard employee or "Uncle Tom" character. He had traveled the world with Rick Blaine because of the mutual respect and affection between them. Sam knew Rick better than anyone, including Ilsa.

There were any number of well-known Negro singer-pianists who could fit the musical requirements of the role, but the part was much too important to assign to a musician with little acting experience. Curtiz and Wallis were intent on finding a man who could act and sing with equal ability. It wouldn't be an easy task, but they were determined to persevere. Their perseverance eventually led them to a man named Dooley Wilson.

Dooley, christened Arthur Wilson, was born in Tyler, Texas, in 1889. Arthur was the youngest of five children fathered by a poor black laborer who died when his children were still quite young. The poverty-stricken Wilsons, mother and children, were all forced to work in order to keep from starving. The youngest son had a talent for singing, and he began to contribute to the meager family income at the age of seven. Young Arthur seldom made more than five dollars a week in nightly appearances in tent shows and church affairs, but his income had risen to as much as eighteen dollars a week by the time he had marked his eighth birthday.

Wilson was sold on a career as a performer. It didn't seem like work to him, and he would later admit that he had never considered doing anything else for a living. He continued to do "one-nighters" as a child performer throughout the southern Midwest before he finally moved to Chicago as a very young man. In the Windy City he landed a job in the black

Pekin Stock Company operated, in part, by Charles Gilpin, who was destined for fame as Eugene O'Neill's *Emperor Jones*. Wilson found that he especially enjoyed the new work which combined acting and singing.

It was in that Illinois stock company that Wilson acquired his nickname, Dooley. There were few playwrights creating roles for black actors or black companies in the early days of the century. The Pekin Stock Company ignored the problem and did ordinary plays, casting them with black actors in "white face" where necessary. The director discovered that Arthur Wilson was able to deliver an incredibly good imitation of an Irish brogue, and Wilson soon began to specialize in Irish roles. In one play, he painted his face white, affected a leprechaunish air, and sang a popular song called "Mr. Dooley." The audience loved it! Wilson and the song became so identified with each other that the performer decided to change his billing. From that time on, Arthur was to be known as Dooley Wilson.

Wilson also learned to play the drums in jazz-conscious Chicago. After leaving the Pekin Stock Company, he traveled to New York and began working with jazz bands in some of the better nightspots in Harlem. On several occasions a young songwriter named Irving Berlin slipped him a sawbuck to play one of his new songs called "Alexander's Ragtime Band."

Dooley formed his own band and decided to explore the world of postwar Europe in the 1920s. He and the Red Devils toured France and found a ready reception in clubs which featured that exciting new American music called "Le Jazz Hot." Dooley and his Red Devils even played a special gig in North Africa on the occasion of a gala party in honor of Lawrence of Arabia—and it was held in Casablanca!

Wilson tired of the foreign scene toward the close of the 1920s and decided to return to the States. Wanting to do some more exploring of his talents as a legitimate actor, he managed to land a job in a New Hampshire summer theater where a young actress named Bette Davis was also starting her career. Back in New York, he found it difficult to get roles of any kind on Broadway. He continued to earn food money by playing drums at the Nest Club in Harlem. Dooley thought he was finally on the way to recognition and solvency when he landed a part in a Broadway play called *The Strangler Fig.* The show closed after seven performances. His first important acting success came on the road where he played the role of Crooks in the national company of the hit play *Of Mice and Men.* That role served as a springboard for his first acting triumph on Broadway. Dooley got the word that a producer was auditioning black actors for a show called *Cabin in the Sky.* Wilson went to an audition and read for a part called "Little Joe." He was surprised to learn that the role was the male lead opposite Ethel Waters, who had already signed to star in the play. Wilson was hired for the part, and his performance as "Little Joe" projected him toward the big time.

Arriving in Hollywood on the strength of his success in *Cabin in the Sky,* he was signed to a contract by Paramount Pictures. When *Cabin* was finally brought to the screen, Wilson's role of "Little Joe" was handed to Eddie Anderson, and Dooley found himself playing a succession of "pullman porter" parts. He had managed to save some of his $150-a-week salary from *Cabin in the Sky* on Broadway and more of the good salary Paramount was paying him.

He and his wife, Estelle, bought a five-room white stucco bangalow with a backyard big enough for a small garden in central Los Angeles. He was fifty-seven years old and happy to be settled and off the road. But he was also anxious about the progress of his acting career in films. Unbeknownst to him, Paramount was also unhappy with their working relationship and was prepared to drop him when the next option came up.

Wilson's agent, worried that his client was about to join the unemployed, excitedly told him that Warner Brothers was looking for a black actor-musician for a good part in their new movie, *Casablanca.* Dooley thought the role sounded right for him, and an appointment was set up with both Hal Wallis and Michael Curtiz. The interview went well. The producer and the director were both taken with Wilson's pixie-like personality, and they were equally impressed by his background. The fact that he had played France, like the man Murray Burnett had based the character Sam on, seemed an amazing coincidence. His experience in the city of Casablanca

131

also did not go unnoticed. However, there was one very big difference between the fictional Sam and the real-life Dooley. Wilson was an accomplished drummer, but he had never learned to play the piano.

Curtiz asked Wilson to read for him. Wilson immediately captured the essence of Rick's buddy, Sam. Dooley also sang a few selections for Wallis and Curtiz, and the two men were pretty well convinced they had found the actor they wanted for the role. Wilson's personality, his singing, and his acting more than made up for his lack of ability at the piano. If he could realistically go through the motions of playing the piano, Wallis could assign a studio musician to dub in the actual playing. Dooley Wilson, the poor boy from Tyler, Chicago, Harlem, Paris, Casablanca, and points in between, would create the role of Sam in *Casablanca*.

Dooley Wilson was one of the last of the major players signed for *Casablanca*. Paramount was eager to obtain as much money as possible for his services, and negotiations went on for some time. They were further complicated because Wilson had been loaned to Loews, Inc., for a movie called *Cairo*. Paramount had no objection to Wilson appearing in the Hal Wallis film, providing he was able to complete his work in the Loews movie first.

The contract, again in letter form, arrived at the Warner studios one day after the *Casablanca* filming had started. Fortunately, Dooley was not in the opening scenes. In terms of money and billing, his contract was a far cry from those of the other actors signed for the film. Warner Brothers was obliged to pay Paramount a minimum of $3,500 for seven week's work. In other words, Dooley Wilson would cost Warner Brothers $500 per week. Paramount would even permit him to work one additional week without pay, providing the studio was again paid on a $500-per-week basis if the overtime ran more than one week. The contract stipulated that Wilson must be furnished with a "suitable" stand-in and that he must receive "appropriate" credit as a featured player. No specific billing was mentioned. Warner Brothers Pictures had gotten a bargain.

With the opening up of the original play into a form suitable for the screen, the writers had created a number of other good small parts. There had been a bit part of a waiter in the original play, and Wallis ordered the Epsteins and Koch to enlarge it to suit the talents of a remarkable actor he intended to hire. He also asked them to write in a meaty small role for a bartender at Rick's. These parts would provide the comedy relief in the plot. The actors he cast for the roles would deliver endearing performances.

Warner Brothers had recently signed an actor with an unforgettable face and the almost unpronounceable name of S. Z. Sakall. Sakall had registered strongly in his first films in America, and Wallis and Curtiz wanted him for the role of Carl, the waiter. Born in Hungary around the turn of the century, Sakall was also a refugee from Hitler's Europe. He became such a lovable, grandfatherly movie personality that his screen billing would be altered to S. Z. "Cuddles" Sakall for the forty films he would make after *Casablanca.*

Sakall, like so many of the others in the *Casablanca* cast, had built a successful career in Europe before Hitler's reign of terror forced him into exile. Widely respected as a fine European comedy actor as a result of the roles he created on stage and screen, he made films in Hungary and Germany before fleeing to England just before the outbreak of war. He also did some work in England for a short period, although he had little knowledge of the language.

Incredibly, Sakall was still unable to speak English when he came to Hollywood in 1940 to make his first film. The picture was *It's a Date,* and it starred one of America's "sweethearts" of the period, Deanna Durbin. Sakall, in the role of a high-strung producer, was forced to learn the role phonetically. Still, his performance was immensely funny, and he was well-launched in his new career. He also came across strongly in the Barbara Stanwyck film *Ball of Fire,* which was a big financial success of the 1941 season.

Although the original play and the first draft of the *Casablanca* scenario contained many witty lines for Bogart and Claude Rains, Wallis knew that the general plot was heavy with tenseness and drama. He was certain that Sakall was the man to bring some needed laughs to the screenplay. He would have some help in the comedy department from the man who undertook the part of the bartender. The reactions of the waiter and the bartender could help in establishing the character of their boss, Rick Blaine, in addition to supplying some brightness to the film.

Sakall's comedic partner in the picture would be another fine actor who had become something of an anonymous institution in American movies. His face was unique and instantly recognizable, but few moviegoers could ever remember his name. That actor, Leonid Kinskey, was hired to portray Sasha, the bartender. Although well-established in films long before the outbreak of World War II, Kinskey was also a political refugee from Europe. Born in St. Petersburg, Russia, in 1903, Kinskey's family left their native land for a new life away from the Communist Revolution.

Leonid Kinskey made his American film debut in 1932 in a picture called *Trouble in Paradise.* He had been blessed with an incredibly flexible face which could change in a wink from boyishly innocent to cunningly malevolent. Coupled with his fine acting talent, the Kinskey face would keep him steadily employed in Hollywood for many decades. He had already appeared in countless films before *Casablanca,* including such important successes as *Duck Soup, Les Miserables, Peter Ibbetson, The General Died at Dawn,* and *The Great Waltz.*

Three roles of great importance in the original play were somewhat reduced in the screenplay. Madeline LeBeau was signed to play Yvonne, Rick's occasional sleep-in girl friend. The roles of Annina and Jan Viereck were altered and made less vital to the basic outcome of the film plot. Their last name was also changed, for some inexplicable reason, from Viereck to Brandel. Still, both roles would be good small parts, and Hal Wallis signed the beautiful, young Joy Page to play Annina, and newcomer Helmut Dantine for the part of Jan. The signing of Dantine was a special coup for Wallis and Curtiz because the young, European-born actor had scored a big success with Greer Garson as the downed German flier in *Mrs. Miniver.*

Philip and Julius Epstein and Howard Koch had done a marvelous job of adapting the play for film, particularly in the beginning of the scenario. They wrote a number of short

134

scenes with new roles which would emphasize the multi-nationality of those in Casablanca in December 1941. Those roles, only bit parts, would be cast with meticulous care. Most of the actors hired to play the parts, like Kinskey and Sakall, had already handled similar roles with such expertise that their faces were instantly recognized by the movie public.

Curt Bois would have two clever scenes as a concerned stranger who "befriends" refugees in order to pick their pockets. Other roles created for the film were members of the staff of Rick's Café Americain. Marcel Dalio, a veteran of countless films, was hired to portray the croupier of Rick's gambling casino. Dan Seymour, an American actor who would later build a successful career as a "young Sydney Greenstreet," was given a fez and asked to play the café doorman, Abdul. John Qualen, another exceptional American character actor who specialized in dialects, was given the role of an underground courier named Berger.

Even the tiniest "atmosphere" parts were cast with care. Whenever possible, Wallis signed actors of national backgrounds appropriate to the refugee situation in Casablanca. Corinna Mura, Ludwig Stossel, Ilka Gruning, Charles La Torre, and Frank Puglia were added to the cast of Casablanca.

The casting process, especially securing the services of Ingrid Bergman, Paul Henreid, Conrad Veidt, and Dooley Wilson, had been a long and arduous one. With Michael Curtiz' aid, Hal Wallis felt he had hired a truly international cast of highly capable actors. Considering the eventual success of Casablanca, his appraisal was conservative. From top to bottom, the cast of Casablanca was one of the best ever assembled.

135

Ten

A preliminary starting date for the filming of *Casablanca* had been set for April 10, 1942, but it proved to be overly optimistic. Wallis was forced to reschedule the start of production for May 25. A number of unexpected problems in casting and other areas would cause him to work with increased vigor to make the May production date. The Epstein brothers had completed a rough draft of a screenplay, and that first master script had been used as the basis for planning. With it, Wallis had worked out the budget for casting, sets, and the myriad details associated with the making of a major motion picture.

Wallis had also put together a first-rate team to head the various off-camera areas of the production. He had named Jerry Wald as his associate producer, and it was Wald's responsibility to help shoulder many of Wallis' extra burdens. Wald would later become an important Hollywood producer in his own right with a number of successful films, including *Mildred Pierce.* Wald's duties would include the responsibility of overseeing the building of the sets under art director Carl Jules Weyl, who had created the settings for *Yankee Doodle Dandy.* Weyl had won an Oscar in 1938 for *Robin Hood.*

Weyl's sets would be aided in their authenticity by the set decorating of George James Hopkins.

Michael Curtiz had asked for Lee Katz as his assistant director, and he was also pleased with the cinematographer that Wallis had selected. Curtiz' last picture, *Yankee Doodle Dandy,* had been filmed by James Wong Howe, but the two men were not overly fond of each other. The cameraman on most of Curtiz' recent movies had been Sol Polito, but Curtiz was content to bow to Wallis' decision to assign Arthur Edeson to *Casablanca.* Edeson seemed to be particularly adept at filming Humphrey Bogart to his best advantage. He had been behind the camera on Bogart's last picture, *Across the Pacific,* and had also been the cameraman on Bogie's first big hit, *The Maltese Falcon.* Wallis envisioned the mood and lighting of *Casablanca* as similar to that of *Falcon,* and he was convinced Edeson was the best man to shoot his new film.

Having promised Selznick that Ingrid Bergman would be beautifully gowned and photographed, Wallis secured the services of Hollywood's top makeup artist, Perc Westmore, to supervise the makeup, and signed the talented Orry-Kelly to create the gowns to be worn by Bergman.

Curtiz wanted to get as much action in the picture as possible by the use of montages and special effects, and so Wallis assigned Don Siegel and James Leicester to search the files for proper war footage for the montages they would create. Lawrence Butler and Willard van Enger went to work early on the special effects which would enhance the basically static film story.

The Epsteins had decided to resort to a fairly standard Hollywood practice of writing in a narration for the opening of the picture. That narration, detailing the refugee trail through Europe to Casablanca and on to Lisbon and the U.S., would be read by actor Lou Marcelle. Major Robert Aisner would represent the War Department as technical adviser on *Casablanca.*

The personnel Wallis got from the Warner music department adds further proof of his intention to make an outstanding film. The man who had created the background music for *Gone With the Wind,* Max Steiner, was assigned to compose the score for *Casablanca*. Hugo Friedhofer would do the orchestrations. Leo F. Forbstein, the head of the music department, would direct the Warner symphony orchestra. Murray Burnett had written his favorite love song, "As Time Goes By," into the script of *Everybody Comes to Rick's,* and nobody objected to leaving it in the film. Burnett and Alison had also included another already published song to be sung by Rick's friend, Sam. That number, "Run Rabbit," was a lively novelty song which inspired Sam's nickname "The Rabbit" in the original script.

Wallis decided that "Run Rabbit" wouldn't be appropriate for *Casablanca.* Dooley Wilson was a fine singer, and Wallis felt the addition of some better music would only strengthen the finished film. He bought the rights for "As Time Goes By" and began to search for other old songs which could be sung by Wilson and Corinna Mura, who would portray another singer in Rick's Café. Warner Brothers paid $500 for the rights to "Shine," written in 1924 by Ford Dabney and Cecil Mack, and Dooley Wilson would give it a knowing new treatment in the film. Warners also purchased the rights to "It Had to Be You," written by Isham Jones and Gus Kahn in 1924, and a relatively recent hit called "Perfidia."

When the filming was about to start, the Warner Brothers press department was composing a release that began, "While *Casablanca,* the Warner Brothers production starring Humphrey Bogart, Ingrid Bergman and Paul Henreid, is not a musical . . . " The press release went on to disclose that a number of songs were being composed especially for *Casablanca,* which would feature several older songs as well. Wallis hired the team of Moe Jerome and Jack Scholl to compose three new numbers for Dooley Wilson, and they produced "That's What Noah Done," "Muse's Call," and "Knock on Wood." "Knock on Wood" was designed to replace the unsatisfactory "Run Rabbit." Everyone concerned felt the catchy novelty tune, the "big song" of the movie, had a good chance of becoming a hit when the film was released. Nobody even dreamed that *Casablanca* would make the long-forgotten "As Time Goes By" an instant hit on its way to becoming a perennial standard.

While Max Steiner's scoring wouldn't begin until after

the filming had been completed, work on the incidental music in the picture started well before the camera began to roll. Elliot Carpenter, a pianist in the studio orchestra, was assigned the job of recording Dooley Wilson's "piano playing." Frank Perkins arranged all of the musical numbers to be used in the scenes in Rick's Café Americain, and Carpenter and a group of studio musicians recorded the songs on the café set well before any of the actors appeared.

Wallis had scheduled his use of the sound stages early in May. Stage 9 would be used for all the filming inside Rick's Café, and the set was ready well before May 25. The airport set was constructed on stage 21, and parts of other stages would be used for the Laszlo quarters and Renault's office. Great use would be made of the Warner back lot for the various exterior scenes. Most of the sets were built, the cast and crew set, and Michael Curtiz was frantic to begin work as the May 25 deadline approached. However, it was generally agreed that the main ingredient of any motion picture—the story—was far from ready.

The Wallis decision to use a three-man team of writers to create the scenario of *Casablanca* was proving to be troublesome. The Epsteins, utilizing the basic plot of *Everybody Comes to Rick's,* had completed a rough draft of the screenplay. Wallis had brought Howard Koch in to add his ideas to it. Unfortunately, for a reason which may never be explained, the three writers seemed to do very little in the way of actual collaboration. Each wrote scenes and presented them to Wallis and Curtiz for their approval. The producer and director had their own ideas about the characters and plot, and the general confusion of opinions made an approved, completed version of the screenplay impossible before the May 25 production date.

Tension had been building as the starting date neared, and several of the principle figures felt the production should be postponed again until the script was in better shape. But Wallis was unwilling to make another postponement: Everything was in readiness except the script, and a postponement would cause him to run over budget. It would also abrogate his contractual agreement with David O. Selznick for the services of Ingrid Bergman.

Nobody seemed to be entirely satisfied with the shooting script on hand, Wallis included. He had a "finished" scenario that obviously needed work. He had to consider the standard movie practice of making script revisions while the shooting was in progress. Such revisions are usually handed out, at the earliest, on the day before the scheduled shooting. It has always been a considerable irritation to actors, in particular, because it gives them little time to memorize and grow comfortable with their lines.

Still, Wallis figured he had a number of things going for him that would help overcome the problem. He had three of the best writers on the lot working on the script whom he would press to accelerate their efforts, and if necessary, he was prepared to assign other writers to particularly troubling scenes. He was also more comfortable with the possibly sticky situation because of the presence of Michael Curtiz. Mike was an old pro who had worked many miracles in the nearly fifteen years Wallis had known him. On more than one occasion the imagination and creative drive of Curtiz had turned a mediocre script into a good movie. Wallis had complete faith in Curtiz, and Curtiz was 100 percent in favor of going ahead as scheduled.

The producer was also confident that his careful casting would pay off during the filming. Bogart, Bergman, and Henreid were all at crucial points in their careers. All three were seasoned professionals in need of a good picture to boost them to greater stardom. They would cooperate. He had filled nearly every role in the picture with a veteran who was well-acquainted with the vagaries of filmmaking. They were all exceptional talents who would have contributions to make in overcoming any lack of polish in their roles.

The first forty pages or so of the shooting script seemed to be in good shape. It would be best to start, get something in the can, and then continue to work on improvements during the filming. Wallis alerted his cast, staff, crew, and Jack L. Warner of his decision. The cameras would roll on *Casablanca* as scheduled—May 25, 1942.

Eleven

A sizeable number of bit players and extras reported to Warner Brothers on the morning of May 25 for the beginning of principal photography on *Casablanca*. Michael Curtiz was prepared to direct them in the opening scene of the film on the realistic exterior settings representing the streets of Casablanca. The first scene to go before the camera was the first live action in the screenplay. *Casablanca* would be filmed in sequence.

There were a number of good reasons Hal Wallis and Michael Curtiz decided to shoot *Casablanca* in consecutive order from the opening to the final scene in the script. Although a rare practice today, many of the major pictures of the era were filmed in that manner. Generally speaking, today's films are shot according to "set-ups"—all scenes taking place on specific sets or locations are shot in a bunch, regardless of the sequence in which they will appear in the edited print of the picture.

Shooting the screenplay from beginning to end would be a boon for the *Casablanca* actors who had started their careers on the stage. They would be permitted to build their characterizations in tempo with the normal dictates of the script, as they would in a stage play. Most of the *Casablanca* filming would be done on the Warner sound stages in Burbank. The use of the back lot, special effects, and stock footage of Paris would take care of the locations. There would be no financial or artistic advantage in not shooting the movie in sequence.

The most important reason that *Casablanca* would be shot in sequence was the unfinished form of its screenplay. Wallis and Curtiz felt confident that the writers had turned in a workable script for the early scenes in the film, but they were not at all satisfied with the last half of it. The writers could work on that problem while the shooting of the first half was in progress. The opening graphics and narration would also be produced later, but the first scene with live action would be filmed on the back lot.

Everybody Comes to Rick's had been written as a one-set play, and all the action was designed to take place in Rick's Café. The opening scene of the movie was strictly the product of screenwriters Julius and Philip Epstein and Howard Koch. They had written a simple scene with relatively little important dialogue, but under Curtiz' direction it was designed to establish immediately the plight of the refugees, the general corruption in the city, and the oppression under the Vichy French government.

That latter fact must be confusing to all but the most history-minded of today's *Casablanca* fans. France, of course, has always been considered an American ally. How could Frenchmen be portrayed cooperating with the Nazis? That question was obviously very much in Michael Curtiz' mind when he filmed the opening scene of the movie. France's grand old patriot, Marshall Henri Philippe Pétain, had decided that a little honor was better than none when his armies collapsed under the Nazi onslaught in the early days of World War II. He and other heroic French generals of World War I agreed to accept the German surrender terms which allowed them a bit of autonomy in their African territories and elsewhere. With German approval, they formed a puppet government in southern France with headquarters in Vichy.

Most Americans and British felt the Vichy French were cowards and "quislings." Michael Curtiz dealt with this feeling in the opening scene of the movie. To underline his point, the threatening forces on the streets of Curtiz' Casablanca were dressed in French uniforms. It was the Vichy *gendarmes* who instigated one of the few pieces of traditional movie action in the picture by asking a refugee for his papers. Curtiz directed the actor to bolt and run as fast as he could toward a nearby building. With his skillful handling of extras, he had the terrified onlookers rush backwards out of the line of fire while the Vichy police coldly shot the man in the back.

Curtiz had been in one of the world's first propaganda film units during World War I, and he demonstrated his skill at the technique in his next sequence. The mortally wounded refugee collapsed in a heap at the bottom of the wall, and Curtiz instructed Arthur Edeson to move his lens slowly upward until it centered on a poster of Marshall Pétain. After the fadeout, to make sure the message registered, Curtiz had his cameraman zero in on the French National motto, *Liberté, Egalité, Fraternité*. With no dialogue at all, Curtiz and Arthur Edeson had spelled out their feelings for the Vichy government and established the danger confronting those who had sought safety in Casablanca.

The screenwriters had moved the exposition about the murder of the two German couriers and the missing letters of transit to the opening moments of the movie. The roundup of suspects has been announced, and the shooting episode adds immediate impact to the building drama. The little scene in which Curt Bois warns the English couple of the unsavory characters in Casablanca, while picking the man's pocket, establishes more of the background as it also provides the first comedy relief.

Curtiz decided to make even more of the hopelessness of the refugee situation. The script called only for a shot of an airplane arriving at the airport. Manipulating his extras as he had in the days of his silent biblical epics, Curtiz instructed them to follow the path of the plane with longing eyes. With a bare minimum of dialogue, Curtiz managed to create a mood of tension, danger, and political intrigue and gave a promise of more violent action than the plot of the film would be able to provide.

143

The opening moments of the picture, including the spinning globe and the narration, covered only eight pages of the script. Curtiz was at home directing crowd scenes, and the filming of the first scenes took only a few days. Fifty days had been allotted to complete the filming of the entire picture. After eight pages, Curtiz was ahead of schedule.

The *Casablanca* screenwriters had decided to follow the opening scenes with the introduction of the lead heavies of the film. Claude Rains and Conrad Veidt would be the first principal actors to face the cameras in Curtiz' second set-up on the airport set. Curtiz also decided to create an incident in the airport scene that would clearly state his feelings about the German-Italian alliance. A gregarious Italian officer is among the party of French and Nazis at the airport. Curtiz directed the French and Germans alike to give the Italian a deliberate "brush off."

The Epsteins gave Claude Rains an opportunity to display his cynical humor in his opening scene with Conrad Veidt. When Veidt asks him what he has done about finding the murderer of the couriers, Rains replies, "Realizing the importance of the case, my men are rounding up *twice* the usual number of suspects." Nobody connected with *Casablanca* had any idea how important that line would become before the filming was completed.

Veidt, as Major Strasser, is also told that the murderer will be caught that evening at Rick's Café. Renault adds, "Everybody comes to Rick's." That line was in the original play and was the inspiration for its title. Curtiz ended the scene with a pan to the sign reading Rick's Café Americain, and his next scene would begin with a dissolve on the exterior of the café.

Humphrey Bogart had not been involved in the opening scenes of the photoplay and had no particular reason to be on the studio grounds. But he had kept himself informed about the filming as well as the progress on the scenario. He had been given the first pages of the revised script and was pleased with the changes in plot construction and his dialogue. The opening scenes were okay. He could only hope that the writers would heed his grievances about the "whiney" aspects of Rick's character.

Bogart had spent years on the stage before coming to Hollywood, and he was pleased by the advance build-up the writers had given his character. He would have a great film "entrance." On Broadway, a proper entrance following a lengthy period when the other cast members talk about the central character, primed the audience to burst into enthusiastic applause at the first sight of the favored star. Loud battles and revisions of dialogue have been precipitated when stars feel deprived of a proper entrance.

Bogart could have no complaints on this point. In *Casablanca*, he was given one of the most memorable "entrances" in the history of film. Starting with the scene between Renault and Strasser at the airport, a great deal of the dialogue deals with the character and eccentricities of Rick Blaine. Strasser says, "I have already heard about this café and also about Monsieur Rick, himself."

After Curtiz focused his camera on the outside of the café, he moved it inside, where he directed his "atmosphere people" to talk about escaping Casablanca. Whispered conversations are overheard in which refugees attempt to sell their jewels to buy exit visas. Others are advised to come back with cash to pay for the hiring of small boats which might make it to Lisbon. S. Z. Sakall is introduced in a conversation with some customers. He is asked by a couple if Rick would accept a drink from them. Sakall quickly establishes one quirk of Rick's personality by informing the people that Rick never drinks with his customers.

Bogart isn't actually introduced on screen until page 14 of the shooting script. Even then, Michael Curtiz decided to make the first visual introduction in a most unusual way. He had the camera pan the nightclub setting, focusing on an employee rushing across the room with a check in his hand. His next shot was a close-up of a table with only a man's hands holding a drink. The employee moves into the frame, and he places the check before the bodyless hands. The check is picked up, studied out of camera range, and returned to the table. One hand turns the check over, and the other produces a pencil. A two-word message is scrawled across the back of the check—"Okay. Rick."

Curtiz then moved his camera back slowly to produce a medium shot of the employee picking up the check and leaving. For the first time, the spectator sees the man everyone has been talking about. Humphrey Bogart, clad in a white tuxedo jacket and black bow tie, sits alone at the table, his face devoid of expression.

Bogie's first lines in the film came on page 15 of the shooting script, when he bluntly ejects a German who seeks admittance to his gambling casino. A similar scene had come later in the stage play, involving Rick with an obnoxious Englishman known to be a habitual passer of bad checks. By changing the intruder from an Englishman to a German, the screenwriters made the scene more timely and also demonstrated Rick Blaine's businesslike neutrality. He was capable of handling undesirable Germans with the same dispatch some might reserve for less formidable patrons. Bogie's Rick was better-dressed and legal, but underneath he was the same tough Bogart that movie audiences were accustomed to seeing.

Michael Curtiz added a tiny piece of business which quickly defined another aspect of the Rick Blaine character. After ejecting the German, Bogie was directed to turn to Dooley Wilson and give him a knowing look. The return smile the look provokes from the black entertainer makes the audience realize that the Bogart character has its pleasant side as well. It will become clear, in time, that Sam is Rick's gentler alter ego.

Rick Blaine's first important scene in *Casablanca* is essentially the same scene that opened *Everybody Comes to Rick's*. For the most part, it would involve only Bogart and Peter Lorre and would be played at a single table on the crowded café set. Before thoroughly rehearsing the scene, Curtiz cornered the two actors and told them the way he wanted them to play it. He was accustomed to action pictures and had a real dread of exposition scenes such as the one they were going to play. The scene was vital to the plot, he told them, but he wanted them to move it along at a fast clip. The entire picture must be well paced.

"We can't go too fast, Mike," Bogie warned him. "I mean, we have to take time to react to what we're saying—to think."

"Sure, think," Curtiz said, "but do not take the long pause. We must make the words go fast to get the pace."

"You mean just throw the lines away?"

"No, no, no! Don't throw away. Jock Varner and Hal Vallis pay too big money to the writers. Just talk them fast. I vill tell you when they go too slow."

Peter Lorre, always ready to attempt a scam on a likely subject, looked at Bogart and gave him a knowing wink. Bogie understood that his friend wanted him to play along when Lorre eagerly interrupted the discussion.

"Excuse me, Bogie, but I think Michael is right. If we do the lines fast enough we can finish before the weekend and not have to worry about violating our contracts. Right, Bogie?"

"That's right, Pete," Bogie agreed. "I never thought about that."

"Why you talking about contract?" the confused Curtiz asked.

"I just wanted to remind you that Bogie and I are not weekend actors."

"I should say not," Bogie added.

"What you mean, weekend actors?"

"Michael, surely you know about our contracts," Lorre smiled. "We're not the only people in the cast with them. With all of your experience you must know there are weekend actors and weekday actors. I'm afraid Bogie and I are not allowed to work on weekends."

Bogart had finally gotten the drift of the impromptu gag and immediately went along with it.

"Sorry I forgot about that, Mike. Yeah, Pete and I only work Monday through Thursday. Nobody's ever going to be able to accuse us of being weekend actors."

Curtiz was both an easy and a dangerous target for a practical joke. He was a tall, strong man widely known for his hot temper. He detested incompetence and he could be a tyrant when he had no respect for an actor. But he did admire Bogart and Lorre and knew that they had both come up the hard way as he had. His single-minded devotion to his work

147

made him more than a little gullible. Never noted for a splendid sense of humor, it never occurred to him that the actors were pulling his leg.

"Is impossible! Actors work only on weekend?"

"Listen, don't blame Pete and me for that. That's not us."

"Weekend actors—Goddam!" Curtiz snorted. "Goddam actor bums!"

Lorre and Bogart were both on the set when Friday came around and Curtiz never let on that he had been fooled by the unusual "clauses" in their contracts. The two schemers agreed that Curtiz was a perfect foil for their practical jokes. Their early days of shooting went smoothly and Curtiz was pleased with their pacing. They decided they could afford to embark on another practical joke they had planned.

Director Curtiz would again be one victim, and a distinguished Warner actor would be the party of the second part. While Curtiz was directing *Casablanca,* Paul Lukas was working on the leading role in Lillian Hellman's anti-Nazi film *Watch on the Rhine.* Lukas and Curtiz had been friends since their early days in Budapest. Lorre and Bogart thought it might be good fun to see if they could foment a feud between the two Hungarians.

When they told Curtiz that they admired and respected Lukas and encouraged the director to fill them in on more details about the actor, Curtiz eagerly obliged. The Curtiz anecdotes were friendly, banal little incidents, but they were enough to give Bogie and Lorre a start.

They then paid regular visits to Lukas at his nearby sound stage, courted him unashamedly, and gained his confidence until they could approach him as "concerned friends." When they hemmed and hawed in obvious embarrassment, saying they didn't like to tell "tales out of school," the confused Lukas urged them to say what was on their minds. Lorre and Bogart finally said they felt obligated, as his friends, to tell him that Curtiz was spreading ugly rumors about him. Using Curtiz' innocent stories as material, they wildly exaggerated them to the point where they became insulting to the sensitive actor. Lukas found it hard to believe

148

that his old friend would spread such vicious rumors about him, but only Curtiz knew of the incidents. Angry, he proceeded to tell Bogie and Lorre every unflattering story he had ever heard about Curtiz. The conspirators then rushed back to the *Casablanca* set to repeat Lukas' assertions.

Bogart and Lorre continued to act as go-betweens with Lukas and Curtiz. The feud grew quite testy before the practical jokers relented and let their victims in on the gag.

There was little time for more such elaborate jokes because Lorre would be finished with his role in the picture early while Bogart was becoming increasingly involved in the problems that were taking shape.

Considering their closeness off screen, Bogart and Lorre did an admirable job of concealing it during their scenes in *Casablanca.* Rick Blaine was the epitome of aloofness as he brushed aside every attempt by Ugarte to proclaim his friendship. Rick's only gesture of courtesy comes when he agrees to hold the all-important letters of transit for Ugarte. The "Bergdorf Goodman device" of Murray Burnett and Joan Alison worked wonderfully in the film. It also provided Rick with his only chance to give a small nod of approval to Ugarte while hinting that he had no sympathy for the Nazis.

On page 20 of the shooting script, many days into the filming, Bogart delivers Rick's line, "I heard a rumor that those German couriers were carrying letters of transit." Ugarte answers, "Yes, I heard that rumor, too. Poor devils." Bogart was directed to look at Lorre steadily, portraying no particular emotion, before saying, "You're right, Ugarte. I am a little more impressed with you."

Nobody on the *Casablanca* set, including the army technical adviser, gave the fictitious letters of transit a second thought. Ironically, the screenwriters did decide to make one change in the original device of Burnett and Alison. Apparently feeling that Charles de Gaulle had become the most famous of all the French leaders, they substituted his signature at the bottom of the letters in place of real-life Vichy leader Marshall Weygand. De Gaulle had been one of the first high military officers to break ranks with the old guard who formed the Vichy government after the French-German armistice in spring 1940, and he became the leader of the Free French with headquarters in Great Britain. The change from Weygand to De Gaulle was one of the few unrealistic changes the screenwriters made in the original play script.

The first serious problem in the actual filming coincided with Dooley Wilson's first big scene. To that point, Wilson had been used mainly as background in the café. At the conclusion of work on the Rick-Ugarte scene, the shooting schedule called for Wilson closeups as he sang and played "Knock on Wood," the number the Warner brass had planned as the big musical hit of *Casablanca.* "Knock on Wood" was an audience-participation song which would lighten the mood following the intense exposition scene between Bogie and Lorre.

All the music had been pre-recorded, and Wilson had studied hard to copy the hand movements of pianist Elliot Carpenter. Wilson became extremely skilled at duplicating Carpenter's fingering and hand movements in synchronization with the recorded music. Normally, in scenes where musicians perform, the music is recorded beforehand and piped onto the set via loudspeakers while the singer "lip-synchs" and the musicians fake their playing.

Wilson was supposed to play and sing at the same time that dialogue was being spoken elsewhere in the café set. That Curtiz directorial technique made the *Casablanca* cabaret scenes more realistic than most, but it also created a problem. The usual process of the sound man cutting the loudspeaker sound during the dialogue would not work. Wilson needed to hear the recorded piano music in order to know when to move his hands as he "played." Eventually, Michael Curtiz solved the problem by moving Carpenter and his piano close to Wilson right out of the range of the camera. That way, Dooley was able to comfortably match his hand movements to those of Carpenter.

Sydney Greenstreet made his initial appearance on the set during the latter stages of Wilson's "Knock on Wood."

Although the Englishman would have relatively little to do during his stint on the picture, Michael Curtiz had been instructed to enhance his role as much as possible. Curtiz directed his cameraman to focus his lens on Greenstreet's corpulent figure as it waddled its way across the nightclub floor. Greenstreet would have every opportunity to make an impression as the mysterious Señor Ferrari.

Hal Wallis and Michael Curtiz wanted to take advantage of Greenstreet's presence as soon as possible, and his character was introduced on page 22 of the film script. The dialogue in the Rick-Ferrari scene closely followed the original Rick-Martinez scene of the play. Ferrari wants to buy Rick's Café, and Rick tells him he has no interest in selling. Ferrari then tells Rick that he would like to steal his entertainer, Sam.

When *Casablanca* was released, the dialogue concerning Sam was considered liberal—almost to the point of daring. Motion pictures generally overlooked American racial attitudes of the early 1940s. Murray Burnett and Joan Alison had consciously created the Rick-Sam relationship as a more human, civilized alternative to the evils of prejudice. They were careful in their script to refer to Sam as the "Negro." At that time, "black" was considered an insulting description.

While the Burnett-Alison approach to the scene was subtle, the screenwriters made it quite pointed. Ferrari says he would like to buy the entertainer as long as the café isn't for sale. Rick snaps back, "I don't buy or sell human beings." Sam turns down Ferrari's offer of employment. Sam is obviously no shuffling lackey, and his loyalty to Rick Blaine is freely given rather than purchased.

Humphrey Bogart's new image as a man who attracts women was established long before Ingrid Bergman's appearance in the film. Following the scene with Ferrari, Rick is shown in a confrontation with a drunken beauty named Yvonne, played by Madeline LeBeau. The scene had been toned down from the original in the play, where the playwrights had Yvonne say, "Rick has no soul, but he's nice to sleep with." The screenwriters deleted the "sleep with" line, but the physical nature of their relationship was clear within the boundaries of the Hollywood moral code.

Curtiz was satisfied with the overall quality of filming on the first twenty-six pages of the shooting script. The opening exterior scenes had helped to establish the mood of the piece, and the scenes inside the café had also gone well. But he was worried that the picture might become too static. At his urging, Wallis instructed his technicians to create a sidewalk café on the exterior of Rick's for the upcoming scene between Rick and Captain Renault. Curtiz wanted to make use of recurring shots of planes landing and taking off at the airport. The hope of the refugees—the means of escape—must not be forgotten. Curtiz wanted to direct it to keep the action flowing between three different sets—the main café, the sidewalk café, and Rick's upstairs office. The Bogart-Rains scene had been doctored by the Epsteins to include lines which would become memorable.

When Rick and Renault were ready to begin their conversation outside the café, Curtiz directed Bogart to let his eyes follow a plane that is taking off, presumably to Lisbon with a connection to America. He also stressed to both actors that he wanted the scene to be fast-paced. The final print proves the actors knew how to take direction. Rains and Bogart deliver their lines with a throwaway pace that comes close to rivaling a scene in a Noel Coward play. The Epstein brothers provided them with some witty dialogue that also clearly defined their similar personalities.

As Rick watches the flight of the plane passing over his café, Renault asks, "What in heaven's name brought you to Casablanca?" Without a beat, Rick answers, "My health. I came to Casablanca for the waters." The puzzled Renault says, "Waters? What waters? We are in the desert." Rick's only comment: "I was misinformed." Brilliantly written and acted, and directed with a dazzling pace, it perfectly establishes the ambivalent relationship of the mysterious café owner and the corrupt Prefect of Police.

Renault warns Rick that he intends to arrest the murderer of the German couriers in his café that evening. Rick seems unperturbed by the news and says, "I stick my neck out for nobody." Renault concedes that Rick's attitude is "a wise foreign policy," another pointed sop to the anti-Vichy feelings of the time. Curtiz kept the dialogue flowing crisply and brought in some movement with the appearance of Marcel Dalio as the croupier, who asks Rick to give him more cash for the casino. Curtiz had Edeson follow the men with his camera as they crossed the interior of the café and mounted the stairs to go into Rick's office.

Burnett and Alison had written Rick as a mysterious figure the authorities knew to be a divorced father and former Paris lawyer who had come to Casablanca because he couldn't return to his native America. The playwrights had also written the character of Victor Laszlo as a wealthy underground fighter whose fortune the Nazis were eager to get. The backgrounds of both characters were changed for the film.

In the office scene, Renault tells Rick that he knows of his background. At Bogart's urging, the screenwriters made Rick Blaine an ex-rebel who fought on the side of the anti-fascist Loyalists during the Spanish Civil War. He was further described as a man who ran guns to the Ethiopians in the fight against the Italians. The new background emphatically established the Bogart character as a man who formerly possessed impeccable democratic principles, in spite of his current attitude as a tired cynic.

Reverting then to the original dialogue of the play, Renault tells Rick about the expected arrival of Victor Laszlo and the fact that he is traveling to Casablanca with a lady. Rick reveals his respect for the legendary underground leader and goads Renault into making a bet with him. The bet covered only 5,000 francs in the play. By raising the ante, the screenwriters were able to give Claude Rains another funny character line in the movie. Bogie offers to bet Rains 20,000 francs that Laszlo will escape again, but Rains persuades him to lower it to 10,000 francs. His excuse—"I am only a *poor* corrupt official."

With his typical flair for action, Curtiz directed the next scene with a maximum amount of physical violence. Ugarte is cornered by the *gendarmes* and tries to shoot his way out of trouble before he is overcome by force. Ugarte and Rick had finally established a bit of rapport by the end of their earlier scene. Lorre had made the Ugarte character likeable, if not admirable, and the audience might expect the café owner to do something to aid him as Ugarte pleads for his help. But Rick reveals no emotion as the police lead Ugarte away. He coldly turns his back and snarls, "I stick my neck out for nobody!" Michael Curtiz deliberately directed his star to play it cool in an attempt to make the audience decide that "Bogie is playing the same old, no-good tough guy."

Another delightful little moment of comedy relief accompanies the entrance of the film's prime villain, Nazi Major Heinrich Strasser. Curtiz encouraged Conrad Veidt to underplay the role, telling the actor that his appearance and manner should threaten sly sadism rather than bombastic brutality. To highlight Veidt's entrance, the screenwriters gave S. Z. Sakall a line that the roly-poly little actor delivered with a wealth of meaning. Renault insists that the waiter give Strasser the best table, and Sakall, jowls aflutter, says, "I have already given him the best, sir—knowing that he is a German and would take it anyway."

Michael Curtiz began to grow agitated about the future filming. He was rapidly running out of what he considered finished pages. He had already told Hal Wallis that he was concerned about the manner in which the past love affair of Rick Blaine and Ilsa Lund was introduced. It had to be done carefully. Simply having the actors talk about it—as they did in the stage script—wouldn't do at all. Curtiz and Wallis decided to flesh-out the script by creating a filmed flashback to show their scenes together in Paris. Julius and Philip Epstein and Howard Koch were already working on it, and Wallis thought it might be wise to bring in another writer with a fresh perspective. He invited Casey Robinson to try his hand at writing the scenes in France. Albert Maltz would also contribute his ideas to the *Casablanca* script, although neither he nor Robinson would receive screen credits.

Curtiz began to press the writers for more and better material. He became involved in some serious disagreements with Howard Koch, in particular. Koch was most interested in highlighting the anti-fascist theme of the screenplay; Curtiz was more concerned with the visual aspects of the film, particularly those scenes that affected the romantic line of the story.

Humphrey Bogart also began to worry about the work that lay ahead of him. He liked Curtiz' direction generally, but wondered if the director wasn't speeding him through his dialogue unnecessarily. The scenes with Bergman were fast approaching, and the lack of finished material did nothing to ease his mind. He was confident he had a "handle" on the man he was playing, and there was no way he would allow the writers to dilute the character when it came to the love scenes. He began inviting Koch and the others to informal meetings in his dressing room. They were friendly talks, usually over drinks. Bogart only wanted to make sure they understood his feelings about the character of Rick Blaine, because that was the only way he intended to play him. If Rick Blaine was a lover, he was going to be a "Bogart-type" lover. The writers considered most of his ideas helpful.

Bogie's already chaotic home life was deteriorating badly. In the beginning he teased his wife about his playing love scenes opposite the beautiful Ingrid Bergman. Mayo's early displays of jealousy had amused him, but now she was drinking more than usual, and her jealousy was becoming worse. Bogie knew that his married life would get less peaceful when Curtiz actually began to shoot the scenes between him and the young actress.

While the writers were working on those all-important scenes between Bogart and Bergman, Curtiz was continuing to turn out his daily quota of film footage. The Ugarte scene had given him a little action, but Curtiz knew that he was faced with nothing but *talk* for many pages. He intended to make that talk as interesting as possible.

The scene involving Rick, Renault, and Strasser provided some interesting talk as well as some sure laugh lines for Bogie. When the Nazi questions him about his nationality, Rick simply replies, "I'm a drunkard." Attempting to discern Rick's political leanings, Strasser asks him how he feels about the Germans in Paris and possibly London. Rick is noncommittal. When Strasser asks Rick if he can imagine the Germans in New York City, the writers gave Bogie a sure-fire laugh. Bogie levels his famous squint at Veidt and replies, "There are certain sections of New York, Major, that I would not advise you to try to invade." That line gets as big a laugh today as it did in 1942.

Bogart was given a few free days when he completed the scene. Curtiz would be shooting the first scenes of his co-stars, Ingrid Bergman and Paul Henreid, and he wouldn't be needed on the set. The leisure time only made him more uneasy, and the idea of spending extra time at home with Mayo and her problems didn't help matters. He had been unable to pry much worthwhile information from Mike Curtiz, so he decided it would be useful to return to the studio for more talks with Hal Wallis and Howard Koch. With no final script to help him, he was anxious to learn what they had planned for him in the upcoming scenes. He was worried that a potentially good story was going to be botched.

Bogart also wanted to watch Bergman at work. He would make it look very casual, so she wouldn't catch on to what he had in mind. His theory of acting was ultra-uncomplicated: "Just *think* it! If you *think* it, you'll *do* it." He wanted to get a line on Bergman's approach before he faced the cameras with her. It might drive Mayo further around the bend, but he was sure it would pay off on the screen.

Twelve

Ingrid Bergman and Paul Henreid made their entrance in *Casablanca* in the seventy-fifth shot of the filming on page 42 of the shooting script. Curtiz decided to pick them up as they approached the entrance of Rick's Café Americain and then follow them inside. The director threw in a marvelous "wild shot" during their entrance, instructing Edeson to shoot a close-up of Sam to catch the astonishment on his face when he first sees Ilsa Lund.

Bergman and Henreid both had mixed emotions as they began their work on *Casablanca*. Convinced the picture would do little to help his career, Henreid was determined to do his best to keep the film from destroying the response he had received for *Now, Voyager*. Bergman, glad to be working again, was intent on banishing all thoughts about the lost role in *For Whom the Bell Tolls*. She had no great expectations for *Casablanca* and only hoped that her confusion about the script would be cleared up before many days passed. She had been given a number of pages for her first scenes but had little idea what would happen afterwards. Hal Wallis had assured her that the script was being revised to strengthen it.

Bergman still wasn't comfortable about the idea of working with Humphrey Bogart. In an attempt to prepare herself, she had made a conscious study of his work. *The Maltese Falcon* was considered his best film, so she asked for a print of it. She ran it over and over, closely watching Bogie's every move, and when she found that he projected very little warmth, she worried that they might be poorly matched as lovers. Of course, she was told she would have two leading men in the picture—Bogart and Henreid. Which man was she supposed to find more attractive? Bogart certainly projected a rugged kind of appeal in *The Maltese Falcon*. Was he like that in real life? She hoped all the stories she had heard were only Hollywood exaggerations—it wouldn't be easy to play love scenes with a hostile leading man. After Bogart and Bergman finally met on the *Casablanca* set, she was relieved. She found Humphrey Bogart quite different from his screen image. He seemed tired and almost shy. She didn't find him overly friendly, but he was courteous and professional in his manner. He was an intriguing man, and she hoped he would lose some of his reserve before the picture was finished.

Through the years, purists have argued that one aspect of the initial Bergman-Henreid entrance detracts from the total realism of *Casablanca*. The audience has already been told that Victor Laszlo is one of Europe's bravest underground leaders who has made a daring escape from a Nazi concentration camp and outsmarted the Germans at every turn. He and his wife have just navigated the tricky turns of the refugee trail described at the beginning of the movie. However, when Victor and Ilsa arrive at Rick's, they give the appearance of two tourists on another leg of an exotic vacation trip. The couple are striking and immaculate; she is dressed in an elegantly simple white formal gown and he wears an off-white tropical suit. The Warner wardrobe department had done nothing to enhance the dangerous mood so carefully built by Michael Curtiz.

The costuming of Bergman and Henreid is another example of how closely the *Casablanca* creators followed many of the dictates of *Everybody Comes to Rick's*. In the play, the stage directions describe Laszlo's appearance but not his costume. The heroine is written as "a tall, lissome brunette with startlingly blue eyes and ivory complexion. She wears a magnificent white gown, and a full-length cape of the same fabric." But Laszlo was described as an extraordinarily wealthy man in the play, and the stage Laszlos weren't required to make their entrances hard on the heels of the grim realism of the opening scenes of the film. A nitpicker would have cause to wonder how the shops of wartime Casablanca could stock such luxurious clothing, or to assume that Laszlo and Lund had traveled the refugee trail loaded down with luggage and a platoon of red caps. Still, Bergman and Henreid made a striking couple and Hollywood's need to "dress" its stars had been satisfied.

Bogart had made a point of watching Bergman work and liked what he saw. She was professional and had a natural way of reading her lines. He watched Curtiz film her from virtually every angle and was convinced she had no "bad" side. Bergman was truly able to project the radiance everyone talked about. After years of brainwashing by Jack Warner, Bogie began to wonder if anyone would buy the idea that a beautiful woman like Bergman would fall in love with him. She was obviously a damned good actress. He had to rely on his own theory: "If she *thought* it," the audience would buy it. But it continued to worry him, and he decided to talk about it with a friend whose opinion he trusted.

His adviser gave him an idea that seemed sensible. He told Bogart he would have a problem holding his own with the talented Swedish actress. Bergman was so young and beautiful that a lot of people would find it hard to take their eyes off her. If Bogie was to keep Bergman from stealing the picture, he had better be prepared to use every trick he had learned in his years in the business. Bogart detested "up-stagers" and had never believed in resorting to tricks in order to hold his own, but he was forty-one years old and concerned that he would look foolish appearing opposite the young beauty. He listened to what the man had to say.

His friend pointed out that Ilsa was not simply in love with Rick; she desperately needed to get close to him because he had possession of the elusive letters of transit. She had to be the aggressor in their relationship—even if she wasn't sincere—in order to get her hands on the letters. Therefore, Bogie should play it cool—let Bergman come to him. He should make her do the chasing as much as possible.

Bogie thought it over and realized that the idea was implicit in the script. He knew he would feel uncomfortable if he was forced to play their scenes as a love sick, middle-aged man. As far as he was concerned, Rick Blaine was a "tough nut" who wouldn't display weakness. He didn't have to worry about being a "lover." The script said Ilsa was in love with him. He'd let Ingrid Bergman worry about it.

The first brief scene in which Bogart and Bergman appear together was directed by Michael Curtiz with remarkable restraint. Bergman and Dooley Wilson, using most of the dialogue and the song from the play, build the mood for Bogart's sudden entrance. Ilsa realizes that the "boy" at the piano is Rick's friend, Sam. Wilson does a fine job of acting when Bergman approaches him. When Ilsa asks him to play "As Time Goes By," Sam hesitates and pretends he doesn't know it, tipping the audience off that the song has some special meaning to Ilsa and Sam—and, in all probability, the cynical Rick.

Curtiz used a series of close-ups, switching between Dooley Wilson and Ingrid Bergman, to heighten the unexplained tension between entertainer and patron. Their expressive faces say more than their words until Sam finally agrees to sing "As Time Goes By." Few songs have been given a more interesting introduction in a movie. Wilson's husky-voiced singing of the sensitive lyrics works in perfect counterpoint to the Curtiz shots of the wistful beauty of the Bergman face. Bogart's slam-bang entrance demanding to know why Sam is playing the forbidden song provides an intriguing conclusion to the reverie.

Under the direction of Michael Curtiz, Bogart brought perfect shading to his surprise at seeing Bergman. It was a highly melodramatic moment that might be expected to provoke laughs from today's less romantic audiences. It never does.

Bogart and Bergman quickly discovered they could work well together. Before the picture was finished, they would form something of a mutual admiration society although they never became really close. Bogart had less time for courteous socializing as the shooting progressed. He spent nearly every lunch hour closeted with Hal Wallis or the writers. His concern about the mental health of Mayo Methot kept him at a professional distance from Ingrid Bergman. As a former actress, Mayo was well aware of the tendencies of some leading men and women to carry their romantic activities beyond the confines of the stage or movie set.

Mayo hounded Bogie every night about his "affair" when he came home from the studio. Bogart was unable to convince his wife that he had no intention of falling for Ingrid Bergman. Mayo began making repeated phone calls to the set which further unsettled the actor. Eventually, she threatened to kill Bogart when she got proof that he was in love with Bergman. Bogie relayed the news to his agents, Sam Jaffe and Mary Baker. The agents, like Bogie, were aware of Mayo's potential for violence. They couldn't persuade Bogart to leave his wife and were powerless to protect him, but they decided to protect themselves, financially. Jaffe and Baker took out a $100,000 insurance policy on the life of Humphrey Bogart. Before *Casablanca* was completed, Mayo would make another attempt on her own life.

The destructive combination of booze and Mayo's insecurity brought Bogie into a confrontation with Jack L. Warner at one point in the *Casablanca* filming. Tired from a busy day at the studio, Bogie was happy to join Mayo for some relaxing drinks before dinner in their West Hollywood home. But the cocktail hour dragged on and the Bogarts didn't have dinner until late in the evening. Afterward, Bogie was anxious to study his lines for the next day's shooting, which would be a light work day for him. Mayo was anxious for more conversation and soon launched into another tirade about Ingrid Bergman, prompting Bogie to simply go to bed. Mayo continued drinking alone and shook her husband awake shortly before daybreak in an attempt to continue the argument. Bogart grabbed his script, threw a topcoat over his pajamas, and drove to the studio.

He had intended to get some more sleep in his studio dressing room but found it impossible and began to drink again. Bogie wasn't due on the set until 11 o'clock, and Mike Curtiz was mildly alarmed when the guard on the gate told

161

him the star had checked in several hours earlier. Curtiz dispatched the assistant director to inquire about him and was informed that Bogart was tipsily trying to ride a bicycle around the lot. All attempts to coax him off the bike had failed. Curtiz was so worried he put in a call to Jack Warner telling him the star of *Casablanca* was drunk and doing crazy things on a bicycle. Bogart could hurt himself.

Warner, a man who was never at ease with his stars, hurried to Bogart's dressing room. He had too much money tied up in the picture to risk any injury to its star. He was surprised to find Bogie, still clad in his pajamas, looking disheveled but none the worse for wear and tear. The star appeared completely sober.

"Goddammit, Bogie," Warner began, "what the hell do you think you've been doing?"

"Riding my bicycle," Bogie smiled.

"But you've been drinking. Don't you know how dangerous that is?"

"That's why I was doing it. I wanted to get some fresh air."

"Listen, I don't care if you bust your ugly face," Warner spluttered. "Well, yes I do, really. But there are hundreds of people depending on you in this picture, and some of them get a pay check that wouldn't handle your liquor bill for two days."

Warner had come up with the magic words. There was no way Humphrey DeForest Bogart would allow anyone to consider him unprofessional. He didn't want anyone to think that he would use his prestige on the lot to take advantage of the so-called "little people." For several seconds he just studied the nervous face of his employer. Finally he said:

"Forget about it, Junior. It'll never happen again."

The scene in which Rick gets drunk and refuses Sam's offer to take him home was the final scene of Act One in the Burnett-Alison play. In fact, the Act One curtain line was Rick's, "Then play it!" as he orders his friend to play "As Time Goes By." Bogart readily recognized the vital importance of the scene to the plot and to his character. It posed a number of acting problems he had never faced on screen, and if he handled it correctly, it could become the best single scene he had ever played on film.

The Rick-Sam scene was one that Bogart had talked a lot about with the writers. It contains one of the lines today's *Casablanca* fans love to quote, and it's likely that Bogart added his own individual touch to it. The passing years have made it difficult to pinpoint which of the talented team of writers came up with any individual line, especially those lines which have become most familiar. One such line has Rick saying, "Of all the gin joints in all the towns in the world, she walks into mine."

Most of the lines in the original play ended up, in one form or another, in the movie script. However, that line was not in the play. It also wasn't in the only master script available when the filming began. At that time the line read, "Of all the cafés in all the towns in the world, she walks into my café." The speech becomes stronger when the word "café" is replaced by the slang term "gin joint." It's probable that Bogart himself suggested the change.

Another famous line in the film, "Here's looking at you, kid," also has the personal Bogart stamp. Bogart says it at least three times in the later stages of *Casablanca*. In the master script the line read, "Here's good luck to you." "Here's looking at you, kid" is far more in character with the Rick Blaine of Humphrey Bogart.

To Bogart, the drunk scene with Sam allowed him to *act* instead of simply *react* as he had been doing in the earlier scenes. Bogie had already discovered that Dooley Wilson was a clever actor as well as a charming man, and he was looking forward to doing the scene with him. Yet he was still faced with some irritating problems. He had to be so unsettled at the beginning of the scene that he would have his head cradled in his arms on the tabletop. Bogart had no desire to appear that "weak." He decided that his motivation would be split evenly between the bottle in front of him and the broken love affair behind him.

Michael Curtiz and Arthur Edeson filmed the scene in light and shadow appropriate to Rick Blaine's somber, if not sober, mood. Curtiz kept the dialogue between Rick and Sam quiet and fast-paced. That approach made it amusing and touching at the same time. The finished print shows Bogart more relaxed and confident than he had been in any scene to that point, and Dooley Wilson matches his believability line for line. The cynical, existential Rick Blaine of the opening scenes vanishes in the shadowy confines of the closed nightclub.

Sam's concern when he first sees Ilsa is justified by Rick's delayed reaction to that unexpected meeting. The thick-skinned owner of Rick's Café Americain is suddenly revealed as a vulnerable man because of his continuing love for Ilsa Lund. Sam's attempts to get him off the booze, to go for a ride or go fishing, make this clear. Sam calls him "Boss," but refuses to follow his orders to play "As Time Goes By." Rick tells him, "You played it for her and you can play it for me." Sam still refuses, and Rick says, "If she can stand it, I can, too!" Only the most detached can remain unmoved when Rick snarls, "Play it," and Sam plays the lovely song. Incidentally, neither the play nor the film contains the line, "Play it *again*, Sam."

The flashback sequence of Rick and Ilsa's Paris idyll proved to be a worthwhile device in bringing *Casablanca* to the screen. The montages of Siegel and Leicester show the marching armies and tanks of the Hilter blitzkrieg as counterpoint to Bergman and Bogart happy together in Paris immediately before the Germans entered. With a minimum of dialogue, Curtiz was able to establish the former stability of the romantic, adult relationship between his hero and heroine.

The mini-episodes of the flashback showed Bogart and Bergman looking their best, seemingly younger than in earlier scenes. The flashback proved beyond doubt that Bogart could play a leading man. Audiences had never seen Bogart as they would see him in the Paris scenes with Bergman—relaxed, playful, even smiling.

Although the various flashback scenes were tiny, they were acted and directed well and built a solid foundation for what many considered the "romantic nonsense" to come. One of those scenes contained the most old-fashioned line of the entire film: Bergman says, "Was that cannon fire—or just my heart pounding?" But she was able to deliver it with conviction. The flashback was already a much-used cinema device when Curtiz employed it in *Casablanca*, but it has seldom been used to better advantage. Curtiz' work was especially clever in the final two scenes of the flashback. In an interesting bit of camera work, Curtiz directed Edeson to film the Paris café's name, *La Belle Aurore,* on the window. Edeson picked it up as a ray of "sunlight" casts it in silhouette on the floor of the café. A troubled Ilsa tells Rick, "Kiss me. Kiss me as though—as though it were the last time." Curtiz had Edeson slowly move his lens downward from the lovers' embrace to a wine glass Ilsa has tipped over. It was an effective bit of symbolism for the scene to follow.

Sam and Rick are shown on a railroad platform, waiting for Ilsa. She had promised to leave Paris with them and marry Rick once they had escaped the Nazi advance. Curtiz had decided to film the scene in a simulated rainstorm. Rick is wearing the same trench coat and snap-brim hat he will wear at the end of the film. Rick is handed a note from Ilsa. After a close-up of Bogart's reaction, Curtiz asked for a tight frame on the note itself. The director wanted the spectator to feel Rick's pain as he reads Ilsa's note saying she can never see him again. Curtiz and Edeson went through many hand-written notes before they got the effect they wanted—heavy rain smearing the handwriting like falling tears. The flashback ends with Bogie at the back of the moving train as he slowly crumples the note and throws it away.

By using the flashback, Curtiz has prepared the way for the first unhindered confrontation between the former lovers. Curtiz returned the plot to the present with a slow dissolve from Rick on the train to him sitting gloomily in the darkened café. It was time for Bergman's first big scene, and Curtiz presented her spectacularly. She looks like an angel in her long white gown, bathed in a single pool of light. She is now completely vulnerable, and Rick is the strong one because of the events revealed in the flashback. He is drunk and bitter and gives her no opportunity to explain her reasons for deserting him. He comes very close to calling her a whore.

Howard Koch, for one, had wanted the flashback sequence to concentrate on Rick's possible involvement in anti-Nazi politics in Paris. He thought the love affair should be a secondary consideration. Few people considered Michael Curtiz a romanticist, but he had insisted that it was the *romance* that must be emphasized during the flashback scenes against a *backdrop* of the war. With the input of several writers in addition to Koch, the Curtiz plan prevailed and the entire screenplay was indelibly strengthened. A film that had started as a wartime melodrama was being transformed into an enduring tale of adult romance.

The establishing scenes of the picture had been shot, and the daily rushes proved that Bogart and Bergman made a realistic love team. Except for the exterior opening, and some adroit rearranging of scenes, the screenplay had pretty much followed the basic line of the play. Following the flashback sequence, however, it was becoming more apparent each day that writing problems posed the biggest threat to *Casablanca.* The cast and director were performing smoothly, but the new pages from Koch, the Epsteins, and others were beginning to slow down to a trickle. Curtiz was convinced he had firmly established the romantic angle. Now he and Wallis agreed to concentrate on the suspense and political intrigue. The writers began a frantic push to keep up with the daily shooting schedule demanded by Michael Curtiz.

Koch and the others gave up their dependence on the play script for a time in order to create new scenes in new locations. Laszlo and Ilsa pay a visit to Renault's headquarters for a meeting with Renault and Strasser and are informed there is no way they can legally leave Casablanca. Victor and Ilsa then approach Señor Ferrari in an attempt to buy the exit visas which would allow them to escape.

The Edeson lens follows Bogart as he makes his way through the bazaars to The Blue Parrot Café, Ferrari's rival bistro. Ferrari intimates that he knows Rick has Ugarte's letters of transit and is willing to pay a high price for them. Rick isn't interested in a deal.

In an amusing scene, Curtiz has an Arab vendor trying to sell Ilsa some linens at his street stall. Played by Frank Puglia, the Arab provides comic relief as he lowers the price by means of pre-marked tags. Curtiz used Puglia's comedy to offset the potential heaviness of the first meeting between Rick and Ilsa since the blowup in the darkened café. Ilsa finally is able to tell Rick that Victor is her husband. When the Laszlos reach The Blue Parrot, Ilsa refuses to leave Casablanca without Victor. Ferrari tells them that Rick has the letters of transit which would enable them both to escape. The brief Ferrari–Laszlo scene helped to "thicken the plot" and also gave Greenstreet an opportunity to use a small piece of business which would become something of a trademark of his acting style. The final shot in the scene shows Greenstreet's glittering eyes following the course of a troublesome housefly. With a malevolent smile, he crushes it with a resounding whack from his handy flyswatter.

The next set-up was the interior of Rick's Café Americain, and Curtiz worked wonders with a whole series of small, well-planned vignettes inside the general action of the packed nightclub. Curtiz chose to direct it like a three-ring circus, with scene overlapping scene as his camera closed in on individual groups. Curt Bois, the pickpocket from the movie's opening scene, is brought back to ply his trade on other unsuspecting visitors to the café. Renault warns Rick about the possiblity of aiding Laszlo and Ilsa. We see Rick's old girlfriend, Yvonne, fraternizing with a Nazi soldier to the annoyance of a Frenchman. In a quick bit of action, Rick breaks up a fight between a German and a Frenchman, immediately before the camera pans to *tête-à-tête* between Renault and Strasser at another table. Renault wryly informs the Nazi, "I blow with the wind and the prevailing wind is from Vichy." Then, it's quickly back to comedy relief as Carl the waiter takes a load off his weary feet and sits down at the table of an Austrian couple to join them in a drink. With good pacing and camera work, Curtiz transformed what could have been a static, "stagey" scene into a cornucopia of action and dialogue that is both amusing and meaningful.

The young refugee couple, Jan and Annina, had been important characters in *Everybody Comes to Rick's*. Rick's attempt to help them get out of Casablanca, where the girl would be safe from the lecherous Captain Renault, had been a motivating influence in the final outcome of the plot. The screenwriters lessened the characters' involvement in the ultimate outcome, but kept the scene between Rick and Annina virtually intact. It became one of Bogart's most relaxed scenes in the film. Annina tells Rick that Renault has promised to allow her and her husband to leave Casablanca, providing she shares a bed with him.

The girl says, "If someone loved you . . . very much, so that your happiness was the only thing in the world that she wanted, and . . . she did a bad thing to make certain of it . . . could you forgive her?" The line is a telling one for Rick, because he begins to comprehend the desperation of Ilsa's predicament. He looks at Annina and then mumbles, "Nobody ever loved me that much."

The screenwriters strengthened Rick's gradual transformation by adding a scene with Jan, played by Helmut Dantine. It also gave Curtiz an opportunity to take his camera onto another set. Rick persuades Jan to try his luck at roulette and advises him to let his money ride on number 22. Rick signals the croupier to allow the young refugee to win until he makes enough money to pay for tickets and the black market exit visas.

The scene demonstrates the uniqueness of Rick Blaine as a movie hero in the era of Hollywood's obsession with simon-pure morality. The man obviously runs a crooked wheel, or he would have been unable to allow Jan to win. Yet, his crookedness is erased by the justness of its cause. Lest he be judged as overly soft, Rick snarls, "Cash it in and don't come back!"

Michael Curtiz added his own touch at the conclusion of the Jan-Rick scene which elevates it to a special moment in the film. His camera focused on an annoyed Renault watching the action and then quickly panned to a close-up of Carl the waiter. S. Z. Sakall views the incident with paternal affection. Curtiz then had Edeson follow the jolly little waiter as he scurried across the nighclub floor to whisper the story to Sasha the bartender. When Rick comes up to them, Sasha surprises him by giving him an impulsive hug and a big kiss. It's a moment that takes only seconds of the total running time, but it remains one of the warmest scenes in all of *Casablanca*.

Rick's new image as a man with a good heart beneath

his stony exterior was only a clever temporary device. Before the audience can get comfortable with it, the writers have the noble Victor Laszlo pay a call on Rick to ask for his help. Victor reminds Rick of his liberal past—his fight for democratic principles in Spain and Ethiopia. But the Bogart character is not prepared to be generous to his rival. He flatly refuses to give Laszlo any help, and his only explanation is a curt, "Ask your wife."

By this point in the filming, new scenes were being written barely in time for each day's shooting. That made it tremendously difficult for the actors to feel secure with their lines—let alone their changing characters. It meant that the *Casablanca* set was in an uproar—many scenes already memorized and scheduled to be shot were changed without warning—other revised scenes had to be shot again.

There was a short break in the action on July 1. Hal Wallis threw the set open for an invited crowd of people who had worked with Michael Curtiz on many past pictures. The *Casablanca* producer hosted a party celebrating the fifteenth anniversary of the director's employment with Warner Brothers Pictures. Curtiz was pleased with the celebration, but he found it difficult to relax because he was too concerned about the progress of his current motion picture. He convinced Wallis to join him and the writers at his ranch for regular Sunday meetings. Perhaps they could successfully pool their ideas about the ending of the film.

Curtiz was embarrassed. He was being forced to tell actors that he couldn't help them because he had no idea what the next day's shooting would bring. He totally confused Humphrey Bogart on one important occasion. Bogart, after another night of little sleep, left his West Hollywood home early in the morning and arrived at the studio where he downed his usual orange juice and took a cold shower. After visiting the makeup department, he strolled onto the set and asked Curtiz what they would be shooting. Curtiz surprised him by saying, "You're going to have a short day. You can go home in a few minutes."

When the camera was ready to roll, Curtiz instructed Bogart to stand on the balcony overlooking the nightclub scene. Bogart was told to just look into the camera lens and nod his head on cue. That would be all he would be required to do for the day. Bogart asked Curtiz why he was supposed to nod—what was he signalling? Curtiz told him not to worry, just nod his head and go home. It wasn't until much later that Bogart learned that his simple nod had motivated one of the most famous scenes in *Casablanca*.

Playwright Murray Burnett still remembers the tears in his eyes as he wrote the "Marseillaise" scene in summer 1940. "It wasn't a scene I had particularly planned or anything," he says. "It just came pouring out of me and moved me to tears as I was writing it." That scene, as it was used in the movie, brings tears and shouts of encouragement from members of today's *Casablanca* audiences who were not yet born in 1940.

The scene was so blatantly contrived to arouse the patriotic fervor of the early 1940s, it should now be the most dated scene in the picture. Yet, the reaction of today's audiences proves that Curtiz' nineteen shots of the sequence were masterfully orchestrated. The scene begins innocently amid the laughter and gaiety of the café interior when a large group of Nazis, seated at one big table, starts singing one of their national songs. Curtiz had Edeson focus the camera on the reactions of the others in the café as the Germans grow louder and more boisterous.

Laszlo demands that the French national anthem be played. Rick's nod signifies his approval and a "singing battle" begins between the Nazis and the French. The scene builds to a tremendous crescendo as Curtiz' camera pans the room and zeroes in for moving close-ups of the refugees and the uniformed French as they join in singing "La Marseillaise" and effectively drown out the Nazi "supermen." The scene, actually much ado about nothing, was terribly effective in 1942 when the German military might seemed invincible. The fact that it still holds up today is a tribute to the talent of Michael Curtiz.

Major Strasser is livid with rage and orders Renault to close the café. The corrupt Frenchman agrees to relay the order to Rick. The next series of shots gives Bogart the chance to act as the straightman for Rains. Bogie asks Rains what legal grounds he has for closing the café. With elaborate mock seriousness, Claude Rains arches an eyebrow and says, "I'm shocked . . . *shocked* to find that gambling is going on here!" Curtiz faded out on the scene with Strasser's ominous warning to Ilsa that she would be wise to leave Casablanca.

The screenwriters wrote some new scenes designed to bring more weight to the role of Paul Henreid. He had come off very well in the "Marseillaise" scene, and Curtiz wanted to strengthen his role to make Ilsa's romantic indecision between Victor and Rick more difficult. Curtiz directed Henreid to act with restraint in his first one-on-one scene with Bergman. Victor expresses only gentle understanding when he surmises that his wife has probably had an affair with Rick Blaine. With a delicate handling of his actors, Curtiz demonstrated that the Laszlo-Lund marriage was based on mutual respect and understanding. The feelings that Ilsa and Rick have shared are dominated by passion. Henreid was permitted to kiss Bergman twice during the course of the scene; both kisses were tender but passionless pecks on the cheek. Victor goes to his dangerous meeting with the underground, and Ilsa knows she has to use whatever means necessary to persuade Rick to give her the letters of transit.

By carefully rearranging scenes from the play, as well as adding new ones, the screenwriters managed to stall this inevitable meeting between Rick and Ilsa. When it finally comes, it is both logical and shattering. Ilsa begs Rick for the letters, but he knows she wants them for Victor, and feels she is further cheapening the love they shared in France. In desperation, she pulls a gun and threatens to shoot him unless he hands over the letters. For the first time in the film, Bogart goes toward Bergman. He coolly takes the gun from her hand, and she collapses in his arms. The scene is Bergman's finest in the picture.

She is completely believable and vulnerable when she tells Bogart she wishes she didn't love him so. Ilsa is finally permitted to tell Rick, and the audience, her reason for leaving the man she loved waiting for her at the desolate train station of the flashback. Rick Blaine can finally empathize with her hopeless inner conflict. Ilsa asks Rick to "do the thinking for both of us." His reply is brief and firm: "All right, I will."

Despite the writers' difficulty in getting finished pages of the script ready for shooting, the plot developments were beginning to move quickly. Henreid and Bogart were scheduled to shoot the very important scene 237 on page 134 of the shooting script. Curtiz considered it the pivotal scene of the entire plot, and he directed both actors to play it with cool intensity.

Laszlo tells Rick that he knows they are both in love with the same woman and urges his rival to use the letters of transit to take Ilsa away to freedom. He will stay on in Casablanca and continue to fight as well as he can. Bogart utilized his "thinking" technique brilliantly in the reading of his simple line, "You love her that much?" The first agreeable meeting between the two men in Ilsa Lund's life ends when the police break in, arrest Laszlo, and take him away. Bogart deliberately obfuscates the effect of the heart-to-heart talk with his reading of the final line in the scene—"It seems that destiny has taken a hand." He says the words flatly, with just a hint of smugness on his face.

Curtiz had directed the quick succession of scenes between his three stars with the hope that the audience would be left gasping in wonderment. Ilsa Lund had admitted that she couldn't fight the conflict any more—that Rick would have to do her thinking. Rick had finally been convinced that Ilsa still loved him. Victor had announced that he would be willing to allow Ilsa to fly to safety with Rick. Only Rick Blaine could resolve the conflict, and Curtiz had directed Bogart to give no inkling of his intentions.

The suspense about the eventual course of the romantic entanglement had to work on screen, because indecision was rife at the Burbank Studios of Warner Brothers Pictures at that moment in summer 1942. The truth of the matter was that the script was being rewritten and otherwise doctored day by day. The screenwriters were still culling ideas and dialogue from *Everybody Comes to Rick's,* and the master script completed by the Epstein brothers. But the momentum of Curtiz' direction and the fine performances of the *Casablanca* cast were causing second thoughts and constant revisions. The suspense built into the film was natural. Everyone was generally pleased with the footage already completed, but nobody from Hal Wallis and Michael Curtiz on down had decided exactly how the film should end.

Thirteen

Ingrid Bergman, in particular, became more frustrated as the fifty-day shooting schedule of *Casablanca* began drawing to a close. Like Michael Curtiz, she was a perfectionist who was worried that she was not giving her best possible performance as Ilsa Lund. She felt trapped by the circumstances of the filming.

It was her first time on the Warner lot, she knew few of the people in the company, and she sensed that some of her coworkers shared her feeling of helplessness. She admired Humphrey Bogart and considered him a very capable actor who took his work seriously. But there had been little time to establish a personal rapport because he seemed to be constantly closeted with Hal Wallis or the writers during their moments away from the camera. Michael Curtiz was a formidable figure who was awesome in his devotion to his work.

Bergman had never before experienced a situation quite like the one that existed on the set of *Casablanca*. She was an actress who liked to devour a script, studying all aspects of her own character and those of others with whom she would have to deal. Only then could she feel free to allow her emotional instincts to take over. She had been given little opportunity to work in her own style on *Casablanca*. As the filming progressed, changes in the master script came so often that she grew confused about exactly where Ilsa Lund was heading in the story.

Bergman understood that a woman could love two men in different ways. But she felt she should know Ilsa's eventual decision in order to play the scenes leading up to it properly. Time and again she asked Michael Curtiz to explain her motivation in a scene. She respected him as a director, but she found that he was seldom able to offer any help. Curtiz was also trapped by the unfinished scenario and couldn't tell her if she would be destined to choose Rick Blaine or Victor Laszlo.

It is possible that the indecision about the ending of *Casablanca* helped the actors give totally believable performances. While Hal Wallis and the writers continued their search for a suitable ending, Curtiz was shooting scenes which closely paralleled the dialogue of the original play. Following the scene in which Laszlo is captured and Rick muses that "destiny has taken a hand," Rick tells Renault that he does indeed have possession of the letters of transit. He informs Renault that he wants to use them to run away with Ilsa. If Renault will help them get away, Rick will set up a trap that will enable Renault to put Laszlo away legally and keep himself in the good graces of his Nazi allies.

To reinforce the idea that Rick is going to double-cross Laszlo, Curtiz again set up his camera in Señor Ferrari's Blue Parrot Café. Rick tells Ferrari that he is now willing to sell his Café Americain because he has decided to leave Casablanca. His only stipulation is that Ferrari must keep Sam at his job. Since Sam has been his only real friend in the story, the one small bow to conscience does little to alter the appearance that Rick is once again looking out for "number one." He had previously told Ferrari that he would never sell the café to him and would never part with Sam unless the entertainer preferred to go. There can be little doubt that Rick intends to leave with Ilsa and honor his agreement with Captain Renault.

Claude Rains' earlier line, "You're the only one in Casablanca with less scruples than I," was evidently a most appropriate description of Rick Blaine. At that point in the

filming Wallis and Curtiz knew that Rick's character development and the direction the story was taking would be a
disappointment to movie audiences who expected a "happy"
ending.

The writers had constructed a tightly knit story of
love, war, and avarice. Curtiz' fast-paced direction and believable performances by the stars and supporting cast caused
Hal Wallis to think that he had the beginning of an excellent
motion picture. But the Bogart character still worried him.
Wallis felt that Bogie was doing a fine job, but his playing of
Rick Blaine was making the film's character far different than
the standard bigger-than-life hero movie audiences expected.
Here was a man as susceptible to temptation as any of them.
He had already declared his credo: "I stick my neck out for
nobody." His decision to turn in Victor Laszlo and run off with
the patriot's wife was convincing. Still, the producer of *Casablanca* was not at all sure it was the way he wanted his film to
end. He continued to meet with his director and writers to
discuss every nuance of a suitable ending for the movie.

Curtiz was beginning to have serious doubts that he
would be able to complete the picture on time, and he was
more tense than usual during the shooting of the final scenes.
Claude Rains fell victim to Curtiz' impatience. The director
became especially irritated with Rains during the shooting of
the scene in Rick's office. He wanted Captain Renault to arrive
at the office eager to finally put away the clever Laszlo.

The scene had been scheduled for early in the morning, and Rains knew he would have difficulty projecting a
sense of urgency because his adrenaline never began to
flow until 11:00 A.M. The scene called for Rains to pound on
the door, Bogart to open it, and Rains to come in. Curtiz told
Rains he wanted him to enter quickly, push past Bogart, and
rush down the hall. This was a big moment for Renault—he
should be keyed-up. They rehearsed the scene several times,
and Curtiz was not pleased. Each time he would scream a
one-word direction at Rains: "Faster!"

Rains decided it would be useless to attempt a ra-
tional explanation of his objections to Curtiz' impatient directing at such an "ungodly hour of the morning." He felt a
dramatic demonstration might better suit his purposes, and

he told Bogart the idea he had in mind. The practical joker in Bogie approved wholeheartedly. After again insisting that Rains make a faster entrance, the disgusted Curtiz ordered the camera to roll for a take. He shouted "action," and Rains knocked on the door. Bogart flung it open and collapsed in laughter as the perspiring Rains entered—on a bicycle!

The Rains-Bogart horseplay managed to relieve the tension, and Claude Rains' entrance appeared fast enough, even without the bike. Rick persuades Renault to call off his *gendarmes* while they await Laszlo's arrival. It seems apparent that Rick Blaine is going ahead with his doublecross. The script, direction, and acting all work to create genuine surprise when Laszlo arrives and Rick pulls a gun on Renault. The incident also provides Renault with another priceless line. Rick reminds the Frenchman that he has a gun pointed right at his heart, and Renault quips, "That is my least vulnerable spot!"

The screenwriters had pretty much followed the dictates of the identical scene in the play. Rick Blaine was going to double-cross Renault instead of Victor Laszlo. The Frenchman points out that Rick's actions are going to place him in a precarious position. That position, of course, would be a relatively normal one in the screen career of Humphrey Bogart. In film after film Bogie had faced electrocution, hanging, and life imprisonment as his penalty for violating the law. As Rick Blaine he was violating the law in *Casablanca;* but this law was an unjust one imposed by the Nazis and their Vichy French puppets. Should Rick suffer because he was moved to "join the fight"? That was the question facing the *Casablanca* creative team.

There were any number of ways *Casablanca* could be ended. *Everybody Comes to Rick's* had Rick holding the Frenchman and Strasser at bay while Ilsa and Laszlo made their way from the café to the airport. After he was certain the couple were safely aboard the plane to Lisbon, he surrendered to Renault, who asked Rick why he had so foolishly broken the law when he knew he would face a certain prison term or death. Referring to their bet that Laszlo would escape again, Rick's curtain line was, "For the folding money, Luis, for the folding money. You owe me five thousand francs."

That ending would certainly be in keeping with Rick Blaine's character, and it could work for the movie. But it bothered Hal Wallis and Michael Curtiz who knew that moviegoers were accustomed to happy endings. The idea of Rick dying a hero's death while helping the Laszlos escape was also discarded. Bogart had made Rick a complex, strong, and likeable character. They felt the average movie fan would identify with Rick and wouldn't like the idea of him languishing in a North African prison, or worse. More importantly, it would still give the Axis forces a kind of symbolic victory. That certainly didn't mesh with Hal Wallis' intention of making a film that would be a positive contribution to the war effort.

Wallis, Curtiz, the Epsteins, Koch, and others had been considering another idea. Conrad Veidt was doing good work as the chief Nazi villain. They had already written Paul Henreid's character into new danger by involving him with the anti-Nazi forces in Casablanca. If they carried the idea a bit further, it would be logical for the frustrated Strasser to kill Laszlo deliberately. There was certainly motivation for the act, and it would strengthen the anti-Nazi feeling that Wallis and Curtiz both wanted. It would also clear the way for a happy ending.

Bergman, in her tempestuous love scene with Bogart, had been brilliant in depicting the emotions of a woman torn between two men. But it would still trouble some if Ilsa deserted her gallant husband to run off with Rick Blaine. That was a very touchy subject in the moral climate of the early 1940s. If Laszlo died heroically, Ilsa would be justified in seeking freedom with her true love, Rick, while continuing to honor the memory of her martyred husband.

The fact that Wallis and Curtiz didn't jump at such an easy solution proves they were not interested in making just another wartime love story. They had both seen the daily rushes and began to realize that they had the makings of something better. *Casablanca* had developed into an intelligent, adult drama beyond their original expectations. It was possible they would cheapen all the fine work that had gone into the weeks of preparation and filming if they settled for the conventional ending.

After completing the original master script, Philip and Julius Epstein had gone back East to continue their work on Frank Capra's film for the government. They had missed the very beginning of the filming, but returned to find the production shaping up well despite its writing problems. Their absence from the studio gave them some new insight into the story line, and they made numerous contributions along with Koch, Robinson, and Maltz. Attending the story conferences on the ending of the script, they understood the feel that Wallis wanted but had been unable to come up with an idea that pleased him.

The Epsteins had put in a full day at the studio, rehashing every possibility for a suitable ending. They continued to discuss the situation as they drove through Cahuenga Pass into Hollywood and turned onto Sunset Boulevard, heading west toward home. Their conversation turned to the marvelous job Claude Rains was doing with their favorite role in the picture, that of Captain Renault. They had written the role so Renault would be likeable despite his blatant amorality. Was it possible that the Renault character might somehow be the key to a more upbeat ending? They had made it clear that Renault had a more genuine affection for Rick than he had for Strasser.

The idea hit them at the same time. They would describe it later as an almost mystical, extrasensory experience. As they approached Coldwater Canyon, they turned to each other and said in unison—"Round up the usual suspects!"

It was a cynical Renault line they had written into the opening moments of the screenplay. They had made that line Renault's standard answer to any illegal incident in Casablanca. Why couldn't he use it again if he felt the conditions warranted it? They hurried into the house and telephoned Hal Wallis. Wallis wasn't sure if their approach would work, but he gave them permission to write the scene. He also asked Howard Koch and others to work on a totally different ending. He would instruct Michael Curtiz to shoot two different endings to see which worked best.

While the writers were frantically creating both endings out of camera range, Curtiz was busy filming the scenes leading up to the conclusion. Wanting to keep the filmed action flowing, he inserted some brief shots of Strasser intercepting Renault's phone call to the airport. Strasser's knowledge of the message, which ordered the gendarmes to honor the letters of transit, worked beautifully in creating a "chase-like" atmosphere.

The camera was moved to the airport set, and the actors were warned to be ready to appear in two different versions of the final scene. At that point, they were only certain that Curtiz would be shooting the beginning moments of the scene with Rick, Renault, Ilsa, and Laszlo at the airport. One male-female couple would probably be boarding the plane for freedom. Ilsa would leave in any event, but the new endings would decide the fates of Rick and Victor. The Epstein version would be shot first.

The reactions of Bergman and Henreid to Bogart's words and deeds would be all-important to the ending Wallis and Curtiz hoped for. Curtiz instructed his property and special effects men to flood the set with the chemically induced smoke which passes for movie fog. The ground cloth was dampened, and Bogart was supplied with his trench coat and snap-brim hat. In many physical ways the atmosphere would be similar to the flashback scene at the train station when Rick had first lost Ilsa.

Because of the way the scene had been written, Ilsa and Laszlo haven't had time to digest the enormity of Rick's crime in taking Renault prisoner until they reach the airport. They could only guess about his intentions. Bergman felt properly motivated to hold out the hope that Rick would still find some way to board the plane. Curtiz concentrated on taking all the backup shots necessary for the beginning of the scene until the Epsteins completed their version. In it, Ilsa and Victor would leave.

Based on Ilsa's line, "You must do the thinking for both of us," the writers had clearly written the scene for Humphrey Bogart. But Bergman's reaction to Bogie's lines, her ability to hang on to every word he uttered, helped him elevate it to a level which would set the standards for bittersweet movie farewell scenes for all time. Bogart's lines, beautifully written and delivered, were made more poetic because of their utter simplicity.

Michael Curtiz suggested that it might be effective for

Bogart to give Bergman one final farewell kiss. Bogart vehemently disagreed, pointing out that his character had already decided to send the woman he loved away for her own good. Under those circumstances there was no way this guy could kiss her. Curtiz was forced to agree, and Rick's farewell "kiss" became a longing look and a final "Here's looking at you, kid."

Curtiz maintained his crisp pace throughout the romantic conclusion of the love triangle which had dominated the plot. But his pacing, coupled with the chiaroscuro lighting and camera work of Edeson, brought a feeling of hope and rightness to a scene which could have been leaden with tragedy. It has become a classic film moment.

With their characters safely on board the airplane, Curtiz told Bergman and Henreid they would not be needed while he completed shooting Bogart, Rains, and Veidt, but they should stand by and be available for the filming of the second ending. They would be called as soon as they were needed. Wallis liked the Epstein ending up to that point. Bogart and Rains also felt that the first part of it had worked well.

The Epstein version of the *Casablanca* denouement was based firmly on the curious relationship between Rick Blaine and Captain Renault. Throughout the photoplay Renault had shown his amused admiration for the antisocial nightclub owner. He had also demonstrated that, although he was willing to obey Strasser's orders, he had no fondness for the Nazi. The Epsteins hoped that Renault's ambivalence about Rick's role in the Laszlo escape could provide the film with an upbeat ending despite possible disappointment about the handling of the romantic triangle.

Curtiz called Bogart, Rains, and Veidt together as they prepared to rehearse the scene where Veidt comes storming onto the landing strip to demand that the departing airplane be halted. The director reminded them to keep the action flowing quickly, and said that he'd shoot the usual cover shots after they had completed the master take.

"When Conrad goes to telephone," the director told Bogie, "you shoot the summabeetch in the back."

"Wait a minute, Mike," Bogie interrupted. "Let's think

about that for a minute. I don't know if this guy would do that. He's not really a killer. That'd be pretty cold-blooded."

"What you care? You can't let him stop airplane. He's no-good bum. Nazi!"

"Yeah, but shooting him in the back would make me the old mad dog again. Why can't he go for his gun, at least. That way it'd be self-defense and we'd get the same results."

"That sounds logical, Mike," Veidt said. "I think it would be in keeping with my character to attempt one last sneak attack."

Curtiz finally gave them permission to rehearse it that way and was pleased with the result. After several rehearsals, he ordered a take. He liked the outcome and took a number of covering takes before proceeding on to the next scene in which the Vichy gendarmes discover the fallen Major Strasser and announce that he has been shot. The line which caused the Epsteins to dream up the new ending—"Round up the usual suspects"—was delivered by Rains with an enigmatic smile following a slight pause. By again utilizing that recurring line, the Epsteins had gotten their hero off the hook and also added another dimension to the character of the rascally but likeable Captain Renault.

Renault's unexpected decision to come to Rick's aid was a delightful development. But Michael Curtiz didn't want the Frenchman's transformation to come too abruptly. After Renault wryly chides Rick for being both a sentimentalist and a patriot, Rick says he thinks it's about time he became a patriot. Curtiz then inserted a piece of business which Claude Rains thought was rather far fetched at the time. The director provided Rains with what looked like a bottle of wine, told him to start to drink and then reconsider and throw the bottle into a nearby trash basket. Renault's line, "Perhaps you're right," was added during the rehearsal.

Curtiz broke the scene to allow his cameraman to take a closeup of the bottle in the trash. The big lens revealed that the discarded bottle was clearly labeled *Vichy* water. Curtiz' inventiveness coupled with Renault's earlier line, "I blow with the wind and the prevailing wind is from Vichy," made it amusingly apparent that the wily Frenchman was about to make a new "meteorological" judgment. Curtiz then instructed Rick and Renault to look up and watch as the plane carrying Ilsa and Victor began to roar its way to freedom.

Realizing that he will have an impossible task hiding Rick's complicity in the Laszlo escape and his shooting of the Nazi major, Renault advises his friend to leave Casablanca. He tells Rick about a Free French garrison at Brazzaville and offers to arrange safe passage for him. Rick registers his surprise at Renault's additional generosity and jokingly warns him that his help wouldn't cancel their bet that Laszlo would escape again. Renault must remember that he still owes him 10,000 francs. Without a pause or change of expression, Renault says, "And that 10,000 francs should pay our expenses."

Rick says, "Our expenses?" The realization of what the Frenchman has said sinks in as they begin their stroll into the fog. Rick says, "Louis, I think this is the beginning of a beautiful friendship."

Mike Curtiz filmed several takes of the final sequence before he said, "Print it!" Hal Wallis was an eager spectator when the rushes were ready to be shown. Curtiz told him that he thought the ending was the best they could do. Wallis watched the scene and agreed. After weeks of struggle, they had their ending for *Casablanca!* The other ending, already prepared for filming, would never go before the camera. The filming of *Casablanca* was completed, except for possible unexpected retakes and any incidental camera work on the montages and special effects. The actors were free to go on to their next projects.

Ingrid Bergman had received news during the filming that had made her happier than she had been at any time since arriving in Hollywood. Paramount Pictures' decision to cast Vera Zorina as Maria in *For Whom the Bell Tolls* had not worked out. The producer and director felt that the features of the famed actress-dancer, in her new short hairstyle, were not suitable for the role of the Spanish guerrilla fighter. The Hemingway film and *Casablanca* had both gone into production in the late spring. After a few weeks, Paramount decided that Zorina should be replaced. David O. Selznick was delighted when the studio approached him with an offer for

Bergman to take over the part when she had completed her scenes in *Casablanca*. Selznick agreed, but added the proviso that his star would require two weeks' rest between pictures.

Ingrid Bergman felt no need for any rest after her work at Warner Brothers. When Hal Wallis informed her that the *Casablanca* filming was completed, she contacted Selznick and told him that she was prepared to leave immediately for the High Sierra location of *For Whom the Bell Tolls*. Selznick first accompanied her to a hairdresser and supervised the cutting of her hair into a becoming, mannishly-short style suitable for her new role.

Bergman's decision to forego the two-week vacation would have a decided impact on the final print of *Casablanca*. Her shorn tresses on the hairdresser's floor would help preserve something which would become an integral part of a very special motion picture.

Fourteen

Owen Marks was the *Casablanca* film editor. Under personal supervision by Hal Wallis and Michael Curtiz, Marks would decide which of the hundreds of close, medium, long, and master shots would appear in the final print. Marks, along with the producer and director, would make the decision on the best way to join together the many reels of exposed film to form a cohesive 102-minute motion picture.

Marks' work would be the all-important final step in the creation of *Casablanca*. However, the improvised way in which the film had been shot figured to make his job a bit easier than normal. A great deal of the usual editing improvements had been made with revisions and retakes during the actual filming. More pressure was taken off Marks' shoulders by Hal Wallis' decision not to rush the film into exhibition. A tentative release date was set for spring 1943, and the editor's only rush priority would be the editing of a rough cut of the film for the music department.

Max Steiner was given a final, revised copy of the screenplay and a rough cut of the film. He would compose the background music designed to enhance the mood and action of every scene in the picture. An old hand at movie scoring, Steiner had strong ideas about his work. Like Michael Curtiz, he was proud and outspoken. Steiner thought the film had good potential and began to plot his score mentally during his viewing of the rough cut. But early into the screening he found one aspect of the picture that troubled him greatly. To his consternation, it continued throughout the film. Max Steiner was convinced it would not be an asset to the movie.

Steiner stormed into Hal Wallis' office to tell him he had made a terrible mistake in selecting the picture's main love song. "As Time Goes By" must be taken out of the film. Steiner felt the old tune was unnecessarily confining in its simplicity. If the lovers' favorite song was going to have such importance in the plot—if it were going to be sung again and again—it should be something with more depth. It should be worthy of a transformation into the main theme of the picture, a vital part of the entire film score. To Steiner, "As Time Goes By" did not have that kind of strength. He could easily write a more appropriate love song. To make a better picture, Steiner felt Wallis should get rid of "As Time Goes By" and reshoot those scenes in which the song was sung and played!

Wallis considered Steiner's idea. The song had been written into *Everybody Comes to Rick's,* and Wallis had thought it a very pleasant tune. Steiner was the first to voice any objection to it. Normally, it wouldn't have been too difficult or costly to retake the few scenes in which the song figured, but a check with David O. Selznick told Wallis that such a procedure would be impossible with *Casablanca.* Ingrid Bergman was already working on *For Whom the Bell Tolls.* More importantly, she had cut her hair. Her drastic change in hairstyle would make it impossible to match any new scenes with those already in the can. Steiner would have to struggle as best he could with "As Time Goes By."

Considering the marvelous ways Steiner used Herman Hupfeld's old pop song, it is difficult to imagine that he had ever felt uneasy with it. But, even in 1942, Steiner was widely recognized as one of the masters of film scoring. His *Casablanca* score would join the one he composed for *Gone With the Wind* as two of his best.

Steiner was also something of a refugee—from the Vienna of a much earlier era. He had left Austria during World War I in order to avoid service in the army, and took up residence in the United States, quickly finding work as an arranger and conductor of Broadway musicals. He had brought with him a background as a conductor, arranger, and composer of operettas in his native Vienna.

He headed west when sound came to the movies and began his film career on the 1929 RKO film musical, *Rio Rita*. As head of RKO's music department, he demonstrated the dramatic impetus that complete background scores could bring to nonmusical sound films. It was Steiner's music which enhanced the drama of the early RKO classic, *King Kong*. After a salary dispute with RKO, he went to work for David O. Selznick but became unhappy when he discovered that Selznick didn't produce enough films to keep him busy. Steiner was a workaholic, and he jumped at the chance to work for the prolific Warner studio. Warner's musical director, Leo F. Forbstein, assigned Steiner to forty-seven films between 1936 and summer 1942.

Steiner's musical education had been steeped in the classics. He had a special feel for the romantic music produced by the great European composers of the previous century, and that, of course, influenced his opinion that "As Time Goes By" was not significant enough to carry the weight of his musical plans for *Casablanca*. Steiner and Erich Wolfgang Korngold were the two principal composers at Warner Brothers, but it was Steiner's music which set the tone for most of the big Warner films. He had a very distinctive style which became as familiar in Warner Brothers dramas as the famed WB logo at the beginning of each movie.

Steiner began working on *Casablanca* after finishing the score for the Hal B. Wallis production, *Now, Voyager*. That score was destined to win a 1942 Academy Award, and Wallis was delighted to have him working on his new picture. *Now, Voyager* was the twelfth Bette Davis film he had scored. A Bette Davis picture without a Max Steiner musical background was unthinkable to Warner Brothers during the late 1930s and early 1940s.

Obviously, a great musical score gives a decided advantage to the screenwriter, director, and actor over their stage counterparts. Many so-so screenplays, unimaginative directors, and untalented actors have been saved from total disgrace by the subliminal aid of an inspired screen score.

The meticulous planning of Hal Wallis had already given *Casablanca* every chance for success. Steiner's score would supply the icing for the cake. The composer listened carefully to Wallis and Curtiz when they explained the moods and emotions they wanted the film to express. Except for the "troublesome" love song, Steiner understood and appreciated their goals.

Steiner proceeded to compose a score for *Casablanca* that particularly heightened the areas where the script was weakest. Steiner's music is instrumental in creating a sense of tension and menace in a film far more devoted to talk than to action. It becomes more of a "war" film because of Steiner's smooth interweaving of "La Marseillaise" and "Deutschland Über Alles." His score was appropriately descriptive and romantic at the same time. It requires a practiced ear to pick out some of Steiner's minute integration of music behind dialogue. One example: Ilsa comes back to visit Rick alone in the darkened café after their first, brief sight of each other earlier. The music behind Rick's drunken, bitter dialogue is heavy and threatening. When Ilsa talks, Steiner's music becomes bright, almost childlike.

Steiner's score was understandably more noticeable in setting up the flashback sequence which preceded the dramatic Bogart-Bergman scene. He utilized "As Time Goes By" to magnificent effect as Bogie drank his booze and allowed his thoughts to return to better days in Paris. The quiet piano version of the melody quickly swelled to a complete symphonic orchestration as the montage of Parisian scenes filled the screen. Steiner musically expressed the carefree happiness of the lovers by incorporating the strains of the hit tune "Perfidia," in addition to "As Time Goes By." His own musical bridges heralded the imminent Nazi presence, and he indicated the impending invasion of Paris by his imposition of the familiar "Deutschland Über Alles." His use of the German and French anthems, or brief pieces of them, add excitement throughout the picture. It is impossible to remain unmoved when "La Marseillaise" swells to a climax at the ending of the picture as Captain Renault and Rick Blaine walk off together in the swirling fog. Steiner must have had second thoughts about "As Time Goes By," because he used that melody in nearly every possible style and tempo. *Casa-*

187

blanca could not have been as good a movie without it.

Wallis and Curtiz were pleased with Steiner's completed score and continued to work with Owen Marks and his staff in the cutting of the final print. Curtiz' work on *Casablanca* was virtually completed, but producer Hal Wallis was in a different situation. He was still faced with the challenge of promoting it into a successful motion picture at the box office.

Wallis knew the quality of the work that had gone into the picture, but only the public could determine its eventual success. The producer was concerned that critics and fans might be disappointed by his first attempt at a war picture. Despite the best efforts of Curtiz and the writers, there was little action in the film. Wallis was aware that other studios had already completed, or were preparing, such combat action movies as *Wake Island, One of Our Aircraft Is Missing, Eagle Squadron,* and *Mrs. Miniver.* All of those pictures contained far more physical excitement and action than *Casablanca.* The public was buying action movies, and his film would have to compete with them at the box office. Bogart and Bergman had given excellent performances, but would the public buy them as a romantic team? He made early plans for an action-oriented ad campaign before the picture's release in 1943.

But a strange thing happened to *Casablanca* on its way to the local movie theater. On November 8, 1942, American and British troops landed on the shores of French North Africa at points in Morocco, including the city of Casablanca. The Allied strategists expected only token resistance from the Vichy French. They encountered nothing like the fierce resistance they would face on the Normandy beaches several years later, but the Allied soldiers would be forced into three days of bitter street fighting before the Battle of Casablanca was won. It was the first significant victory against Adolf Hitler and his Nazis since the official beginning of the war in September 1939.

The happy news was too much for Hal Wallis, the one-time Warner press agent, to resist. Here was a natural, unpurchasable promotion for his new motion picture. The biggest battle of the war had just been won in the city which had supplied the title for his film. He approached Jack Warner and told him he would like to release *Casablanca* as soon as possible, stating that he and Curtiz could work overtime with Owen Marks to complete the final polishing. Jack Warner emphatically agreed.

A Warner Brothers press release dated November 1942 told part of the story:

Warner Brothers studio has rushed a print of Casablanca *to New York for earliest possible shipment to the U.S. armed forces now seeing the city and situation which inspired the Humphrey Bogart-Ingrid Bergman-Paul Henreid starring picture.*

The Hal B. Wallis Production which was directed by Michael Curtiz is one of the most timely parallels of current history to emerge from the studio which is famed for the timeliness of its product. Immediate delivery of the feature to Casablanca will enable the soldiers to be the first to see the story they are living on the screen.

The press release wasn't designed to win any prizes for journalistic accuracy. *Casablanca* had little, if anything, to do with the story the American G.I.s were living in Morocco. But the studio had made its point. It would have been impossible to release a motion picture with a more timely title. One Hollywood columnist suggested that the War Department would be wise to check with Warner Brothers before planning any future invasions. If the soldiers in Casablanca were going to see a rushed finished print of the movie, so would the civilian populace of New York City. *Casablanca* was booked for a special advance showing at Warner's Hollywood Theater in Manhattan on November 26, 1942.

Hal Wallis had attended an earlier sneak preview of the film at Huntington Beach, California, that did nothing to increase his confidence about *Casablanca*—its reception was less than enthusiastic. One of the exhibitors in the preview audience even suggested that Wallis should change the title, saying that *Casablanca* sounded too much like Carta Blanca, a popular beer of the day. With the movie set for its formal premiere before the tough New York critics, Wallis could only hope that recent real-life events in Morocco would have a positive effect on his filmed fiction. His concern was unwarranted; the reviews were generally enthusiastic.

The *New York Times* described *Casablanca* in glowing terms:

The Warners here have a picture which makes the spine tingle and the heart take a leap . . . The crackling dialogue which has been packed into this film . . . is of the best. . . . The performances of the actors are all of the first order, but especially those of Mr. Bogart and Miss Bergman . . . One of the year's most exciting and trenchant films.

A month later, the *Times'* Bosley Crowther would include *Casablanca* in his list of the ten best films of 1942 with the comment:

This tough and exciting melodrama possesses . . . the sure virtue of being highly entertaining and intellectually stimulating to boot. Humphrey Bogart gives a shrewd performance in it as the boniface of the Casablanca casino, and Ingrid Bergman, Dooley Wilson, Claude Rains and Conrad Veidt are in its excellent cast.

The New York *Herald-Tribune,* though not as enthusiastic as *The Times,* also gave the movie a good notice. The *Tribune* called *Casablanca* "a melodrama with a capital M," but admitted that the love story was moving, "if at times 'slushy.'" Bogart came off very well in the review, which said that he "was never better." The notice was less complimentary to Bogie's co-stars, Ingrid Bergman and Paul Henreid, damning them with the faint praise that they were "decorative and convincing." The now-defunct newspaper waxed eloquent over the talents of Claude Rains and stressed its belief that Warner Brothers should immediately build Dooley Wilson "into a featured, if not star, player."

Casablanca's real money review appeared in the November 28 issue of *The Showmen's Trade Review,* a trade paper read by distributors and exhibitors all over the country. A good review in *The Showmen's Trade Review* would mean that theaters across the nation would be eager to book and exploit the values of the movie. On a page head-

190

ed with the legend "Box Office Slant," the review said, in part:

It may be the prominence Casablanca *enjoys in current news, but somehow or other the picture takes a stranglehold on the emotions in the opening scene. The character backgrounds are quickly established . . . the vicious intrigue, black market operatives, thieves and vandals who prey on the unfortunates willing to relinquish virtue, wealth, and position in order to secure the coveted privileges of passage to America. On to this vividly colorful and highly interesting tapestry of circumstances is laid a captivating array of heart tugs, thrills, pathos, suspense, terror, glamour, excitement and revelry, masterfully embellished with lilting songs and leavening sidelights. Throughout, the spectator is kept aware of the fact that the inner working of a woman's heart and the torment of a man's soul are being laid bare. Each of the dominant screen characters cleverly avoids any clue as to the exact positions they will assume as the story unfolds, and many surprising and pleasing reversals of expected performance take place before the highly-satisfactory climax.* Casablanca *probably is as fine an example of the care and secrecy that prevails in the widely-publicized but little-known "underground" as it is possible for pictures to portray. Humphrey Bogart chalks up another ace performance as a fellow with a world-hardened front and a soft heart, while Ingrid Bergman's performance as the heroine gives new understanding to the complexities of feminine nature. Paul Henreid does a swell job. . . . Claude Rains is as usual without fault. . . . Sydney Greenstreet and Peter Lorre score in the menace department. The subordinate players, the direction, the technical departments and all the factors, including the song they will all be whistling, contribute to make this an absorbing and entertaining photoplay.*

The trade paper's capsule review under the heading "Audience Slant" summed up the picture's potential impact: "As sweet a package of grand, all-around entertainment as has been seen in a long time." Its "Box Office Slant" read: "Title, cast, story and production all presage stratospheric receipts."

The prediction of *The Showmen's Trade Review* proved to be accurate, even before the picture went into national release. The rave reviews, enthusiastic word-of-mouth promotion, plus a timely ad campaign made *Casablanca* an immediate hit at the 1,500-seat Hollywood Theater in New York. In a matter of days, even the standing room was sold out, and the picture enjoyed a solid ten-week run, grossing $255,000.

The Warner Brothers technicians had finished enough prints of *Casablanca* to enable the picture to go into national release in February 1943, at about the same time it was ending its run at the Hollywood Theater in New York. The national reviews were also enthusiastic, and the movie did fantastic business across the country. Some 200 movie houses showed *Casablanca* during its first national run. By the end of 1943, *Casablanca* had enriched Warner Brothers by $3,700,000. At that time, the studios did not release accurate film grossings, but *Casablanca* was easily one of the top money-making films of the 1942–43 season.

The rush release of the film caused some confusion when it came time to name the best pictures of the year. Despite its general release date in 1943, the New York critics decided that *Casablanca* should be judged as a 1942 release since it had opened in the city in November of that year. *Casablanca* did not do as well as expected when it came time for the official awards of the New York Film Critics. That group, dedicated to promoting "worthwhile films and the craft of film criticism," decided that Noel Coward's *In Which We Serve* was the best picture of 1942. *Wake Island* was a close runnerup. One of Hal Wallis' pre-release worries had been justified by the critics; both films were heavy on action. The New York critics named John Farrow best director for his work on *Wake Island*. James Cagney won the male acting honors for *Yankee Doodle Dandy,* and Agnes Moorehead was named the best actress for *The Magnificent Ambersons.* Humphrey Bogart got two votes for his work in *Casablanca* and *Across the Pacific,* and Ingrid Bergman picked up a single best actress vote for *Casablanca.*

Casablanca's first mentions on the national awards scene came through the offices of the National Board of

Review, an independent organization considered to be the oldest in awarding "best picture" prizes. That board judged *Casablanca* as a 1943 release and placed it well down on its ten-best list, sandwiched in between something called *The Hard Way* and *Lassie Come Home*. Michael Curtiz was named one of the three best directors of 1943 for his handling of *Casablanca* and *This Is the Army*, but none of the *Casablanca* actors made the National Board of Review list.

Humphrey Bogart was delighted with his public reception for *Casablanca*. His next picture for Warners was *Action in the North Atlantic*. Although he didn't have Ingrid Bergman as his leading lady, he did have a worthy co-star in Raymond Massey. While *Action in the North Atlantic* would never rival *Casablanca* in popular appeal, it always remained one of Bogie's favorite films because of the wild practical jokes he and Massey, who were great friends, pulled on each other and anyone else who seemed a likely pigeon during its filming.

Although Mayo Methot no longer had any reason to be jealous of Ingrid Bergman, Bogart's home life continued to be rocky. The director of *Action in the North Atlantic* was forced to find new ways to photograph its star because of the classic shiner Mayo had given her husband. In general, the motion-picture industry was mystified at Bogie's new-found success as a screen lover. Reporters began to besiege him more than ever. His answer to questions about the reasons behind his new romantic image were straightforward.

He told one interviewer, "I didn't do anything I've never done before. When the camera moves in on that Bergman face, and she's saying she loves you, it would make anybody look romantic."

Ingrid Bergman was also being asked questions— how it felt to work opposite Bogart, how it felt to kiss him. She told interviewers that they had been so busy working on the film that there had been little time for any socializing: "I kissed him, but I never really knew him." She was surprised by the enthusiastic reception *Casablanca* had received. Her reviews had been good, and she was relieved that the film might actually help her career. She was, however, certain that *For Whom the Bell Tolls* was the picture that would bring her the most acclaim, and she was looking forward to the release of the Hemingway story. She had felt comfortable on the Paramount movie, while the chaotic conditions on the *Casablanca* filming had only left her tired and confused.

The Allied invasion of North Africa wasn't the only unexpected boost *Casablanca* would receive. The public wasn't advised of it until later, but Roosevelt and Churchill had selected Casablanca as the site of one of their historic wartime meetings. Bogart was also interested in seeing the city that had, in a roundabout way, contributed so much to his burgeoning career. He got the opportunity late in 1943 when he signed on for a USO tour which would play American outposts in North Africa. Bogie agreed to take his wife with him on the tour, prompting old buddy Peter Lorre to predict that the battling Bogarts would no doubt be the main participants in a "Second Battle of Casablanca." Lorre's quip proved to be true, and the Bogart family brawls became an international legend.

Back in the States again, Bogart found that the popularity of *Casablanca* was still growing. The picture was even being touted as the possible winner of a number of Academy Awards, including one as best actor for Humphrey Bogart. Bogart never seriously considered himself a good bet to win an Oscar, but he was flattered by the talk. He had obviously come a long way since his days as an office boy for William A. Brady, Sr.

The war had definitely affected the operations of the Academy of Motion Picture Arts and Sciences. The surprise attack on Pearl Harbor had caused the Academy to cancel its award ceremony which had been scheduled for December 1941. Academy President Bette Davis resigned when the organization refused to open the rescheduled ceremony to the public as a benefit for the Red Cross, and it wasn't until February 1942 that the presentations were finally made. The winners of films released in 1942 were not announced until the late winter 1943, and the Oscars were made of gilded plaster rather than the usual gold-plated bronze. Awards for pictures released in 1943 would not be made until March 1944.

Since *Casablanca* didn't go into general release until

February 1943, the Academy's board of governors ruled that *Casablanca* would be judged with the films of that year. That decision probably helped the Hal Wallis picture in its quest for the Oscar. It would have stiff competition as it was, but in 1942 it would have competed with such exceptional films as *Random Harvest, The Magnificent Ambersons, Yankee Doodle Dandy, King's Row,* and *Mrs. Miniver.*

It was announced that the 1943 Academy Award ceremonies would be thrown open to the public for the first time. In the past, the ceremonies had been a members-only affair, with the awards handed out at a dinner in a hotel banquet room. This time Grauman's Chinese Theater would host the ceremonies, with formal presentations made on the stage of the theater. The impact of *Casablanca* had moved Hollywood, and the picture had been nominated for six awards. The Hal Wallis production had obviously scored better inside the industry than it had with either the New York Film Critics or the National Board of Review.

Casablanca was one of ten films nominated as the best picture of the year. Michael Curtiz was one of five directors in contention for the award as best director. Julius J. Epstein, Philip G. Epstein, and Howard Koch were among the nominees for writing the best screenplay. Arthur Edeson would compete with nine others for the best black-and-white cinematography of 1943. Claude Rains was nominated as a contender for the Oscar in the category of best supporting actor.

Two of *Casablanca's* stars were also prepared to take a lively interest in the voting. Humphrey Bogart had won a nomination as best actor, and Ingrid Bergman would be contending for the best actress award. Bogart would rise or fall on his personal popularity and the quality of his work in *Casablanca.* True to David O. Selznick's prediction, Bergman had been nominated for her portrayal of Maria in *For Whom the Bell Tolls.*

Fifteen

The Twentieth Century-Fox film about the miracle at Lourdes, *The Song of Bernadette,* became the odds-on favorite to capture the lion's share of the 1943 Academy Awards. The moving story of the young French girl who sees a vision of the Virgin Mary in a cave had been nominated for nine awards, including best picture, best actress, best director, and best screenplay.

Casablanca's six nominations tied it with *For Whom the Bell Tolls* and the Columbia comedy, *The More the Merrier,* for second place. Although *Casablanca* had proved itself a tremendously popular picture with the public, its success in Academy nominations was a surprise. Few figured it would actually win many Oscars, since it was going up against strong entries in every category. The Academy members are supposed to vote solely on the merits of individual and collective accomplishments, but industry politics and favoritism were as much a part of the proceedings in 1943 as they are today. The early consensus was that *Casablanca* was a fine, entertaining picture but hardly on the artistic level of several of its peers.

Hal Wallis was afraid the advance predictions might be correct when the first *Casablanca* nominee lost. Arthur

Edeson, who had done such a magnificent job of cinematography amid the light and shadows, would not win the 1943 Oscar for that category. Arthur Miller won the award for his black-and-white camera work on *The Song of Bernadette.* The *Bernadette* interior decorators had won an Oscar for their work earlier in the ceremonies, and Alfred Newman's score for that picture had also been named the winner. The Fox picture was already leading *Casablanca,* three Oscars to none.

The first *Casablanca* win came in a category which could not have been anticipated during the filming. The award was given for work in the area that had caused most of the problems. There were five nominees for the writing of a screenplay from nonoriginal sources. The were Dashiell Hammett for *Watch on the Rhine,* George Seaton for *The Song of Bernadette,* Richard Flournoy, Lewis R. Foster, Frank Ross, and Robert Russell for *The More the Merrier,* Nunnally Johnson for *Holy Matrimony,* and the Epsteins and Howard Koch for *Casablanca.*

As Hal Wallis waited for the envelope to be opened, he had reason to recall the troubles that the script had caused him. There were many times when he had been close to wasting $30,000 per day of Jack Warner's money because the writers were slow in coming up with material for the actors to perform. In the beginning many at Warners had written off the Murray Burnett-Joan Alison source play as so much sentimental nonsense. Many people had contributed to the writing of the scenario, but the Writers' Guild had settled on the Epsteins and Koch to receive the screen credits. Wallis felt they had earned the recognition. Howard Koch, among others, was totally unprepared for the announcement that he and Julius and Philip Epstein had won the Oscar for writing the best screenplay of 1943.

Claude Rains lost to Charles Coburn in the race for the Academy Award for best supporting actor. Coburn had impressed everyone with his clever comedy portrayal in *The More the Merrier.* Ingrid Bergman faced formidable opposition in her battle to win as best actress for her performance in *For Whom the Bell Tolls.* The other nominees were Jean Arthur for *The More the Merrier,* Joan Fontaine for *The*

Constant Nymph, Greer Garson for *Madame Curie,* and Jennifer Jones for *The Song of Bernadette.* Ironically, it was David Selznick's *other* protegée, Jennifer Jones, who took home the Oscar.

Humphrey Bogart thought his chances of winning the Oscar were slim. He had never been a "back-slapper," and he knew as well as anybody that the Oscar race was as much a popularity contest as it was a critical judgment by a body of his peers. He felt he had given a good performance in *Casablanca,* but he thought that Paul Lukas had been magnificent as the dignified anti-Nazi in *Watch on the Rhine.* Gary Cooper in *For Whom the Bell Tolls,* Walter Pidgeon in *Madame Curie,* and Mickey Rooney in *The Human Comedy* had all turned in impressive performances and were more popular in the industry than Bogart was. Bogie didn't win the Oscar for *Casablanca.* Paul Lukas, the man he and Peter Lorre had teased into a near fist fight with Michael Curtiz, got his "small measure of revenge" by carrying off the coveted statuette.

The *Casablanca* principals had come away empty-handed in three of their first four attempts at an Academy Award. There were only two categories left, best director and best picture. Michael Curtiz was up against Clarence Brown for *The Human Comedy,* Henry King for *The Song of Bernadette,* Ernst Lubitsch for *Heaven Can Wait,* and George Stevens for *The More the Merrier.* Henry King was considered the favorite, and Michael Curtiz was the most surprised man in the theater when his name was called out as the winner for his direction of *Casablanca.*

Mike Curtiz' pride, earnestness, and his inability to handle the English syntax were all apparent when he climbed on the stage to accept his award. The tall, muscular director rubbed his forefinger against his hawkish nose, took a deep breath, and said, "So many times I have a speech ready . . . but no dice. Always a bridesmaid, never a *mother.* Now I win . . . I have no speech!" The "mother" line provided the biggest laugh of the evening.

There was a growing rumble of excitement in the audience as it waited for the awarding of the Academy's most important prize. *Song of Bernadette* was still the favorite in the best picture category. The Fox picture had already won Oscars for best actress, best cinematography, best musical score, and best set decoration. But the excitement was caused by the sudden resurgence of *Casablanca.* The Wallis movie had won the award for the best screenplay (other than an original), and its director had been named the best of the year. With the best story and the best direction, *Casablanca* had to be considered a very strong contender. But *Bernadette* had already won the Golden Globe Award as the best picture of 1943, and the Golden Globes had been prophetic in naming Jones and Lukas as best actress and actor.

The nominees for the best picture of 1943 were *Casablanca, For Whom the Bell Tolls, Heaven Can Wait, The Human Comedy, In Which We Serve* (the New York Film Critics' winner in 1942), *Madame Curie, The More the Merrier, The Ox Bow Incident* (winner of the National Board of Review prize), *The Song of Bernadette,* and *Watch on the Rhine. Watch on the Rhine* had already won the New York Film Critics Award as the best picture of 1943. It was also a product of Warner Brothers Pictures, and it was likely that the Warner voters would split their ballots between it and *Casablanca,* which would lessen the chance of either picture to win.

When the winner was announced, the unlikely had happened. *Casablanca,* made from an unproduced play and beset by troubles from beginning to end, had been named the best picture of 1943. *Casablanca* had earned its Oscar, and it was an especially happy night for Hal Wallis.

In 1980, Paul Henreid would say there were all too many myths about *Casablanca.* Among the ones he wanted to refute was that the film had started production as only a "B melodrama." Henreid said nobody on the picture ever felt that way about it, although they never expected it would become a classic. Henreid stressed his belief that Michael Curtiz had been generally overlooked as a great director. He considered Curtiz "among the top seven, or so, directors of all time." But he emphasized that Hal Wallis was the guiding genius behind the success of *Casablanca.* "All the fame and glory of *Casablanca* belongs to Hal Wallis."

Hal Wallis made two trips to the stage of Grauman's Chinese Theater on that night in March 1944—one, as producer of *Casablanca,* to accept the Oscar for the best picture of 1943, and the other to accept the Irving Thalberg Memorial Award for his outstanding contribution to the art of motion pictures. It was an unprecedented moment of recognition by his peers in the movie business.

The Thalberg award was, and is, considered perhaps the highest honor the industry can bestow on any of its members. Not necessarily presented every year or for any one picture, the award given to Wallis in spring 1944 was only the fifth time it had been presented, and he became its first two-time winner.

In a year of good motion pictures, *Casablanca* had broken box-office records and received the ultimate honor of winning the Academy Award as the best picture of 1943. It remains Hal Wallis' all-time favorite, and it became the launching pad for spectacular film careers. *Casablanca* provided Mike Curtiz his only chance to make a speech accepting an Oscar for best director, but his four nominations place him well up on the list of successful directors. Curtiz' versatility and tremendous output kept him from receiving the full recognition he deserves as one of the very best directors in his field.

Paul Henreid was correct in his fear that *Casablanca* could hurt his career more than help it. Rick Blaine was obviously the leading male role in the picture, and nothing the noble Victor could do would stand up to the compelling interest of the Bogart character. Henreid "flew off" with Bergman, but the audience knew that she really wanted to stay with Bogie. Still, Henreid has enjoyed a fine career, starring in, for example, *Song of Love* opposite Katharine Hepburn and *Of Human Bondage* with Eleanor Parker.

His combination contracts with Warners and RKO, he claims, often left him at a disadvantage in getting better roles. He also points out that the sudden awareness of foreign accents after World War II kept his career from fulfilling its early promise.

It is possible that no picture in the history of film has had such an excellent cast, from top to bottom, as the one Hal Wallis hired for *Casablanca.* Claude Rains, of course, went on to make a number of good motion pictures after *Casablanca,* including a Technicolor version of George Bernard Shaw's *Caesar and Cleopatra* with Rains as an aging Julius Caesar. Conrad Veidt died in 1943, the year *Casablanca* went into national release. His good friend, Paul Henreid, says, "He died at the age of fifty while playing golf, one of the things he enjoyed most. He died right on the golf course." Sydney Greenstreet went on to portray a number of interesting roles, including the repulsive executive who badgers Clark Gable in *The Hucksters*. Peter Lorre rejoined his pal Bogie and Claude Rains in another Warner picture called *Passage to Marseilles,* which the studio vainly hoped would be as successful as *Casablanca.* Before his death, Lorre would be forced to caricature himself in stock heavy parts in cheap horror movies. S. Z. "Cuddles" Sakall profited greatly from his comedic bits in *Casablanca* and made a number of pictures in which he kept audiences laughing with his delightfully befuddled characterizations. Leonid Kinskey has outlived most of the cast and still does occasional comedy roles in films and television when he isn't presiding over his own acting classes in southern California.

After *Casablanca* was released, music stores were swamped by people asking for Dooley Wilson's recording of "As Time Goes By." Unfortunately, Warner Brothers did not yet own a recording company, and no sound track album was produced. A ruling by James Petrillo, then czar of the tough American Federation of Musicians, kept Dooley from capitalizing on his instant fame and popularity with "As Time Goes By." Wilson contributed much to the movie but profited from it less than any of the main players. Shortly after the film went into general release, the Warner mail department called Wilson to tell him he was getting stacks of letters. Warners claimed that Wilson's fan mail count was running higher than Clark Gable's. Still, his fame was short-lived. During the 1970s a popular trivia question was, "Who was the man who played Sam in *Casablanca?*" Dooley joined Frank Sinatra for the singer's film debut in *Higher and Higher* but never again found a role to equal Sam in *Casablanca.*

Ingrid Bergman's disappointment about losing the Oscar for her work in *For Whom the Bell Tolls* was assuaged by the enormous popularity she gained from *Casablanca.* It, rather than the Paramount picture, sparked the real turning point in her career. Even today, musicians break into the strains of "As Time Goes By" when she walks into a cabaret. She would receive five more Academy Award nominations after 1943 and would win the Oscar a year after *Casablanca* for her portrayal of Charles Boyer's tormented wife in *Gaslight*. She received another Oscar as best actress for *Anastasia* in 1956 and picked up still another Academy Award as best supporting actress for a cameo role in *Murder on the Orient Express* in 1974. But she remains most closely identified with *Casablanca*.

Until *Casablanca*, Ingrid Bergman's name had never appeared in any poll of America's favorite actresses. She had never received so much as an honorable-mention listing. But following her success in *Casablanca*, she zoomed to the number three position of most popular female stars in the poll published by *Box Office Barometer*. Although Ingrid Bergman has had a distinguished career in motion pictures, and has played more spectacular roles in more expensive movies, she has never appeared in a film which has approached the popularity of the one she almost didn't make—*Casablanca*.

Humphrey Bogart would not pick up his first and only Oscar until many years after he had been passed over for the award in March 1944. There is no doubt, however, that *Casablanca* and "Rick Blaine" were the cornerstones of the Bogart career. The Bogie legend started when he first donned a trench coat and played a "good guy" in John Huston's *The Maltese Falcon*. However, Bogie's Sam Spade was only the fuse of the popularity time bomb that exploded when he played Rick Blaine. *Falcon* pushed Bogie into a low position on the honorable-mention list of box-office draws in an exhibitor's poll in 1942—the first time he had ever made any such list. Yet after the release of *Casablanca* he became the fifth biggest male star in the business, according to *Box Office Barometer*. Only Bing Crosby, Gary Cooper, Spencer Tracy, and Cary Grant were more popular among America's movie spectators. Bogart finished seventh in the theater owners' poll of all screen personalities, male and female, after his success in *Casablanca*. In 1943 Betty Grable, Bob Hope, Abbott and Costello, Bing Crosby, Gary Cooper, and Greer

Garson were the only stars to inspire more ticket sales than Humphrey Bogart.

His astounding success as a world-weary lover, after years of playing second-rate gangsters of little dimension, had to give him immense satisfaction. He had proved his point after trying since 1935 to convince Jack Warner that he was capable of playing many different kinds of roles, including romantic ones.

Following *Casablanca,* Bogart went on to give fine performances in a number of films like *To Have and Have Not, The Big Sleep, Treasure of the Sierra Madre, The Desperate Hours,* and *The Caine Mutiny.* After years of frustration, he had earned an opportunity to show his acting ability in a wide variety of characterizations. His earthy, funny portrayal of the scroungy riverboat skipper in *The African Queen* with Katharine Hepburn in 1951 brought him the Oscar. But it was Bogie as Rick Blaine—hunched over the bottle of booze in his darkened café while Sam played "As Time Goes By," and slouched in the hat and trench coat against the swirling fog of the Casablanca airport—that audiences around the world remember best.

The most forgotten contributors to *Casablanca* remain Murray Burnett and Joan Alison. They forfeited all rights to the property when they sold *Everybody Comes to Rick's* to Warner Brothers on January 12, 1942. Their names appeared on one line of the film's credit frame, but it did little to explain their vital role in the creation of the film. The critics didn't help. One national critic referred to the play in 1943 as "the world's worst." That critic, and very few others, have ever read the play. A close comparison of the play and the finished screenplay reveals that the overall setting, plot, characters, song, and much of the dialogue in the movie came directly from the play. Joan Alison claims that the screenwriters used seventy-two of the original ninety-seven pages of the play script in the scenario of *Casablanca.*

In 1942 Burnett and Alison saw *Casablanca* during its original run at the Hollywood Theater in New York and were thrilled at the job Hal Wallis and Warner Brothers had done in bringing their play to the screen. The film company had captured the essence of what they had hoped to say when they wrote the stage piece. Secretly, they had envisioned Clark Gable and Carole Lombard in the leads, but they were more than satisfied with the performances turned in by Humphrey Bogart and Ingrid Bergman. Both Burnett and Alison landed jobs as Hollywood screenwriters as a result of the success of *Casablanca*. Burnett later returned to writing for the Broadway stage and works today in television production in New York, while Joan Alison is semi-retired.

An analysis of the original play and the screenplay reveals that Burnett, Alison, Philip Epstein, Julius Epstein, and Howard Koch all deserve credit for the success of the *Casablanca* story. The Epsteins and Koch, who received Academy Awards for writing the best screenplay of 1943, deserved that distinction because of their arduous care in shaping, polishing, and expanding the original play to make it suitable for the screen. But Burnett and Alison must not be forgotten as the writers who started it all. Without their basic plot, characters, setting, and idea of using "As Time Goes By," there would have been no *Casablanca.*

The motion-picture industry has always been, first and foremost, a profit-making business. Great success by a motion picture breeds imitation in sequels and remakes, a practice that has been so blatant in recent years that film companies now often give their follow-ups numbers instead of names—witness *Godfather II, Jaws II,* and *Rocky II.*

A Warner Brothers plan to make a sequel was announced in *Box Office Barometer* shortly after *Casablanca*'s release in early 1943. The item reported that the new film would be called *Brazzaville,* and its stars would be Humphrey Bogart, Geraldine Fitzgerald, and Sydney Greenstreet.

It's possible the Epsteins and Hal Wallis had that idea in the back of their minds when they rewrote the final scene of *Casablanca,* in which Claude Rains tells Bogart that they'll head for a Free French garrison in Brazzaville. In the sequel it was planned to have Geraldine Fitzgerald play a Red Cross nurse working at the African headquarters of the Free French. The trade paper article reported that the producer, director, original source story, and screenplay were all "not set." After much discussion, it was decided to abandon the project. Movie fans would have to rely on their own imaginations to determine the eventual fate of Rick Blaine, Captain Renault, and the others.

In the 1950s Warner Brothers decided to join instead of fight the new medium of television. The head man of Warner TV, Bill Orr, felt that *Casablanca* might make a winning TV series. But the gamble proved disastrous, and the ill-fated series ran a minimum number of weeks. Of course, the studio did permit capsule versions of the script to be broadcast on radio and television after its release. Warner Brothers sold the radio broadcast rights of *Casablanca* to the B10W Company for $1,000, and a one-shot condensed version of the film script was broadcast on the "Phillip Morris Program" on September 3, 1943. In 1955, Warner Brothers received $3,000 from the J. Walter Thompson Advertising Agency for the one-time TV rights to *Casablanca,* and a shortened version of the film was broadcast on "The Lux Video Theater" live over the NBC network. Coast-to-coast TV broadcasts were not possible at the time, and kinescopes were used on KFSD in San Diego, KRCA in Los Angeles, KMJ in Fresno, KRON in San Francisco, KHQ in Spokane, KOMO in Seattle, KPPV in Portland, and KEY-T in Santa Barbara. One of the stipulations of the agreement was that the kinescopes must be destroyed immediately after the broadcast.

Murray Burnett and Joan Alison's *Everybody Comes to Rick's* finally got a stage production, although neither of the playwrights participated in the negotiations. On May 15, 1946, Warner Brothers granted Sara Stamm the rights to produce the play, under the title *Casablanca,* at the Casino Theater in Newport, Rhode Island, for a run between August 12 and August 17 of that year. The studio legal department advised her that she was not being authorized to use the names of the authors in connection with the play. She was charged no royalty and was told she could make any changes in the play that she cared to, as long as the changes were listed and sent to Warner Brothers where they would become the property of the studio.

Alan J. Lerner and Frederick Loewe wanted to transform *Casablanca* into a Broadway musical in the early 1950s. In a letter to Monte Proser and Jack Small, dated March 14, 1952, Lerner and Loewe said that they were prepared to complete the music and lyrics of the stage musical within eighteen months. They were under the impression that Proser and Small had obtained "certain rights" from Warner Brothers in bringing the film to the stage and agreed to give them equal billing in the producing scheme. Unfortunately Proser and Small had not yet worked out a final deal with Warner Brothers, and the negotiations dragged on for months. Harry Mayer, the top-notch executive who headed Warners' New York story and talent departments, finally broke off negotiations on May 22, 1952, saying he didn't feel they were getting any closer to an agreement. Thus, the 1942 *Casablanca* of Humphrey Bogart, Ingrid Bergman, and Paul Henreid remains the one and only original article.

The underlying message in *Casablanca* was no more earthshaking or new in 1942 than it is today. But the ability to express simple truths with honesty and believability has been the special province of all great drama since the ancient Greeks. Many of today's *Casablanca* buffs say they love the film because it depicts a happier time when everyone stood together and the choices were not so complicated. Whatever the reasons, *Casablanca*'s ideas about personal and political responsibilities continue to haunt us. A columnist for the New York *Daily News* reminded us of that on February 25, 1980, in an article about an astounding American victory in the Winter Olympics.

Describing the national rejoicing when the young American hockey team upset the highly-favored Russian team, Peter Coutros wrote:

A group of revelers in a Philadelphia bar broke spontaneously into the "Star-Spangled Banner" after watching the game on TV. . . . The vision of all those people standing up in a gin mill and singing homage to their country brought to mind Paul Henreid. Henreid, Humphrey Bogart and Ingrid Bergman and a movie called Casablanca. *Bogie was Rick, an expatriate Yank who ran a bar frequented by Henreid, a Free French fighter. . . . At one point in the film, the Nazis who are running Casablanca in cahoots with the Vichy regime, get up in Rick's place and start singing their Nazi songs. This gauls the Gaullist Henreid so he demands that the band play the "Marseillaise." Rick . . . gives the band a nod and they comply and pretty soon sounds of the French anthem overwhelm the Nazis. . . . There must have been the spirit of Paul Henreid in that bar the other night, a defiance set to martial music meant to be heard in Moscow.*

The Coutros article, written some thirty-eight years after the filming, is another indication that the spirit of *Casablanca* lives on. A simple, 102-minute screen entertainment has become a legend despite misleading stories that have sprung up around it over the years. The offhand explanation that *Casablanca*'s success was a quirk—that it just "happened"—simply does not hold up. *Casablanca* was an example of filmmaking at its finest. Its continuing appeal is the result of the labor of a carefully-assembled team of workers whose only aim was to make a good, commercial motion picture.

Webster's Dictionary defines the word inimitable as "not capable of being imitated: matchless." The words fit *Casablanca*. The uniqueness of the 1942 film makes it unlikely that anyone will ever attempt a remake. The story could be updated, of course, and there are capable actors today who could give believable performances in the parts played by Bogart, Bergman, Henreid, Rains, Wilson and the others. But the *feel* would not be the same. The least-envied actor in the world would be the unfortunate chosen to play the role created by Humphrey Bogart.

It is impossible to forget the Rick Blaine of Humphrey Bogart. Long years after his death, Bogie and *Casablanca* have both been elevated to a rare level in the pantheon of cinematic greatness. Bogie, the man, would have been startled by the hoopla, even as he was surprised when he came to realize how many industry friends and admirers he had shortly before his death. Bogie, the actor, would probably have given most of the credit to those who buy the tickets. Chances are, seated at the helm of his yacht *Santana* with a good breeze spanking the canvas, he would have hoisted a glass in your direction.

"Here's looking at you, kid."

207

Index

211

215